Clouds of White Sail

Clouds of White Sail

Fishermen, Racing, and the End of an Era

Michael Wayne Santos

LEXINGTON BOOKS
Lanham • Boulder • New York • London

Published in paperback in 2020 by Lexington Books by permission of Associated University Presses. All rights reserved.

Published by Lexington Books
An imprint of The Rowman & Littlefield Publishing Group, Inc.
4501 Forbes Boulevard, Suite 200, Lanham, Maryland 20706
www.rowman.com

6 Tinworth Street, London SE11 5AL, United Kingdom

Originally published as *Caught in Irons: North Atlantic Fishermen in the Last Days of Sail* by Susquehanna University Press.

The hardcover edition of the book was catalogued by the Library of Congress as follows:

Santos, Michael Wayne.
    Caught in irons : North Atlantic fishermen in the last days of sail / Michael Wayne Santos.
    p. cm.
    Includes bibliographical references (p.).
    1. Fisheries—North Atlantic Ocean—History. 2. Fishers—North Atlantic Ocean—History. 3. Fishers—North Atlantic Ocean—Social life and Customs. I. Title.

SH213.5 .S26 2002
338.3'727'091634—dc21   2001034492

To my wife, Mary Colin, for her love and support in all aspects of my life.
To my son, Nathaniel, so that he may better understand a part of his heritage.
And to the fishermen, whose story this is.

Contents

Acknowledgments

THIS BOOK GREW OUT OF RESEARCH DONE WHILE I WAS ON SABBATICAL AT Mystic Seaport Museum in the fall of 1993. In addition to the library staffs at the Seaport and the other repositories that I visited in the course of my research, I especially want to thank Nancy d'Estang in the Seaport's Shipyard Research Department. Her support and enthusiasm for this project was unfaltering. Fred Calabretta graciously shared every relevant oral history in the Seaport's collection with me. Andy German read an earlier version of the manuscript and did all that he could to encourage its publication. Barry Thomas, in the Small Boat Shop, put up with my incompetence while I came to a fuller understanding of the boatbuilder's craft. My dad, Joaquim Santos, provided both a base of operations for research trips to Gloucester and much-welcomed companionship during a six-month separation from my wife and son. Lynchburg College's financial assistance defrayed many of the costs associated with researching, writing, and publishing this book. My in-laws, Oris and Margaret Hyder, helped underwrite the costs of illustrating the text. My participation in the Frank C. Munson Institute of American Maritime Studies in the summer of 1994 gave me the broader context I needed to focus and define the research. The Munson faculty, and the students that I studied with, deserve special recognition. Their insights helped me better understand America's unique relationship with the sea. Finally, my readers and the editorial staff at Susquehanna University Press thoughtfully read the original manuscript and made innumerable suggestions for improvement. They disabused me of my residual romanticism, asked the right questions, and still managed to remain encouraging about the significance of the project.

Clouds of White Sail

Introduction
Romanticism and Reality:
Fishermen as Workers and Heroes

BY THE FIRST DECADE OF THE TWENTIETH CENTURY, MOST AMERICAN WORK-
ers seemed to have succumbed to the consequences of industrialization. For
some, such as textile workers, changes had come early. For others, like miners and steelworkers, a process begun in the 1880s slowly transformed them
from craftsmen to semiskilled machine tenders. In either case, while the
nineteenth century was characterized by workers with a high degree of control over their labor, in the twentieth century machines set the pace.[1]

When the scale of production increased, the intimate connections between owner and employee disappeared. As one industrialist lamented, "[At
one time] I knew every man . . . I could call him by name and shake hands
with him . . . and the [office] door was always open. When I left the active
management . . . we had . . . some thirty thousand employees, and the men
who worked . . . would have stood just about as much chance to get in to see
any one with his grievance as he would to get into the Kingdom of Heaven."[2]

In some cases, the problem was exacerbated by the influx of new workers
from the countryside and overseas. In many cities and towns during the
nineteenth century, cross-class empathy had reinforced worker autonomy
on the job so that workers and their lower-middle-class neighbors shared a
cultural life organized around sports, saloons, and theaters.[3] As new technologies redefined the workplace, cities grew more heterogeneous. No
longer able to dictate working conditions or define the community's cultural life, workers became isolated from each other by skill and ethnicity,
and from the members of the middling classes with whom they used to associate.[4]

North Atlantic fishermen, romanticized in Rudyard Kipling's novel *Captains Courageous*,[5] and by James Connolly's many articles in popular maga-
zines of the day, seemed exempt from this process. After all, these men made
their living from the sea, and as such were free of the drudgery and routine
of factory work. They were, by all accounts, independent, tough-minded,
and rugged. They risked their lives in an epic struggle against nature, and
their bravery was a way of life, a job requirement.

13

They were matter-of-fact, and in some cases even taciturn, about the danger. A fisherman simply did what needed to be done with no fuss or brag. It took a special person to fish from a dory on the Grand Banks, or to captain a schooner in a howling gale carrying nearly every stitch of canvas. It was commonly held that such men were not likely to become victims of wage slavery like their landlubber contemporaries.

However, this assumption overlooked the fact that, stripped of its romanticism, the pitching deck of a schooner was a place of work, in many ways no different from the coal face in a mine or the shop floor of a factory. The bottom line was that someone other than the fisherman, miner, or factory worker owned the means of production. Although the owner needed his workers' skills, he, or some rival, also had a strong incentive to find a more efficient way of getting the job done. It was just the nature of capitalism.

That fact became obvious in the fishing industry in 1905, when a group of Boston investors organized the Bay State Fishing Company to build the steel-hulled beam trawler *Spray,* which was modeled on the steamers used in the North Sea. Within two years the company turned a profit, and by 1912 it owned six trawlers. Each vessel averaged forty-nine trips and two million tons of fish that year.[6]

Concerned, the all-sail fishermen pushed for a bill to outlaw the landing of fish caught by trawlers. Their argument was threefold: the new method depleted fish stocks; it marked the beginning of industrial fishing; and ultimately it would lead to monopoly. The last two points were particularly telling. As the debate over beam trawling unfolded, it became obvious that fishermen were well aware of the dynamics redefining work in other industries, and they wanted no part of it.

According to Frank Nunan, a spokesman for the fishermen, the backers of the Bay State Fishing Company planned "to control the fish business; to have their own wharf; to have their own store for fitting out steamers; to have ice houses, railways, and lastly, to sell their own fish."[7]

Like entrepreneurs in steel and other industries, the Bay State executives, at least in Nunan's mind, were attempting to horizontally integrate the industry to maximize control and profitability. Clearly, the leadership at U.S. Steel had learned the value of having everything from raw materials, to transportation, to processing facilities, under a clearly delineated corporate hierarchy.

However, this integration had come at a cost to the workers employed in U.S. Steel's various subsidiaries. Unions had been busted, worker autonomy had been lost, and skill had been diluted to the point where almost everyone in the mill was a semiskilled machine tender, easily trained and easily replaced.[8] As Nunan put it, "It is labor and independence against something not right."[9]

Right or not, the outcome seemed a foregone conclusion. The U.S. Commission of Fisheries admitted as much when it issued its report on trawling in 1914. As the investigators put it:

We believe that the unregulated use of otter trawls will inevitably result in the practical displacement of the less efficient line fishery, and that this will induce a change in the character of the men manning the fleet, as the substitution of steam for sail power has changed the type of crews in the merchant marine and in the Navy. There is also the probability, in fact almost the certainty, that the change would result in a reduction in the number of individual vessel owners and the concentration of ownership of fishing craft in the hands of a comparatively small number of firms and corporations. Whether or not these changes be desirable is a matter to be judged by the same criteria governing opinion respecting similar phenomena affecting other industries.[10]

For the government, as for most of society, opinion clearly favored change, or, at the very least, held that any debate of the issue was merely academic. In a statement that could have been applied to the study of any industry at the time, the 1914 Fisheries Commission Report noted that "The consideration of broad subjects of social welfare should be divorced from special application, and we do not regard them as germane. . . ."[11]

Because middle-class Americans and government bureaucrats were not directly impacted by the changes redefining American industry, of course the matter was not "germane" to them. Yet, for the workers whose way of life was being altered, it was more than germane. It was a frontal assault on work and community patterns that had existed for generations. Fishermen, miners, steelworkers, and others had no choice but to resist as best they could. In the end, though, the outcome was the same.

As one steelworker told an investigator looking into working conditions in Pittsburgh, "The galling thing about it all is the necessity of accepting in silence any treatment that the Corporation may see fit to give. We have no right to independent action, and when we are wronged there is no redress."[12]

Captain Nunan warned fishermen of the same thing in a slightly more colorful way. Noting what would happen on the day before Christmas or before a big storm, he quoted an imaginary conversation between a fisherman and his wife that would take place if the Bay State Fishing Company got its way. "Well, wife, the fish company says I must go out tonight. You know I am hired and I must go, for if I don't there is someone to take my place on the wharf. Goodbye. Think of me tomorrow."[13]

By 1920, Nunan's scenario had become reality for many New England fishermen. Even for those who continued to fish aboard schooners, auxiliary power changed both the nature of work and the shipboard routine. As in so many sectors of the economy, progress and technology redefined the fisheries in short order, turning skilled men into relics.

Fishermen were going the way of steelworkers, miners, and textile workers. Had fate not intervened, few Americans would likely have noticed, much less cared. Certainly, there was never great public outcry lamenting the passage of skilled workers from the smokestack industries.

Then again, there was little that seemed romantic about tending a furnace of molten pig iron or operating a loom. Average Americans did not want to envision themselves laboring in a factory, mill, or mine. Where was the adventure, the glamor in those workplaces? What possible marketable public entertainment could be developed to showcase and celebrate the working-class traditions of steelworkers, miners, or weavers?

Fishermen, on the other hand, labored in a more exotic setting. Their vessels were beautiful, the stuff of a Currier and Ives print. There was no wonder, then, that when William H. Dennis proposed an international fishermen's race in 1920, it captured widespread public interest and enthusiasm. The story goes that Dennis, editor of the *Halifax* (Nova Scotia) *Herald* and a former senator in the provincial parliament, sat in his office reading a packet of papers when his eye caught news of the cancellation of an America's Cup Race because of a twenty-three-knot wind.[14]

"Twenty-three knots!" he reportedly chortled. "Why *our* fishermen down in Lunenburg would wonder if it was worth their while to hoist sail in a light breeze like that!"

Apparently still tickled with the notion, Dennis met his friends H. R. Silver, Reg Corbett, and Harry de Wolf, all prominent Halifax businessmen, for lunch. The foursome got a good laugh from the whole affair, and soon began thinking about a "real competition" between "real sailors, real fishermen." With the annual Fall Fishermen's Carnival coming up, what better time for a regatta. Before long, they traveled to Lunenburg, won support among the skippers of that town's salt bank fleet, and the race was on.

From this it seemed only logical to issue a challenge to Gloucester (Mass.) and to create an International Series that would pit the best of Nova Scotia against their Yankee counterparts. A trophy was commissioned, and a subscription was organized to raise $5,000 in prize money.

For Dennis, the fishermen were romantic stereotypes cut from the mold of Rudyard Kipling's *Captains Courageous*. In organizing the *Halifax Herald* series, he was reported to have rationalized the races as a means of giving "our men down in Lunenburg a chance to show their heels to those lily-livered millionaires down there." Just as Captain Disko Troop showed spoiled, rich, young Harvey Cheyne a thing or two about life in Kipling's fictitious tale, Dennis expected life to imitate art.

Many in the popular press picked up the theme. The fishermen's races were supposed to be straightforward and unpretentious, just like the men who participated in them. As such, they became symbols of an older, more innocent time that stood in sharp contrast to the crass materialism and pretense of the era. That the all-sail fishermen were also becoming obsolete only added to their romantic appeal. The same public that had barely noted their impending displacement by the trawler fleet less than ten years before now trumpeted their races as "proof that the age of sail is not ended."[15]

Media hype aside, the 1920 international series was a throwback to an earlier period, perhaps in large part because the impromptu nature of the Canadian challenge gave little time for anything else. Officials in Gloucester were given one week to accept the challenge and name the boat that would race. The American contender was expected to be in Halifax ready to compete by the end of October.

Taking whatever they could get, American race officials settled on the fourteen-year-old *Esperanto*, which just happened to be the only all-sail vessel then in port. With no time for much else, *Esperanto*'s hold was emptied, and she was brought into trim. She was hauled out on the marine railway, her underbody scrubbed, and a fresh coat of paint applied. Leaving Gloucester on October 25 to a cacophony of cheers, sirens, and bells, she returned on November 7 a champion, having defeated the Canadian contender *Delawana*, two races to none.

Yachting magazine spoke for many when it declared, "This championship race appears destined to become a classic."[16] What made it a classic was its purity as working-class sport. The 1920 races were in keeping with the spirit of the first races organized by Tom McManus in the late nineteenth century.[17] When McManus conceived the idea of a formal fishermen's race in 1886, he knew quite well that for a race to have any hope of legitimacy with the fishermen, let alone attract their participation and interest, it had to be kept simple. It should have no fancy yachting rules, ratings, and the like. A straight-out, boat-for-boat free-for-all, with the only rules being the rules of the road, was what was necessary. Inasmuch as possible, an official race needed to replicate the everyday reality of life on the Banks. As McManus put it:

> I called the captains of the entered vessels together, and instructed them to take off all the dories except two (which were necessary in case of accident) and to haul out, clean and paint their vessels' bottoms. This arrangement put them all on an equal footing. All were cautioned to be at the starting line at a given time. When the races were over it was simply necessary to put their dories back in the nests, take on ice, bait and provisions and they were all ready to go to their different businesses. Thus expense and unnecessary delay were obviated.[18]

McManus realized that, although the heroic images of writers like Kipling and Connolly were grounded in truth, for the fishermen, winning a community-sponsored race was irrelevant when measured against the realities of making a living.

Informal racing to and from the Banks had long been part of the fishermen's culture. Indeed, racing was a logical extension of a worldview grounded in practical concerns and simple pleasures. Paid on a shares system, fishermen had a clear incentive to be the first in to market, because the first vessel in got the best price. With all hands sharing equally in the profits of a voyage, everyone had a stake in pulling together and driving the ship as hard as possible.

Besides, it was fun. There was something about being aboard a schooner on the homeward run, with the wind piping up and the sea boiling over the rail, that quickened the pulse and made it all worthwhile. As one fisherman recalled, "You get the trickle on the rail . . . and you've really got a good sailing breeze . . . you're at your top speed. . . . Oh, it was a lot of fun. . . . You're livin' then."[19]

A fisherman knew what was necessary to survive at sea under all sorts of conditions, and was proud of doing what it took without having to be told.[20] A race put him to the test, allowed him to prove himself. For the captain, it was a matter of honor to carry a full press of sail in the teeth of a gale, and woe to the skipper who doused his canvas first in a head-to-head confrontation with a rival vessel in a blow.[21] Because a captain's reputation as a "highliner" (a big money-maker) guaranteed that he attracted a good crew and kept it,[22] impromptu races to and from the Banks enhanced reputations. They also made for good yarning during "mug-ups" (coffee breaks) in the fo'c'sle.

Community-sponsored races served much the same purpose as the informal events that happened on the way to and from the fishing grounds. They were fun, allowed for a test of seamanship, made for great stories, earned the crew a little extra money, and appealed to the romanticism in everyone. In short, they reflected the culture that created them.

Like most working-class towns in the nineteenth century, Gloucester's social life was dominated by its primary industry, and the values of its workers. After all, nearly everyone in town was a fisherman, knew a fisherman, or worked for a firm ancillary to the fisheries. Even those who did not, like yachtsmen and the summer residents and monied interests on affluent Eastern Point, took an interest in goings-on down on the wharves because they considered themselves part of the community. To the youth of the town, as well as to its leaders, the fishermen were heroes. The master mariners who skippered the fleet were pillars of the community, civic leaders in their own right.[23]

In 1920, however, this community was in flux. The all-sail fishery was in decline. Men who had grown up in the business found themselves with an unpalatable choice: move into beam trawling, retire, or continue to work on one of the declining number of schooners that still practiced dory fishing.

Like skilled workers in other industries, so much of their identity was tied up in what they did that there really was no choice. "The older guys," remarked one fisherman, "were the last to go [out of dory fishing]. It was their life. . . . They were 70 years old, some of those men. Sixty was nothing. . . . Which was kind of old to be jumping around in a little dory."[24] Their reasoning for hanging on was tied to something Captain Nunan had said: the independence of labor. On the schooner, "you were free. You didn't have a boss over your shoulder all day long. . . . You were more or less on your own." Besides, "on a steamer you went out in storms," something you'd never do in a schooner.[25]

For the skippers, the reason to hold on was even more compelling. They had worked their way up from the fo'c'sle. Their reputations had been built on their ability to drive a vessel and her men and to make money. Auxiliary power and beam trawling made their skills irrelevant. What did it matter if one knew how to carry a full press of sail in a gale when a diesel engine could get one home? Why should one be able to "think like a codfish" when all one's vessel had to do was drag a net across the ocean floor?

Gloucester's reputation as the premier fishing port in North America had been built on the labors of her all-sail fleet. Her glory days, however, were behind her. By the early twentieth century, Boston had displaced her. Her civic leaders were well aware of the change, and resented its implications for their community.

Had William Dennis not issued his challenge in 1920, the story would likely have turned out like so many others where the local industry underwent dramatic change. Working-class culture would have been replaced by a more homogeneous mass culture. It happened in textile towns, mining villages, and iron manufacturing centers.

Workers lost control of their labor, their community life was transformed, and they were assimilated into the broad-based activities being created by the newly emerging leisure industry. As professional baseball displaced amateur, and movies became popular, workers gradually abandoned their commitment to their own cultural values and reshaped their tastes and habits to conform to the dominant culture. The transformation was subtle and always gradual, but inevitably mitigated the frustration and discontent that accompanied the displacement of skill and the redefinition of work.[26]

For Gloucester and its fishermen, the 1920 races provided a unique opportunity to turn the process on its head. Widespread public interest and the desire to make international racing an annual event allowed business and political leaders in the community to halt Gloucester's slide while showcasing her heritage, all with an incredible payoff in tourist dollars.

For the captains, the races met a more fundamental need. By racing, they could hold on to their status in the community and affirm their importance to the fisheries at a time when both were in question. As Charles Sabel, an expert in skilled worker behavior observed, when skilled men begin to slide down the skill hierarchy, they tend to cling to their old sources of identity.[27] Here they were being asked to demonstrate their skills as sail carriers for an international audience and in defense of national honor. How could they resist?

For the average fisherman, there was no such recourse. They lacked the clout in the community to shape decisions, and were therefore excluded from the process. In the name of fielding the best, the race crew that took *Esperanto* north included seven captains. Only one, her current master, had been aboard her before the trip to Halifax. Made up of a cross section of Gloucester's elite, ranging from politicians, to vessel owners and processors, to skippers, the American Race Committee was content to let the spotlight fall on the master mariners who had helped establish the city's reputation. The fo'c'sle crowd was not considered.

That was just as well. The skippers were far more reputable and easy to deal with than their crews, who tended to drink and carouse more than was approved of by polite society. Because the races were a popular event, there was a clear need to put one's best foot forward.

With the help of William Dennis and the press, Gloucester and its captains had unintentionally co-opted the mass culture by integrating a portion of their own traditions into the public psyche. The working-class dimensions of fishermen's races attracted middle- and upper-class citizens who could fancy themselves aboard the pitching deck of a fishing schooner. It appealed to a society enamored by the growing popularity of sports. It also fed the fervent sense of nationalism on both sides of the U.S.-Canadian border.

Unfortunately, officially sanctioned racing had never been a large part of the fishermen's heritage. Before 1920, there had been only five races in the United States and two in Canada. Participation and interest in these events were sporadic and localized, with vessels just as likely to forgo a race if the fishing was good. The races that really counted, and that fed so much of the fo'c'sle yarning, were the unofficial brushes on the way to and from the Banks.

In an era when technology had made sail obsolete, however, Gloucester and its captains had to take what they could get. What other one-industry town and its workers got the chance to successfully resist the ravages of industrial capitalism while being lionized for perpetuating a working-class alternative to mass culture?

The problem was that, ultimately, international racing was a product of that culture. As such, the public imposed its own set of assumptions on the races, expecting fishermen to be living incarnations of the "Captains Courageous," while conforming to rules of sportsmanship and fair play that had little to do with the fishermen's life experiences.

The outcome should have been predictable, yet international fishermen's races continued off and on until 1938. Not surprisingly, the simplicity of form of the 1920 contest was never duplicated. Beginning in 1921, Americans and Canadians became caught up in a fever to build winning racing schooners that, as Howard Chapelle aptly pointed out, "were economic failures, requiring subsidies to allow them to exist in both racing and fishing, without complete conversion to power."[28] The races became farces, and the captains became either romanticized caricatures of themselves or unsportsmanlike bores, depending on how well they conformed to popular expectations.

Still, the master mariners persisted in the charade because, as skilled workers, it was the only way they could hold on to their status. If someone was willing to construct a high-quality schooner for them, who were they to argue? Indeed, it was the only way for men who were still committed to sail to have an all-sail vessel built for them. Fishing companies were either building auxiliaries, or by the mid-1920s were investing in diesel-powered draggers and trawlers. The trade-off for the fishing captains was giving up control to men with little or no vested interest in the fisheries—yachtsmen and sportsmen with a desire to win the *Halifax Herald* Trophy. In the short run, it seemed like a small enough price to pay.

After all, the captains were like a vessel caught in irons. The winds of change had shifted toward power, leaving no hope for advancement in the old fishery. A sailboat is said to be caught in irons when it is headed directly into the wind and cannot move. The only option is for her crew to extend the sails to one side of the boat, put the tiller to the opposite side, and let the wind push her backwards until she is beam to the wind and can sail again. The *Halifax Herald* Races offered skippers a chance to do the same thing. It was, however, only a temporary fix. Like workers in other industries, the Gloucestermen succumbed to the inevitable onslaught of technology and mainstream American culture, even as that culture perpetuated their myth.

This is the truly interesting part of the fishermen's races that has heretofore been ignored. Books about the races have tended to deal with them in a vacuum, concentrating on the results of contests and the personalities of the participants. When they talked at all about developments in the industry, it was usually a passing comment about the impact of trawlers and power on the schooner fleet.[29]

Studies of the industry, meanwhile, have focused on the nature of work, community dynamics, and the economic and technological developments that redefined the industry. Part of this last topic was tied up with vessel design, and later the introduction of the otter trawl.[30] When industry-focused sources dealt with the races at all, it was usually as an afterthought; such was the case with Joe Garland's provocative but overly short chapter in *Down to the Sea*.[31] Bill Dunne addressed the races in greater detail, but his study was about vessel designer Tom McManus, and the races were only one part of that larger story.[32]

What is unique about this book is its interpretation. The races are not so much the focus of the study as a window into the changing economic and social times that redefined the North Atlantic fisheries, and for that matter, the society as a whole. They were part of the larger waterfront culture that created them, and later, of the popular culture that romanticized them. Both these facts defined how they were organized, who participated, and how events transpired. Fishermen and their communities were able to temporarily resist the incursions of new technology while simultaneously indulging in the modern boosterism of promoting a major sporting event. Indeed, such contradictions reflected the more general confusion of the era.

By attempting to bridge the artificial gap between maritime and labor history, this book seeks to create a coherent interpretation of working-class life among the fishermen in the last days of sail. To do that, we begin with a look at the oral traditions of the fishermen, with an eye to understanding the informal work rules and attitudes that defined the fishermen's culture in the late-nineteenth and early-twentieth centuries. By putting the Gloucestermen's "competitive spirit" into context, one can better grasp the dynamics of work, leisure, and class in Gloucester, and the significance of the early fishermen's races.

This understanding provides a baseline against which to measure the impact of changing corporate structures and the introduction of new technology. As they did in all industry, these changes redefined nineteenth-century realities and required major adaptations by workers and their communities. In the case of the fishermen, it was an attempt to cope with these dislocations that at least in part informed how the international races played themselves out during the 1920s and 1930s.

Stripped of their social and economic context, the races seem like anomalies, strange and inexplicable quirks in an era of strange and inexplicable quirks. Such a perspective, however, does a disservice to the men who participated in them. That is a shame, because the men from the last days of sail were interesting in and of themselves, without any of the embellishments of James Connolly, the popular press, or local community boosters. Their struggles with a rapidly changing world, unpredictable economics, uncontrollable technology, and uncertain values are the real story of the fishermen's races, and, ultimately, understanding that story is the purpose of this book.

1

Competition and Working-Class Tradition among the Gloucestermen

In the late-nineteenth and early-twentieth centuries, Gloucester fishermen home from the Banks tended to congregate on Fishermen's Corner, just across the street from the Master Mariners' Hall on Main Street. Here they chewed the fat about their most recent trips, complained about the cooks' grub, or hung around waiting for a skipper who needed someone to fill a site. They were all different: tall, short, mustachioed, clean-shaven. Some spoke with the broken English of the Portuguese, others with the unique cadence of the Nova Scotian. Yet, for all their distinctiveness, they shared a common countenance, a quiet self-confidence that was obvious to even the most casual passerby.

Across the street, above Wetherell's Drug Store, skippers gathered in the big lounging room of the Master Mariners' headquarters. The motif was practical and utilitarian, perfect for the needs of the men who used the room. The walls were decorated with charts of the fishing banks and photographs of famous schooners. Some of the captains played pool, others cards. A handful sat in easy chairs scattered about the hall, or looked out the windows at the goings-on down on Main Street. Like the fishermen across the way, the skippers were loafing—taking some time to relax, connect with old friends, catch up on gossip, and talk shop.

According to James Connolly, these men had an "independence of spirit [that was] the inevitable outcome of [their] calling and . . . inheritance. . . . [W]hen a man has been a fisherman, his father before him a fisherman and his people before that for several generations fishermen,—that man has got something that isn't deserting him in a hurry."[1]

Hyperbole aside, Connolly understood that a fisherman's sense of himself came from a connection with his past. Like all skilled workers, fishermen knew their heritage and were proud of it. This was especially true of the captains, who were the most highly skilled of the fishermen and had made their mark in the business through a combination of hard work, intelligence, and perseverance. The fo'c'sle crowd tended to be more transient, and occasionally less respectable, but these men still understood and

23

When fishermen were in port, a wide variety of activities awaited them. From hanging around Fishermen's Corner, to drinking and carousing, there was plenty to do. Of course, there was always the work of getting ready for the next trip. Here a man sits on the foredeck of a schooner splicing rope. (Photograph courtesy of Mystic Seaport Museum, L. Francis Herreshoff Collection, Mystic, Connecticut)

accepted the values defined by the skippers' culture, in large part because they knew that crewing for a good captain meant more money.

This fact was supplemented by the reality that fishing was at its heart a family business. Whether skipper or crew, most men had not made a conscious decision to enter the fisheries. Rather, it had been part of a family tradition handed down from father to son and reinforced by the nature of the towns and villages where they had grown up. For the boys especially, the wharves were a favorite hangout after school, or instead of school in some cases. The waterfront culture got in the blood early, in many cases tempting a whole new generation to "go down to the sea."

Remembering how he got into fishing, one man said:

> When I was a little kid we started hanging out around the docks, running errands for the cooks and they'd pay us off with fish and we'd take the fish uptown and peddle it. And later we started scrubbing binboards. . . . [O]ne of the skippers, when we were twelve, gave four of us an old dory and he helped us fix it up and we were longlining blackbacks and cod fish in the harbor. . . . I loved these vessels [the schooners], God, I loved them. . . . I was hanging around the docks all the time . . . [and] I went [fishing] the first summer when I was . . . thirteen years old . . . dory fishing for halibut in the *Killarney*.[2]

Such experiences repeated themselves frequently. A retired captain wistfully recalled, "I was born in 1911 and I think in 1916 I was down on the wharf going from boat to boat and I was only 5 years old. And I was going ever since." He went to sea at age fourteen, leaving for seven weeks without telling his mother where he had gone. His reason for wanting to go fishing was simple: "If it's good enough for my father it's good enough for me."[3]

Migrating from Nova Scotia and Newfoundland, many of the fishermen out of Gloucester represented upwards of a hundred years of family experience in the fisheries. For such men, formal education was irrelevant, because there was only one occupation realistically open to them.[4] As one man from Aquaforte, Newfoundland, recalled, "As soon as you could work at something you quit [school]. There wasn't too much to be educated for."[5]

Although their choice of fishing seemed inevitable, there was nonetheless an attractiveness to it that made these men more than mere pawns of fate. In a story similar to that repeated by countless immigrants to Gloucester, another Newfoundlander noted that, from an early age, he had "water in his blood." Instead of going to school, he "somehow or other ended up hanging around at the wharves all the time."[6]

Of course there was pride in knowing that one could set one's own goals without having to be told what to do. Not every man could be a fisherman, and those who could not were weeded out early, and fast. In a system that promoted cooperation and mutual responsibility, there was likewise accountability. There was an "unwritten law" that everyone accepted but no one discussed—everyone pulled his weight, with no arguments and no complaints.[7]

Old-timers showed youngsters aboard a vessel how to do things *once*. After that they were on their own, which meant, one man remembered, "You learned a lot by yourself."[8] Another observed that aboard a schooner "you didn't grow up" so much as you were "rushed up."[9] Such a rough apprenticeship bred self-reliance and self-confidence among those that passed muster, but it also encouraged a sense of cooperation. Eager youngsters wanted to please their shipmates and impress them as being worthy of trust as fo'c'sle equals. The experienced hands, meanwhile, were not above correcting the new fellows when they made mistakes, if they showed themselves to be reliable and hardworking.

In the end, "It was up to your pride," noted a fisherman. "It was up to yourself. If you didn't do it, you knew you were going to get it. So you wanted to be as good as the other guy."[10] Such an ethic had a leveling effect aboard the fishing schooner. According to a Boston man who went fishing at age nine, "It didn't make any difference where you came from, as long as you knew your business . . . and they could find out in no time whether you knew your business or not."[11]

Knowing what you were doing was essential to survival, because, as one fisherman put it, "you live together out there. . . . [I]f you can't trust a man alongside of you, you don't want him there. . . . A good shipmate . . . knows his business, doesn't say nothing . . . when you're working it's team work."[12] This was especially true for the skipper, who had to be counted on to know where his dorymen and their trawls were, especially on the Grand Banks, where sudden fogs often separated men from their vessels.[13]

Like skilled workers in other high-risk occupations, the shared dangers fed craft identity and a sense of solidarity. Indeed, to listen to nineteenth-century miners and fishermen was to hear the same themes. John Brophy, who grew up in the coal mines of western Pennsylvania and learned his trade alongside his father, believed that "one of the great satisfactions that a miner had . . . [was] that he was his own boss within his workplace." Informal work rules and pride "inclined [a miner] to lose face with his fellow workmen if he misses his turn because of poor workmanship."

"The miner in my day," Brophy went on, "was aware that all knowledge didn't start with his generation." Miners before him had experienced what he had, and "had passed this knowledge on to their children, and their children had passed it on." Coming from four generations of English miners on one side of his family, Brophy had a "strong sense of pride" in this inheritance.[14]

This sense of connectedness with the past created what Charles Sabel characterized as a craftsman "proud of his fellowship with his companions whose skill he respects."[15] It was clearly perpetuated by an oral tradition that recounted stories and folklore that showcased values of independence, competence, and pride.

Listening to such stories led James Connolly to remark that if one hung around Fishermen's Corner or the Master Mariners' Hall long enough, one could come to believe "that the main interests of [Gloucester's] people were not so much the catching and marketing of fish from the banks as they were the building and racing home of fast fishing schooners."[16] A cursory observation of fo'c'sle yarning seemed to bear him out.

One fisherman recalled that, as a boy in the early 1880s, he went mackerel seining with his dad aboard the *Astoria*. It was there that he learned about the famed *Sarah H. Prior* and her skipper Tom McLaughlin. The crew was fond of yarning about both. The *Prior*, they declared, "was the ablest vessel to carry sail in a blow, and the smartest sailer by the wind in a fresh breeze." Of McLaughlin, they said that he was not only a smart fisherman, but a great sail master as well. Many times he would turn for home with a hold full of haddock and the wind "blowing a heavy nor'wester." "With a long hard beat ahead of him . . . he would set her 'four-lowers' and drive her for all she was worth."[17]

Every fisherman had heard the stories countless times before, but never seemed to tire of listening to them, or recounting them himself. Charlie

Harty was known among the fishermen as "the greatest man to trim and sail a vessel out o' Gloucester." Reportedly, he loved nothing better than sailing, even to the point of missing meals to stay at the wheel of his vessel during a race with one of his rivals in the seining fleet.

Joe Silva, a young immigrant from the Azores, was captain of the *Governor Russell* when he refused to douse sail when challenged by Maurice Whalen of the *Harry L. Belden*. It was blowing "like stink," and the helmsman asked Silva when they should take in the main. Silva got a piece of chalk, walked to the weather side, and made a mark about a foot from the rail. "There," he said. "When she rolls down to there call me." With that he went below, having won the nickname "Roll Down Joe."[18]

Nor was Silva the only one who reveled in the glory that came from flying every stitch of canvas. Skippers won nicknames for such incidents all the time. Captain Gippern of the *Hesperis,* for example, was known as "Strings," because he had once been quoted as saying, "My canvas will be all strings before I'll take it down."[19]

Even the *Atlantic Fisherman,* the self-proclaimed "home paper of the fishermen," devoted space to fo'c'sle gossip. As late as September 1922, for example, readers learned that Captain "Paddy" Mack, of the recently launched *Mahaska,* had sent word to the South Boston Fish Pier that his craft was the fastest in Nova Scotia. Mack boasted that he had "whipped" *Bluenose* to windward "each time they came together in anything like a breeze."[20] Not to be outdone, Captain Albert Pico, of the *Elizabeth Howard,* arrived in Boston on November 25, 1922, after a record run of 350 miles in thirty-one hours.[21]

At the heart of all these stories was not so much an obsession with "building and racing fast fishing boats" as valuing those things necessary to making a living. Middle-class readers of Connolly's stories might be enthralled by tales of derring-do, but, to the fishing captain and his crew, the ability to carry sail and win races home from the Banks was an economic imperative.

Stories of successful races almost always ended with a discussion of the crew's take as a result of the victory. The oft-repeated stories about Sol Jacobs's determination and grit were usually told to explain why he was the number one highline skipper except for a year or two in the mid-1880s.[22]

Captain Al Miller loved to tell the story of when he beat Marty Welch and the *Lucania,* despite having his foretopsail and balloon jib carried away. The first into market, he got the buyers to pay ten cents a pound, selling his whole catch of 60,000 pounds for $6000, or $152 share per man.[23] Races made reputations because they tested a skipper's skills, and that, when all was said and done, translated into money.

Still there was more to it than that. There was a state of mind, an ephemeral longing for something larger than self that most fishermen understood instinctively. The Portuguese called it *saudade.*[24] For Lunenburgers, it was *sehnsucht.*[25] Whatever one called it, the feeling was tied to the vessel and her combination of beauty and function, and was especially strong among the fishing captains.

To a skipper, his vessel was his livelihood, but she was also his protection in stormy and unpredictable seas. That she was weatherly and fast endeared the schooner to her master for practical reasons. That she could have these qualities while simultaneously being beautiful melted his soul. Fishing captains were, as one contemporary described Clayt Morrissey, skipper of the 1922 racer *Henry Ford*, "hard as nails, determined, good natured."[26] Yet, they could become "kinda sentimental when it came to [their] vessels," as Angus Walters, feisty captain of the Canadian champion *Bluenose*, put it.[27]

There was a unique bond between man and vessel that could be understood by only a few outside the master mariners' fraternity. Certainly, the sense of *saudade* helps explain the outpouring of anger from fishing captains that accompanied L. Francis Herreshoff's scathing critique of the Gloucester schooner in 1922. Coming on the heels of a heated debate the previous year about what constituted a "bona fide fishing vessel," Herreshoff's arrogance rankled many skippers who were tired of yachtsmen and their know-it-all attitude.

Writing to the *Atlantic Fisherman*, the famed yacht designer noted that it was a shame:

> . . . that in the years gone by so little paint was used on the frames and inside planking of Gloucester schooners as they were being built!
> . . . Now they are rotten in the bilge and are the nightmares of the insurance companies, who know if they touch bottom but once, their whole keel will fall out, as most of them are only held together with Portland cement. No wonder the average age of the fishing schooner is only seven years! No wonder there are so many widows in Gloucester and no wonder it is hard to get people to put their money into such death traps!
> . . . It certainly is a pity that so little pride is taken in the Gloucester schooners of today by their crews. . . .[28]

Whether his critique of the vessels was valid or not is irrelevant. Herreshoff had grossly miscalculated the degree of pride among the Gloucestermen. Over the course of the next two months, letters condemning Herreshoff's ignorance and pointing to the stellar record of the fishing schooner poured in.[29] Captain George H. Peeples, president of the Gloucester Master Mariners' Association, wrote, "Is it possible there are men on our Atlantic Seaboard who know so little about the Gloucester fishing schooner? If there are, it is well to inform them that the Maine- and Massachusetts-designed and built fishing schooner is not only the best constructed, but the finest sea boat in the world." Peeples cited several examples of the extraordinary performance and ability of Gloucester vessels, concluding that such a litany was no doubt pointless.

We could tell Mr. Herreshoff of 12-ton boats loaded with ice weathering 80 mile [per hour] hurricanes without losing a rope yarn—but, of course, he would not understand.

We could also tell him of racing from Bay of Islands in vessels loaded decks to the water and making good time at that. . . .

No, Francis, there is nothing the matter with our Gloucester schooners. No need of gas motors to enable them to swing off or tack. I have seen them turn that trick in a whole gale under foresail alone.

Other letters picked up and elaborated on these themes. Pointing to the countless songs and stories written about Gloucester fishermen, one writer mused whether such widespread interest would have been shown "if the 'Gloucester schooner' had not been the wonderful vessel she is? A type capable of weathering any gale on the seven seas that ever blew; a vessel to always attract the eye and hold the attention of 'men who go down to the sea in ships' in any port she may happen to drop anchor; such is the Gloucester schooner and more."

Peeples's letter especially hit on a theme long present in fishermen's folklore: the superiority of the Gloucester fishing schooner under "real racing conditions." Yachts were fast, but only in fair weather. When a twenty-three-knot breeze could cancel a race, as it did in the 1920 America's Cup Series, one had to wonder about the seaworthiness of the yachts that men like Herreshoff built, or the courage of those who sailed them.

Although no fishing skipper could have become a member of a fancy yacht club, few if any would have wanted to. They were members of their own fraternity, and no yachtsmen need apply. This reverse classism was one of the reasons fishermen took great pride in yarning about the time that Tom McLaughlin of the *Sarah H. Prior* beat a yacht on the run into Boston.

The story goes that, as the *Prior* neared Cape Cod, she fell in with a big schooner yacht bound for Boston. With the wind fresh, the yacht was under single reefs, while the *Prior* had her four lowers set. McLaughlin decided to have some fun. He sailed up across the yacht's stern, then passed her to windward.

With the *Prior* about half a mile ahead, McLaughlin spun his wheel up, jibed, and sailed under the yacht's lee. Back astern of her, McLaughlin tacked, crossed her wake, and passed her again to weather. Now a mile ahead of the yacht, he announced to his crew, "I've heard a lot o' talk 'bout that yacht being a great sailer! She's no sailer, for the *Prior* can sail rings 'round 'er!"

By the time the yacht got in, *Prior* had been sitting alongside T Wharf for awhile. The yachtsman was furious. He went up to his ship broker's office on State Street, ready to sell his vessel. When asked why, he replied, "I don't want any yacht that a fisherman can beat as badly as we got beaten today."

When asked what fisherman, the yachtsman replied, "The *Sarah H. Prior.*"

"Pshaw!" the broker retorted. "You don't need to feel badly about that, for the *Sarah H. Prior* is called the ablest fisherman in a blow, and the fastest sailer by the wind, out of Boston."

Still, the yachtsman was inconsolable, and he sold his vessel.[30]

Although the tale was likely exaggerated, as was much of fishermen's lore, it pointed up the lesson that Peeples tried to teach Herreshoff nearly forty years later: Gloucester schooners could outsail any vessel anywhere in the world. Oft-told stories like that about McLaughlin's triumph, and his own experience aboard countless fishing schooners, gave Peeples all the evidence he needed to prove his case.

In 1922, the *Atlantic Fisherman* published a poem that, like their tales, captured the spirit and code by which the fishermen lived. Entitled "The Fisherman's Way," it observed:

> The rules, whut there is, are fair, and square,
> "Each man is expected to do his share."
> Ef he don't wa'al, sumbody parts his hair
> For that is the fisherman's way
> . . . .
> They don't stop to figger out which is worst,
> To swamp and go down er die of thirst,
> But say "Damn the man thet gives in first."
> Fer that is the fisherman's way.[31]

The fisherman's competitive spirit transcended most everything he did. In addition to the money, fishing meant a rush of adrenaline unequaled by most experiences ashore. Among the mackerel seiners, for example, there was just as much excitement in a race of seine boats to capture a school of fish as between two schooners on the homeward run.

Raymond McFarland, who went fishing with his uncle, Captain John McFarland, aboard the *Yosemite*, vividly described one such contest.[32] The *Yosemite, Senator Lodge,* and another schooner were idly jogging back and forth one morning, when a cry from *Yosemite's* masthead aroused everyone on her deck. There was a school, about a mile and a half away! All hands leaped into action, and in an instant the seine boat was away. However, Captain John Mills, aboard the *Lodge,* was faster. His watch had spotted the school first, and he was already away by the time *Yosemite's* crew was scrambling with their oars.

Aboard *Yosemite,* the cook yelled after the men in the seine boat, "You fellows ain't going to let John Mills get that school, are you?" The words were unnecessary, for as McFarland recalled:

> No man at the oars, especially when a keen race is on, needs to be urged to his best. Surely, on this morning, we had no wish to be reminded of the

power in our rival's boat. The seine-boats were fairly leaping from the quiet waters as they rushed towards a common goal. . . . We did not know our own power and endurance. Competition is a revealer and quickener of one's spirit.

As both boats raced on, the captains stood tall in their sterns, eyes fixed on the school, guiding the boats with a sure hand toward their quest. Their quiet confidence and steady leadership inspired their crews. "We bowed over the ash blades," McFarland remembered, "we straightened our backs as one man, fairly lifting the bow on the seine-boat clear of the water. What a thrill to feel the arm muscles bulge into full roundness when we snapped the oars against our bodies! We were answering the challenge of John Mills."

With only a furlong to go, the boats closed on each other fast. Mills, to starboard of the *Yosemite*'s boat, crossed her bow, clearing it by barely a boat length. *Lodge*'s boat got there first, but Captain Mills had miscalculated. To set his seine net, he had to turn his boat and maneuver into position. Captain McFarland had kept his boat on a course that required no such adjustment. As he yelled, "Let go your twine!" the net hit the water, and the race was over.

As Mills's crew rested on their oars and cursed the *Yosemite* men, the latter bent to their work with a passion. As McFarland tells it:

Gone was fatigue, we were kings of the sea! . . . We had won a great race fairly, against the best men that Gloucester could furnish. That was honor enough for us and five generations of descendants.

Even more mundane activities, like baiting trawl, brought out the fishermen's competitive edge. In 1914 there were some who wanted to hold a contest on Boston's T Wharf to see if Gloucester, Boston, Provincetown, or Portland fishermen were the fastest baiters. The average fisherman could bait a tub of trawl with five hundred hooks in thirty minutes in a cold hold. Some, it was reputed, could do it in twenty. Although an official contest never took place, there were doubtless many unofficial ones held between fishermen on their own vessels and between crews of rival schooners.[33]

A hard-fought victory, in a race between two seine boats, while baiting up, or between two schooners on the run to market, had its rewards, but the satisfaction was often made sweeter in the retelling. Small wonder that the gossip on Fishermen's Corner, at the Master Mariners' Hall, and in the fo'c'sle was peppered with stories of competition. Indeed, it was the fishermen's oral traditions that fostered a sense of fellowship that Charles Sabel identified as common among all skilled workers. Quite simply, fishermen's stories perpetuated a value system, kept alive traditions, and defined a sense of self. In short, it created a unique working-class culture, as distinct and real as that of any other skilled group.

Of course, as with workers elsewhere in the nineteenth century, community patterns did much to reinforce the fishermen's culture. The fishermen and their stories were so much a part of Gloucester's social fabric, for example, that even those not directly connected to the fisheries were able to articulate the Gloucestermen's sense of themselves. Why else would the Master Mariners have asked Arthur L. Millett, a Gloucester newspaper man, to write the foreword to the Master Mariners' Association's *Yearbook?* Waxing eloquent, Millett summarized the commonly held view of the Gloucester fishing captain:

> The Master Mariner on the deck of his craft is in his real element. Here he matches his wits and judgment against the most exasperating calms and the worst hurricanes that the elements can deal out and meets these vicissitudes with a resourcefulness unparalleled. Generally he is the winner. Sometimes, sad to say, too often perhaps, the strength of man can not prevail against the awful power of the elements, and having done his best, he takes the inevitable like the *MAN* he is. . . . His judgment is uncanny at times. He is always alert and no opportunity for a "big trip" is missed. We are all familiar with the hustler who never loses a chance to "set," who "drives her" home in the dead of winter against a howling nor'wester and strikes the big market. Nobody begrudges him the golden shower that rewards his efforts. He has earned every nickel of it.[34]

In Gloucester, the fishermen, and especially the master mariners, were heroes. Without them the city, quite simply, would not exist. The master mariners were well aware of that fact, although the average fisherman may not always have been so sure, especially when he had been arrested on a "drunk and disorderly" charge.

Even so, community dynamics in Gloucester were an outgrowth of the waterfront culture that had created the city. As such, fishermen, and in particular, the captains, were able to identify themselves as more than mere employees. They were neighbors, business associates, and even friends, equal in their own minds, at least, to the vessel owners and nouveau riche of Eastern Point.

2

Class, Community, and the Fishermen of Gloucester

As INDUSTRIALIZATION CAUSED MASSIVE DISLOCATIONS IN AMERICAN SOCIETY during the late-nineteenth century, Gloucester seemed a peaceful throwback to an earlier time. It is probably no coincidence that many of the movers and shakers of the new industrial era escaped to Cape Ann in the summer months to renew themselves. From the romanticism associated with the white-sailed fishing schooners entering and leaving the harbor, to the fishermen, who, in Rudyard Kipling's words, had become "used to all manner of questions from those idle imbeciles called summer boarders," Gloucester had much to recommend it. Ironically, though, the fishermen's culture that so enchanted many affluent visitors stood as a significant pocket of resistance to the industrial order that they were helping to create.

Indeed, community relations in Gloucester reflected patterns identified by Herbert Gutman, who showed that industrialism and its values were resisted in small towns dominated by one or two industries.[1] Making up a large proportion of a town's total population, industrial laborers shopped in the small stores owned by the community's middle class and lived close to them. Whereas in large metropolitan areas workers were dealt with as factors of production, in small towns daily contact and personal relationships mitigated against such attitudes, predisposing small businessmen to see workers simply as fellow citizens, and to treat them accordingly.

In Gloucester, such events as vessel launchings and trial trips brought skippers, fishermen, vessel owners, builders, and even the occasional yachtsman together on a fairly regular basis. Although their motivations for participating in these activities obviously differed, each in his own way was drawn by an interest in boats and the water. When a highly touted schooner was involved, interest was especially high.

Fredonia's launching on April 16, 1889, was typical. A large crowd flocked to Essex to see her take the plunge, including what the *Gloucester Times* termed "a barge load from the Master Mariners' Association."[2] That Charlie Harty, one of the most respected of Gloucester's skippers, was to be her master naturally added to the general interest in the new vessel. More than that, though, *Fredonia* was a Ned Burgess boat. Burgess had designed three America's Cup winners between 1885 and 1887, and his *Carrie E. Phillips* had already changed the standards by which fishing schooners were measured.

As an added bonus, a new vessel for George E. Thurston was sitting on the ways at Arthur D. Story's Yard ready to be launched. Anticipation ran high as people milled about chatting, excited by the prospects of seeing two schooners hit the water within minutes of each other. With a shout of "Here comes the tug boat!" shipyard crews knocked out the keel blocks on the two schooners and settled them into their cradles.[3] All was ready for the christening. Crews stood by ready to cut through the blocks holding the vessels on the ways.

Over in the Moses Adams Yard, where *Fredonia* sat, the foreman ordered, "Stop at your first mark!" With that the ship's carpenters began to work, sawing to the first mark on the ways. Then there was a break, and then the next command: "Take your second mark!" This time the men cut to within an inch of the block's end.

The tension in the air became palpable. Clenching his fists, the foreman yelled, "Saw away!" With a loud crack, *Fredonia* began sliding down the ways, and, with that, pandemonium broke out. As a champagne bottle was cracked across her bow, the Guy Brothers Minstrel Band began to play, and the assembled crowd cheered, "There she goes!"

At 11:45 A.M., she settled into the Essex River. The tug that was to tow her to Gloucester to be rigged let go a resounding blast from her whistle. Two minutes later, the schooner over at the Story Yard took the plunge and received a similar reception.

Launchings were commonplace, but when vessels like *Fredonia* were involved, they became local happenings. With schooners the talk of the town in Gloucester anyway, waterfront sages were always alert to those that promised to be special or unique.[4]

Such interest made trial trips big community events as well. The wives and children of everyone affiliated with a vessel got dressed in their Sunday best and were on board for the occasion. If the schooner was highly touted, prominent citizens turned out in force, including a goodly number of the master mariners who happened to be in port. When this happened, the Gloucester Cornet Band was usually on hand to add to the festivities.

Although launchings and trial trips were often an excuse for a party, they also generated gossip about vessels that made reputations. Except for the yachtsmen and summer residents, whose interest in such events grew from their passion for boats or their penchant for local color, most city residents—regardless of class—had an economic stake in the doings on the waterfront. Paid on shares, fishermen wanted to crew aboard fast boats with highline skippers, who, for their part, wanted to captain first-rate vessels. Owners, naturally, wanted the best men and schooners because that meant profit.

This created a commonality of interest that permeated the fo'c'sle and defined life ashore. Because everyone in the society had a vested interest in the same industry, class differences, although relevant, were ameliorated by the personal relations that informed community life. As in Gutman's towns, the economic fortunes of middle-class citizens were tied to that of ordinary workers in such a way that cross-class empathy—if not always understanding—was possible. This was especially true for the fishing captains.

The relationship of vessel owners and skippers is particularly instructive in this regard. As a means of attracting and keeping good men, it was common practice for owners to build a boat for what Thomas J. Carroll, president of Gorton-Pew Fisheries Company, termed "worthy" individuals.[5] Good skippers, those who could bring in good money, were offered shares in their vessel.

Since the captain and crew were paid based on what the vessel produced, partnership for the skipper meant additional revenue. He not only received his cut as the captain, but partook of an owner's share as well. These arrangements led to long-term associations between fish companies and their captains, and no doubt encouraged a sense of mutual understanding and respect not evident in industries like iron and steel that were leading the way in redefining labor-management relations in the late-nineteenth and early-twentieth centuries. Certainly, the job structure that persisted in the fishing industry was reminiscent of an older, more personalized style that existed in many industries before the Civil War.

Patterns of work were reinforced by the old New England work ethic, which seemed to infect nearly all those affiliated with the region's oldest industry. No doubt the size of Gloucester and Essex, where nearly everyone knew each other and were engaged in similar pursuits, contributed to creating a shared perspective. Whatever the reason, people in Essex and Gloucester went at life the same way.

Arthur D. Story, one of Essex's most successful shipbuilders, for example, ran his yard much as a fishing captain would his schooner. As his son recalled:

> He was not a hard man to work for, and ran the business with as few words as possible. He didn't interfere with a man who knew his work and was doing it, asking only a good day's work for a day's pay. There was not a time, however, even though he didn't say much, that he was not aware of just what every man was doing. He held the theory . . . that he should only have to tell a man once what he wanted done.[6]

Those men who did their jobs well, either in the shipyard or aboard ship, were noticed, and if they had any ambition, they could usually rise. Such was the case with Frank E. Davis. A native Gloucesterite and the son and grandson of fishermen, Davis began his career as a fisherman but aspired to more.[7]

In 1885 he established the Frank E. Davis Fish Company as a mail-order business. With a flair for the dramatic, a commitment to high quality, and a belief in fair dealing, Davis turned his fledgling firm into a national, and eventually an international, corporation. In the process, he managed to send his son, Arthur, to the Massachusetts Institute of Technology, and he successfully ran for mayor of Gloucester. Still, he was never far from his roots. With his firm headquartered down on Central Wharf, Davis had regular contact with the fishermen and skippers who visited his shop.

If Davis was a sort of Horatio Alger, he was not alone. The rewards for conforming to dominant community values were open to Americans and immigrants alike. Men from the Canadian Maritime Provinces, Scandinavia, Ireland, and the Portuguese Azores often became captains and business leaders in Gloucester. Unlike their counterparts who found work in New England's textile mills and shoe factories, these immigrants brought skills with them from the old country that were readily marketable in the fisheries. The Irish of Fingal Coast had long experience in fishing and its related businesses before coming to the United States. Likewise, Nova Scotians, Newfoundlanders, Azoreans, and Scandinavians had been fishermen for generations before immigrating.

Because of a shortage of American labor after 1850, skilled immigrants filled a real need in the fisheries. For a variety of reasons, including an unwillingness by American fathers to let their sons go fishing, an increased availability of public education, and a rise in industrial jobs, only 58% of Massachusetts fishermen in 1885 had been born in the United States. By 1890, 53% of New England's fishermen were British provincials or Canadians, 20% were Scandinavians, 15% were native-born Americans, and 2% were Portuguese.[8]

Some of the Portuguese rose quickly. Manuel Domingoes, for example, came to America from Pico, in the Azores, not knowing how to read or write. "All he knew," his son later recalled, "was fishing."[9] Finding friends on "Portygee Hill," he was able to make contacts and get a site with the famed Portuguese skipper Frank Cooney, one of the fleet's highliners. Over the years, Domingoes proved himself a hard worker and an able seaman, and he eventually became a schooner captain.

In 1914, after years of command, he was asked to head up United Fisheries, which had been started two years earlier by a group of Portuguese skippers and fishermen who had pooled their resources to organize a vessel supply firm. Domingoes sold his boat and ran the company until 1947, when he retired and turned the reigns over to his son. Like other Portuguese immigrants to Gloucester, his aspirations had been simple—to own a home and provide for his family. Becoming one of the city's leading businessmen was an unexpected fringe benefit.

Joe Mesquita, another Azorean, was also an influential citizen, serving as a bridge between the Portuguese and Anglo communities.[10] Indeed, he was equally accessible to both. It was common knowledge that when a civic organization in Gloucester needed the help or cooperation of the folks up on "Portygee Hill," they saw Mesquita first. Likewise, newly arrived immigrants who needed a job could count on Mesquita to find them work.

Mesquita's influence came from his status among Gloucester's skippers. He was one of the most popular members of the Master Mariners' Association. Often yarning late into the night, he kept his audience spellbound for hours on end. A card shark, he was always in demand at the tables up in the Mariners' rooms.

Certainly, the respect that he commanded beyond the Portuguese community had much to do with the widespread enthusiasm with which the Crowning Service was received in Gloucester. After a steamer ran down his *Mary P. Mesquita* in 1901, Mesquita decided to bring the ceremony, popular in the Azores, to Gloucester in thanksgiving for his crew's deliverance. In towns where ethnic lines were more rigidly drawn, such a decision would hardly have merited notice beyond "Portygee Hill." When Mesquita sent to Portugal for a silver crown, however, he knew that he could count on the support not only of his own men, but of his fellow captains and their crews, many of them Nova Scotians, Newfoundlanders, Scandinavians, and Americans.

In July 1901, while the ceremony was taking place back in the old country, Mesquita and his fourteen crewmen marched through the streets of Gloucester in their yellow oilskins and sou'westers, ending their parade at the altar of the Church of Our Lady of Good Voyage. As each man knelt in turn, the crown was held over his head while the choir sang the *Magnificat*. The process was repeated fourteen times, once for each surviving member of the *Mary P. Mesquita*'s crew.

The assembled crowd that morning included a broad cross section of society. Summer residents from Manchester and Pigeon Cove, artists from Rocky Neck, and businessmen and officials from Gloucester and Boston mixed freely with master mariners and fishermen. After the ceremony, a feast was held, lasting through the afternoon and into the evening. Everyone ate his fill, and after supper an auction was held to benefit the poor. Finally, lots were drawn to determine who would carry the crown in next year's procession.

The ceremony became an annual event in Gloucester. Thousands of people turned out each year to watch the pageantry of color, flags, religious banners, and marching bands escort a long line of fishing captains and the crown bearer to the church, and then partake of the good food and camaraderie of the afternoon feast. Although the service was no doubt good for

Gloucester tourism, its focus and intent remained religious, working-class, and ethnic. Summer residents and Boston elites could attend because it was fun, but in so doing they rubbed elbows with fishermen, went to Catholic Mass, and ate *lingica* (a type of Portuguese sausage). In short, they encountered Gloucester's Portuguese community on its own terms.

Granted, the interactions that occurred during the ceremony were brief and superficial. However, they formed impressions that went a long way in shaping community dynamics. Having partaken of Portuguese hospitality, middle- and upper-class citizens found it hard to negatively stigmatize these immigrants, even if they still tended to stereotype them. Captain Charlton L. Smith spoke for many when he wrote:

> A "PORTYGEE" is a natural born fisherman. Indeed, many who are in the know . . . claim that he is not equaled at that arduous calling by the men of any other race. . . .
> The thrift, honor and good citizenship of these adopted sons is common knowledge to any who have visited much or have lived at our fishing ports.[11]

The Portuguese captains especially helped build connections within the ethnically diverse Gloucester community, not so much by assimilating as by proving their strength and competency as fishermen, businessmen, and citizens.

The Portuguese were not the only ones for whom this formula worked. The vast majority of the city's fishermen and schooner captains were from Nova Scotia and Newfoundland. Sol Jacobs, the so-called "King of the Mackerel Seiners," was born in Twillingate, Newfoundland. Marty Welch, who won the first *Halifax Herald* series in 1920, was a native of Digby County, Nova Scotia. Alden Geele, who reportedly landed more big trips of salt fish than any other skipper in history, hailed from Shelburne, Nova Scotia.[12]

Because they brought a skill that was readily transferable to the American fishing industry, the so-called "white washed Yankees" of the Maritimes were able to assimilate into American culture without major adaptation of their old country folkways. Unlike other ethnic groups who had to confront the harsh realities of urban industrial America, the Nova Scotians found life in Gloucester little different from what they had left behind, except for greater economic opportunity. Because of the mobility implicit in their jobs, moreover, their ties to home remained stronger than those of most other immigrants, who were denied regular physical contact with folks in the old country.

Men like Mesquita, Welch, and Jacobs succeeded in New England's fisheries because they were able to fit into its culture. Their background made it easy at a time when a labor shortage necessitated their presence. Their values, attitudes, and expectations dovetailed nicely with those of the dominant Yankee culture, while the shared interest in a big catch promoted by the shares system encouraged their acceptance and, in many cases, their upward mobility.

Gloucester's self-made men had their feet in two worlds. They were at ease talking to bankers as well as fishermen, not only because they had to to be successful, but also because their experience transcended both realities. If master mariners were highly skilled workers, many were also businessmen.

Because Gloucester was a small town, its business community was small and interconnected. Businessmen were expected to be leaders, with a sense of responsibility for, and understanding of, community expectations and values. It is true, of course, that few if any fishing captains were invited out to affluent Eastern Point, where John J. Pew and Nathaniel Gorton built sprawling homes, and where it was possible to hobnob with the likes of Henry Clark Rouse, the railroad tycoon and yachtsman. Certainly, it is doubtful if Benjamin A. Smith, who later headed up Gorton-Pew, ever asked members of the Master Mariners' Association to join his wealthy friends for an outing aboard his yacht. However, in their workaday world, Gorton, Pew, and Smith had to deal with Marty Welch, Manuel Domingoes, and all the rest.

Occasionally, business relationships spilled over into other areas. The water, after all, was not only where most people made their living, it was where they played. Until at least the late-nineteenth century, it was common throughout the United States for working people to organize "yacht clubs" to race all manner of small watercraft. Amateur yachtsmen, professional watermen, and hired captains and crews mixed it up with bricklayers, carpenters, and salesmen, with a minimum of rules to spoil the fun.

In 1896, the East Gloucester Yacht Club was organized, continuing the tradition of what one researcher has termed "blue collar yachting."[13] Boatbuilder and motor mechanic Percy Wheeler; Captain Albert Gosbee, a carpenter and the Humane Society's lifesaving chief; and Freeman H. Brown, a fish skinner, were the club's chief organizers.[14] Wheeler was elected commodore and Gosbee vice commodore. Archibald Fenton, boatbuilder and designer, was designated fleet captain, and Scott Call, a spar maker, was elected secretary. Other founding members included carriage maker and ship smith Alex McCurdy, policeman John G. Mehlman, woodworker Joseph Merchant, mason Sidney Pomoroy, carpenter Horace Sargent, J. Warren Wonson, deputy collector of customs, and Melvin Haskell. The club's headquarters was the old fish house on Wonson Wharf at Smoky Point.

Club-sponsored events were simple and fun. The first official cruise ended at Plum Island with a clambake. Evening sails and cruises lasting anywhere from three days to two weeks supplemented regularly scheduled regattas. The annual Chowder Race ended each season, with Officer Mehlman whipping up large helpings of his famous fish chowder and steamed clams. With an initiation fee of one dollar and annual dues of two, club membership was open to anyone. By 1900, the club had fifty members, a curious mix of local working men, wealthy East Point residents, their children, and summer people. The only bond among them was a shared interest in boats.

Opportunities for such cross-class associations were many and varied in Gloucester. For example, a fondness for the fisherman-type schooner, which was reputed to be faster and more weatherly than the seagoing yacht, led many yachtsmen to build boats modeled on fishing schooner designs.[15] Visiting the Tarr and James Yard in Essex to supervise construction of their vessels, yachtsmen often had the opportunity to see firsthand what went into construction of a fishing schooner, and, on occasion, to chat with fishing skippers overseeing the finishing touches on their crafts.[16]

Sometimes relationships developed through a third party. Such was the case with Captain Charlie Harty, who got J. Malcolm Forbes to build *Fredonia* for him. In keeping with the old adage, "It's who you know," both Harty and Forbes knew Tom McManus, the father of the fishermen's races. All three had a keen interest in building fast boats, though for different reasons.

Forbes had organized the syndicate that commissioned Ned Burgess to design *Puritan*, the 1885 America's Cup winner, and her successors in 1886 and 1887, *Mayflower* and *Volunteer*.[17] McManus's family had been a driving force in developing innovative and fast fishing schooners since the 1860s, and Tom's brother Charley had made *Puritan*'s sails. When Tom conceived the idea of an organized fishermen's race in 1886, he had gone to Forbes for financial backing. McManus's shop on Commercial Wharf was, in the words of one historian, "a general clearing house for all news of fishing and yachting. Here were to be met the captains of fishing vessels . . . the yacht skippers . . . [and other] notables [like] D. J. Lawlor, Arthur Story, Mils Wood, 'Nels' Sibley, John McPhail. . . ."[18]

For his part, Harty, like many Gloucester skippers, was bothered that, because of the McManus-inspired innovations, the fleet's fastest boats—the *John H. McManus*, *Sarah H. Prior*, and *Carrie E. Phillips*—all hailed from Boston. He and fishing captain turned designer Mel McClain, who had designed Harty's current command, the *I. J. Merritt, Jr.*, issued a challenge in early 1888 to race either the *McManus* or the *Prior* (neither wanted any part of the just-launched *Phillips*). After Harty and McManus met, the two men broadened the challenge to the entire fleet. Having helped sponsor the first fishermen's race in 1886, Forbes naturally jumped at the chance to serve as referee for the race.[19]

With all these ties in place, it was not hard for Harty to get Forbes to underwrite the building of *Fredonia*, especially after he agreed that she should first race the Boston pilot boat *Hesper*, which Forbes had been interested in beating for quite some time. So it was that *Fredonia* was launched flying the Eastern Yacht Club burgee, and, after beating *Hesper*, took Forbes for a cruise to the Azores before Harty had the chance to take her fishing. It was a small enough price for Harty to pay to get a first-rate vessel.[20]

If McManus was a link between the fishermen and the elite of his day, so too was James Connolly. Indeed, it was Connolly's influence that brought famed sail carrier Tommie Bohlin and yachtsman Dr. Lewis A. Stimson together in a long-term partnership.[21] In 1905, German Emperor Wilhelm II offered a cup for a transatlantic race. The New York Yacht Club accepted the challenge, announcing that the race would be open to any yacht of more than 100 tons. She could be any size above that, of any design or rig, though no time allowance would be made for vessels of different classes. Whether they realized it or not, the New York Yacht Club was setting out the conditions for a fishermen's race—a boat-for-boat showdown, winner take all.

Stimson's schooner yacht, *Fleur-de-Lys*, was only 92 tons, but he wanted to race her under the command of "a real sea-going captain," hoping that she would show well. The New York Yacht Club amended its restrictions, and all that was left was for Stimson to find his captain. At a meeting with Connolly, arranged by the editor of *Scribner's Magazine*, the doctor laid out his criteria. "I'm looking for one of your sail carriers," he said, "somebody who won't want to tie up his mainsail every time he sees a black cloud on the horizon. He should be a clever sailing master also."

Connolly immediately thought of Maurice Whalen and Tommie Bohlin. With Whalen out fishing, he approached Bohlin. The response he got was predictable. Making a face, Bohlin incredulously asked, "Yachting?"

Connolly did a hard sell, explaining that Stimson was a regular guy and the *Fleur-de-Lys* was a Burgess boat designed on a fisherman's model. Except for her yachting skylight and the binnacle stand on her quarter deck, Connolly argued, she could pass as a real fishing boat.

Connolly's argument did the trick, and Bohlin took the job. He drove the *Fleur-de-Lys* as hard as she had ever been driven in her life. She averaged 12½ knots for three days on end, just under 13 knots for two days and two nights, and 9¾ knots for the entire passage. Although the three-masted schooner *Atlantic* won the race, *Fleur-de-Lys* broke the sailing record for yachts of her size, making the crossing in 14 days, 9 hours, and 43 minutes.

The race confirmed Stimson's stereotype of the Gloucester fishing captain generally, and his admiration for Bohlin personally. Although Bohlin and his fellow skippers usually did not cotton to yachtsmen, Stimson's appreciation of boats and his down-to-earth manner allowed Bohlin to make an exception in this case. Another reason was that Stimson was willing to pay him good money to do what he loved. From 1905 until his death in 1910, Bohlin was on Stimson's payroll. Every summer the captain and doctor went yachting. In the winter, Bohlin took a leave of absence at full pay and returned to fishing.

Such incidents suggest that the world created by Rudyard Kipling in *Captains Courageous* was not so far from the truth. Intentional or not, there was a fitting symbolism in the way Harvey Cheyne, Jr., ended up on the *We're Here*. Falling from a steamer bound for Europe, the young man was plucked from the sea and thrown in among fishermen, who disabused him of his pretensions and showed him the value of hard work and self-respect. In real life, the summer residents and industrial and financial titans who lived on Eastern Point had likewise fallen into the midst of the Gloucestermen after the Civil War.[22]

When Thomas Niles died, a syndicate known as the Eastern Point Associates bought his large farm from the trustees of his estate. They subdivided the property, laid out streets, and developed plans for building a vacation hotel. Eastern Point would be a haven, simultaneously a quaint residential summer resort and a permanent home for some of the wealthiest oilmen, financiers, and railroad magnates in the country, men very much like Harvey Cheyne, Sr.

Both Cheynes, Jr. and Sr., learned much about what really counted from the fishermen. Perhaps so too did the Eastern Point crowd that interacted with their neighbors at the East Gloucester Yacht Club, at vessel launchings, at crowning ceremonies, and at any number of other community events.

Yet, as in real life, it was a two-way street. If Captain Disko Troop helped make a man of Harvey, Jr., then Harvey's dad returned the favor by helping Disko's son get a spot aboard one of his tea clippers. The partnership was one of mutual benefit, made easier because Harvey, Jr., and his father had proven themselves regular guys. In a very real way, there are shades here of the relationship between Charles Harty and J. Malcolm Forbes, or of Tommie Bohlin and Dr. Stimson.

Beyond the symbolism, Kipling clearly understood the routine of shipboard life, accurately describing the hardship, camaraderie, friendly rivalry between crews, and the yarning of the fo'c'sle. His understanding was especially remarkable considering that his only experience aboard a fishing schooner left him seasick. Kipling's *Captains Courageous* suggests just how easy it was for anyone with even half an interest to grasp the fundamentals of the fishermen's culture that so permeated Gloucester life.

None of this is to suggest that Gloucester was some sort of working-class utopia. It was not. Fishing crews experienced a different reality from their captains. In many ways marginalized, crewmen had their own culture, and its rougher aspects were often an affront to polite society. Indeed, if bridges existed between classes and ethnic groups, they were seldom, if ever, crossed by common fishermen.

Average fishermen viewed themselves as simple men, with simple pleasures. They were, in the words of one oldtimer, "rough and ready guys." When they hit shore, they tended to drink a lot, but it was only "a release from working on your nerves all the time while you were out."[23] For some-one who had never been to sea, or survived the rigors of fishing from a dory, it was difficult to appreciate the fishermen's need to blow off steam when they came ashore.

The time of greatest concern was when a large portion of the fleet was in. Then, it was not uncommon for two or three hundred schooners to be in port, unleashing hundreds of crewmen on the city. Each man sought his own diversion. One local resident recalled, "Gloucester made Dodge City in the days of the Old West look tame."[24] A man could get drunk at any number of saloons. From there he might wander over to Rogers or Hancock Street, or maybe head down to the Old Harbor Wharf. As one old captain recalled, "Every house down along here was a whore house. . . . [They'd] call you right in, call you off the streets!"[25]

A freshly paid fisherman after a good trip might have over a hundred dollars in his pocket, making him easy pickings for the denizens of these establishments. Raymond McFarland remembered one time, after the crew of the *Yosemite* received its shares, that a shipmate named Peavers disappeared into "Martha's Joint," never to be heard from again. With the vessel ready to cast off, he was nowhere to be found. When one of the crew told the captain where he had last been seen, the skipper put the man's duffel ashore and went looking for a replacement.[26]

Such behavior appalled Gloucester's pious, and kept its police force busy. If a fisherman were arrested, it was worth noting his profession in the paper, though occupation seemed irrelevant when listing other lawbreakers. This attitude reflected a general assumption that fishermen ashore tended to be troublemakers, and needed to be controlled. Sweeps of the waterfront filled the city's jail on a fairly regular basis, confirming the assumption. Usually the fishermen were drunk and disorderly, though, occasionally, more serious crimes were involved.[27]

One of the more comical "crime waves" perpetrated by fishermen was the pilfering of fruit. Newspapers noted that the return of any large portion of the fleet gave owners of fruit trees "great apprehension." After squandering their wages on tobacco, liquor, and women, fishermen had the audacity to stage midnight raids on the apple trees of decent citizens. Things were only brought under control when the *Cape Ann Advertiser* announced: "The citizens have rigged spring-guns under the fruit trees on their land."[28]

Fortunately, most people in Gloucester sought less drastic solutions to the "fishermen problem." Many civic leaders felt an obligation to do something to redeem the wayward fishermen who frequented their port. For many of the more devout, the fishermen were simply lost souls, far from home and easily tempted by the dens of iniquity along the waterfront.

In the late 1880s, periodic letters to the editor of the *Gloucester Times* extolled the advantages of creating a "fishermen's clubhouse" as a means of promoting temperance.[29] By giving the fishermen someplace to go, and creating a home away from home for those transients from other ports, such a club would keep sailors from going astray. As one writer calling himself "Moral Suasion" concluded, "[L]et us reflect upon the good we all may do by a single act or word. Save the fallen, make strong the weak and so fulfil [sic] the law of Christ." Proposals called for a company of about a hundred well-wishers to build or retrofit an existing building with sleeping facilities, a reading room, bowling alley, rifle gallery, bath, and canteen. Provision would be made for an orchestra and music, and for meals to be served by stewards and waiters. As the writer "Cosmopolitan" put it, "The club house should afford opportunities for fun for those who want it and quiet for those who prefer that."

The dream came true in 1892, with the founding of the Gloucester Fishermen's Institute, just in time for the city's 250th Anniversary celebration. A veritable Who's Who of Gloucester society was behind the enterprise. Reflecting their rationale for creating the Institute, the Rev. Emanuel C. Charlton wrote in the Chaplain's Annual Report:

> The Gloucester Fishermen's Institute . . . is a beacon light of hope and life for the brave men, who by their toil and daring have taken their lives in their hands, while from the ocean's depth they have provided the choicest dainties for our tables, and contributed so largely towards the wealth of our city.
>
> The wise, careful and liberal maintenance of this work will be an undisputable evidence that the folks at home care for the men that toil for them on the sea, and that the Christians, philanthropists, and humanitarians are as wise, prudent, earnest and determined to bless and save the toilers of the deep, as the saloonists, landsharks, and harpies, who systematically, zealously and effectively work without cessation to rob, blast, and destroy them.[30]

This work necessitated making "numerous calls, sometimes in houses of vice and degradation, where no minister or Christian worker has ever entered," reported Charlton in 1894. In an effort to be "the confidential friend of the young and innocent, a loving brother to the erring wanderer, a faithful counselor to those in trouble, a friend to sinners," the chaplain visited the police station each and every Sunday morning.[31]

By 1896, the work continued apace. Pressure from community leaders involved with the Fishermen's Institute led to prohibition and a report of "moral improvement" among the fishermen.[32] In reality, anyone who wanted a drink knew where to find it, usually at one of the "recreation parlors" down on Front Street.[33]

If some of the middle-class morality seemed out of place in the rough-and-tumble world of the fishermen, the Institute still met a need along the waterfront, and so gained friends among the fishermen. Supported by generous donations from summer boarders as well as local residents, the Fishermen's Institute provided nourishing food and snacks, a well-stocked reading room, a navigation school, and regular religious services. It also served as a place to write letters and receive mail. In only its second year, more than 100,000 fishermen visited the Institute, and by 1895 the chaplain complained, "We have entirely outgrown our present quarters, and must make speedy provisions for enlarging our borders."[34]

Such success speaks volumes. Even with their tendency to moralize and preach, and their inability to understand the fishermen's penchant for drinking, supporters of the Fishermen's Institute appreciated enough of the fishermen's condition to develop viable programs to serve them. The community dynamics that brought classes and ethnic groups together so regularly no doubt did much to generate the empathy necessary to make the Institute a priority with many of its wealthy and middle-class patrons. Put simply, even as they condemned the wayward conduct of the fishermen, supporters of the Institute felt an obligation to them that elites in large cities failed to muster for their working classes.

Collectively, vessel launchings, ethnic celebrations, business dealings, and institutions like the East Gloucester Yacht Club and the Fishermen's Institute created a climate that made it easy for Tom McManus to organize community-sponsored fishermen's races in the late-nineteenth century. Indeed, the personal relationships and shared interest in vessels and the water that were necessary to make organized fishermen's races possible had been in place long before McManus conceived the idea.

As with most events in Gloucester, yachtsmen and other elites provided the money to underwrite the cost of racing, but depended on the cooperation of the fishing captains to make them successful. That meant that the races held before 1920 were generally a mixed bag. Gloucester's working-class character, clearly reflective of the realities in Gutman's towns where class and economic structure insulated laborers from the demands of the country's industrial elite, was the reason why.

3

The Early Races, 1886–1913

When tom mcmanus set up the first fishermen's race in 1886, he clearly understood the fishermen's mindset. His family had been fixtures in Boston's market fishery since his father, John McManus, emigrated from Ireland in 1846.[1] Upon his arrival, the elder McManus had worked as a hand on winter cod fishing trips to supplement his income as a journeyman sailmaker. The experience taught him the dangers of life at sea and motivated him to find an alternative to the fast but unstable clipper schooners then in vogue in the fisheries. In 1864, John, his fishing captain brother-in-law Dick Leonard, and designer Dennison J. Lawlor pooled their talents and resources to build *Sylph,* a fast boat with innovative lines that helped transform Boston's Irish fishing fleet.

John continued to dabble in vessel design, taking his sons, including young Tom, on frequent tours of the shipyards, and carefully explaining the intricacies of vessel construction as he went. These experiences helped define the course of Tom's life. By the time he was a teenager, he had acquired a considerable knowledge of boat design, and had honed a talent for whittling scale models. At home on the Boston waterfront, Tom and his brothers knew the fishermen and their ways intimately, counting many of them as personal friends. Not surprisingly, when Tom opened his fish brokerage in 1877, his shop became a hangout for the local waterfront crowd.

By 1881 Tom's true calling was becoming apparent. In that year, John commissioned Lawlor to design the *Sarah H. Prior,* a clipper-bowed schooner with a deep draft that was far more stable than her shallower-draft Gloucester sisters. While the latter were fast, they were top-heavy and easily knocked on their beam-ends in a gale. According to government statistics, between 1864 and 1881, a total of 1,620 Gloucester fishermen were lost as a result.[2] Motivated by the appalling loss of life, the McManuses devoted themselves to the *Prior* project with a passion, with Tom and Lawlor designing her model and molds.

Thus began Tom's apprenticeship in vessel design, an apprenticeship that eventually led to a career as one of the most prolific fishing vessel designers in American history. In many ways a visionary, McManus, like his fa-

46

ther, was motivated by a desire to build boats that would be both safe and profitable.[3] In 1885 he and Lawlor teamed to design a vessel explicitly to beat the *Prior.* The result was the plum-stemmed *John H. McManus,* named for Tom's father.

By April of 1886, circumstances were right to see just how well they had done. With a fish-handlers' strike in full swing, captains and crews milled about the wharves aimlessly, inevitably turning up at Tom McManus's fish store on Atlantic Avenue to yarn and shoot the breeze. Not surprisingly, talk soon turned to the relative merits of the *Prior* and the *McManus.* Each had her partisans. Some argued that the *Sarah H. Prior* was an "Old War Horse" who had proved herself queen of the fleet, and could certainly do it again against the newer *McManus.* Other waterfront sages were not so sure. They liked the new schooner's lines and her turn of speed.

Tom was used to such debates. They had been the stuff of conversation for as long as he had frequented the docks, and certainly argument over the relative merits of this vessel or that had been a staple at his shop since it opened. However, he had a vested interest in this particular discussion, and so was born the idea for the first formal fishermen's race.[4]

McManus asked J. Malcolm Forbes to help sponsor the contest. Forbes pledged $100 and promised to put up a cup worth an additional $100 if the Boston pilot boat *Hesper* were allowed to race. McManus agreed, and he got Forbes to help him raise additional funds from several other Eastern Yacht Club members. Caught up in the enthusiasm, other yachtsmen joined in, as did several wholesale fish dealers. Before long, McManus had a $1500 pot and a $100 trophy.

All his efforts were nearly for naught, however. *Hesper's* entry aroused the fishermen's ire. A pilot boat had no place in a fishermen's race, they fumed. At 104 feet long, she was at least ten feet longer than her rivals, and everyone knew the old maxim, a good big boat will always beat a good small one. Over the two years since her launching, *Hesper* had proven that axiom enough times in informal brushes with fishing schooners to convince the fishermen that she was a ringer.

Besides, this race of McManus's could hardly be called a fishermen's race. A short, offshore contest was the sort of thing that pilot boat crews did everyday to make their living. Speeding out of Boston Harbor to meet incoming ships was a lot different than driving a schooner home from the Banks with a full trip of fish. That being the case, *Hesper* had an additional advantage. The final straw was the pilots' insistence on carrying a balloon jib topsail. The fishermen were adamant—*Hesper* should be disqualified.

McManus realized the implications of their decision. If the *Hesper* were barred, Forbes would likely withdraw his support. Without him, the race initiative would probably collapse. On the other hand, if *Hesper* raced, the fishermen would not. Going down to the wharves to talk to the skippers, Mc-

Manus got right to the point. "You fellers aren't sailing for the Cup," he said. "It's the money you're after!"

This seemed to settle the matter. Only Captain Sylvester Whalen, of the *Julia E. Whalen,* and Captain Tom Cornell, of the *William Parnell O'Hara,* withdrew, though it is not clear that *Hesper* was the reason. The rest of the field agreed to let *Hesper* participate, on the condition that the most she could win was the cup.

The incident illustrated the dynamic at work in most of the dealings between fishermen and yachtsmen during this period. What motivated the fishermen to race and what led men like Forbes to put up money were clearly different, yet as with other community events, they cooperated to make the race a success. For the fishermen, the reason was simple—they willingly abided by the wishes of those who paid the freight, so long as they saw a benefit in doing so. If Forbes wanted *Hesper* to race, he had to accept the fishermen's terms. The presence of McManus made compromise easier, although ultimately the fishermen remained in control of just how much they were willing to concede.

After all, they saw no great incentive to participate beyond fun, extra money, and bragging rights. Fifteen hundred dollars for an afternoon was nice, but they knew full well that putting bread on the table had little to do with sailing around a triangular course from Boston Light to Davis Ledge Buoy off Minot's Light, to Half Way Rock off Marblehead, and back to Boston Light. Such a race could be interesting, to be sure, but only a fool, or a yachtsman, would take it very seriously.

McManus understood all this, and he gave the fishermen a practical reason to race. Between the prize money and side bets to be won, a winning crew stood to pick up a considerable amount of cash. Certainly no fisherman would waste his time trying to win a cup. Appeals to sportsmanship, the spirit of competition, or any of the other nonsense that tended to motivate yachtsmen had no place in a mediation of the *Hesper* situation, and McManus knew it. More than likely, such a line of reasoning did not even occur to him.

The gap between fishermen's and yachtsmen's attitudes was further illustrated when it came to the rules governing racing. George A. Goddard, a former measurer for the Eastern Yacht Club, was named referee of the contest and given use of the outside tug *Elsie.* As it turned out, his position was largely ceremonial. With no instructions, there was nothing Goddard could do about the three fouls committed during the race, nor should he have expected to. This was, after all, a fishermen's race; if no one called fouls in races to and from the Banks, no one should be calling them in this contest either.

More than anything else, the race was an excuse for a party. J. Malcolm Forbes was a guest aboard the *Hesper* and had the time of his life, as did the crowds aboard the *Prior* and *McManus*, who had paid five dollars a ticket. With more than two thousand people milling about the docks, the schooners did not leave T and Commerce Wharves until 10:45 A.M. on May 1, over an hour later than scheduled. The festive atmosphere was contagious, and in some ways reminiscent of the excitement and enthusiasm surrounding trial trips.

Ten vessels came to the starting line: *Belle J. Neal, Edith Emery, Emily P. Wright, Gertie S. Windsor, Hattie I. Phillips, Hesper, John H. McManus, Sarah H. Prior, William Emerson,* and *Augusta E. Herrick.* The last was a centerboarder, 114 feet long, out of Maine; her captain, Bill Herrick, had sailed down hoping to be allowed to race over the course for fun. Although the *Herrick* was something of a curiosity, the real interest focused on the *Prior, McManus,* and *Hesper.*

As things turned out, the race did nothing to resolve the arguments that characterized fo'c'sle conversation and dockside chatter. If anything, it fueled the debates. To no one's surprise, *Hesper* won the trophy, with *McManus* nipping *Prior* in light winds to take the first-place prize money. Still, many fishermen were not convinced of *McManus's* superiority. They contended that, given rough seas and a heavy wind, the *Prior* would have sailed away from the field. For them, the real test would be to pit the vessels head-to-head in a "smoky sou'wester," with the wind piping up between 35 and 40 knots.

The McManus family's continued commitment to producing safe and fast fishing schooners led to another race in 1888.[5] For a long time, fishermen and owners had been skeptical about deep-draft schooners, arguing that in Gloucester, especially, the harbor necessitated a shoal draft, and, despite their danger, the old-style vessels had proven themselves fast. Although *McManus* had gone a long way to silence the objections, the McManus family was not satisfied. They wanted to take her type to the next logical level.

Naturally they turned to Ned Burgess to design their new boat. Charley McManus had become friendly with Burgess when the latter came to him to make *Puritan's* sails. McManus's invention of a new type of sailcloth with predictable shape retention had not only helped give *Puritan* her edge, it had sealed the relationship between Burgess and the McManuses.

Because Charley was sick, the work of assisting Burgess fell on Tom, who had already proven himself helping Lawlor. The collaboration produced a schooner with sharp lines and deep draft. Plum-stemmed, the *Carrie E. Phillips* had a strong rocker keel and unique fittings and rigging that set her apart from anything else in the fishing fleet.[6] Among other things, her bowsprit consisted of only one spar, her shrouds were made of steel wire rather than iron roundstock, she carried a single large jib, had quarter lifts on her main boom, and a double mainsheet.

By the time she was launched in November of 1887, the *Phillips* had created quite a stir along the waterfront. Fast to windward, she proved to be an able sail carrier in a strong breeze, and, by the spring of 1888, she had justified all the attention she had received while under construction at the Arthur D. Story Yard in Essex. It was therefore big news when Captain Tim Cole of the *Roulette* arrived in Newport, R.I., claiming to have beaten both the *McManus* and the *Phillips* on a run in from the Banks.

This prompted Charlie Harty and Mel McClain to issue their challenge to *McManus* and *Prior*. Seizing the opportunity, Tom McManus accepted on behalf of the *McManus*, and he convinced Harty to open the competition to "all vessels of the fishing fleet, barring the *Carrie E. Phillips*." Because Harty knew a ringer when he saw one, he was adamant about keeping the *Phillips* out. Still, after a week, he relented and the new Burgess schooner was allowed to compete.

Five boats raced on April 5, 1888, the *John H. McManus, Carrie E. Phillips, I. J. Merritt, Jr., Roulette,* and *Carrie W. Babson*. Most waterfront wags felt that the outcome was a foregone conclusion, and they were right. The *Phillips* won, but Charlie Harty took great satisfaction in finishing second, and beating the *McManus*.

The race gave the fishermen something to argue over, and, by October of 1888, speculation was rife about the prospects for 1889. John Cannon's new schooner *Susan R. Stone* attracted a lot of attention and led to speculation that, if another race were held in the spring, she would likely give the *Phillips* a run for her money.

Of course, the *Stone* was not the only likely challenger. The *Julia Costa* was a fast boat in her own right, and likely to trim both the *Stone* and the *Phillips* if conditions were right. Rumor had it that another Burgess schooner would be built in time for an 1889 race. Another story made the rounds that a syndicate of Boston owners was determined to build a vessel in case "a certain skipper's services can be obtained."[7] As with any sporting event, such gossip was half the fun, and along the waterfront, where boats were both a means of making a living and a way of life, it was a passion.

Although a bona fide fishermen's race did not materialize in 1889, interest in the newly launched *Fredonia* was high enough to sustain enthusiasm for a hybrid contest between Burgess's latest and *Hesper*.[8] Indeed, *Fredonia* received so much attention for her victory in that race that she totally eclipsed her sister, the *Nellie Dixon*. Truth be told, the *Dixon* was the model for what became known as the *Fredonia*-type schooner, the design that more than any other revolutionized fishing boat development. In fact, the only difference between the *Dixon* and *Fredonia* was that the *Dixon* went directly to the Banks after being fitted out instead of taking a stint as J. Malcolm Forbes's yacht.

Forbes's involvement with the fishermen had drawn the interest of his friends at the Eastern Yacht Club since the first race in 1886, and not just to provide monetary support. As referee for the 1888 contest, Forbes had selected Henry S. Hovey of the Eastern to act as judge for the Gloucester boats. Hovey must have enjoyed the experience, because he agreed to chair a Regatta Committee that would oversee both a fishermen's race and a small-boat competition to help commemorate Gloucester's 250th Anniversary in 1892.[9]

Hovey often watched the comings and goings of the fishing schooners from his summer cottage at Gloucester's Freshwater Cove, or from aboard his 109-foot schooner *Fortuna*. Like Forbes, he apparently enjoyed the no-holds-barred simplicity of the fishermen's contests. Inspired by the possibilities, Hovey helped raise prize money from his yachting cronies and offered a silver cup worth $300 to the winner of the large-vessel class. He planned to allow his beautiful schooner to serve as the judges' boat while he entertained friends aboard.

Hovey's enthusiasm was contagious, and, before long, talk around the Eastern's clubhouse turned to the relative merits of Tommie Bohlin's *Nannie C.* and Charlie Harty's *Grayling*. Of course, some members were partial to Maurice Whalen's plum-stemmed *Harry L. Belden,* while others felt Sol Jacobs's *Ethel B.* would make a good run at the lead.

In the weeks before the race, Eastern members sounded an awful lot like the boys down at Fishermen's Corner or the skippers up in the Master Mariners' Hall. Gloucester and Marblehead were abuzz with race talk. Ten schooners were entered, seven in the large-vessel division (over 80 feet waterline length), and three in the small (60 to 80 feet on the waterline). All were fast, and their skippers notorious sail carriers. Among the big schooner entrants were Maurice Whalen's *Harry L. Belden,* Sol Jacobs's *Ethel B. Jacobs,* Rube Cameron's *Joseph Rowe,* Charlie Harty's *Grayling,* Tommie Bohlin's *Nannie C. Bohlin,* John McDonald's *James G. Blaine,* and Charlie Olsen's *James S. Steele.* The small-vessel class included two Mel McClain designs, the *Caviare,* skippered by Frank Stevens, and the darling of the fleet, *Lottie S. Haskins,* a quick and handy vessel launched in 1890. The *Elsie F. Rowe* rounded out the field.[10]

With the exception of Whalen, most of the participants were in port at least a week before the race. The waterfront was a beehive of activity, which only added to the excitement in town. Vessels were hauled out and their bottoms cleaned and painted. Crews were kept busy painting rails, hatch coamings, and deckhouses, or replacing sheets and halyards. By race day, many of the schooners looked as sharp as some of the yachts out of Marblehead.

As things turned out, such preparation proved futile, for it was Whalen and the *Belden* that stole the show. Indeed, had Connolly or Kipling attempted to write a story capturing the essence of a fishermen's race as working-class sport, he could have concocted no fiction to rival the 1892 race.

Whalen was out seining, and since the mackerel were plentiful, he decided to follow the fish until the last minute. On Sunday, August 21, five days before the race, he told his crew that they would be heading home the next day. With any sort of breeze, they would be in Gloucester in plenty of time to haul out and paint *Belden*'s bottom. Of course, Murphy's Law being what it is, she was becalmed for the next two days. On Wednesday morning, with the wind freshening, *Belden* began the run for home.

Under her four lowers and both her topsails, she made upwards of fourteen knots through the day on Thursday. By ten o'clock that evening, a mere thirteen hours before the race was set to begin, she pulled up alongside the wharf. As the crew made ready to go ashore, Whalen reminded them to be back early the next morning. They were going to race, as she was, with her hold full of mackerel.

It was a fortunate turn of events. As the schooners left for the starting line on Race Day, Friday, August 26, winds ashore were blowing at 54 miles an hour. Out to sea, it was blowing even harder. The mackerel in her hold gave *Belden* the added ballast she needed to stand up to the weather. With the *Jacobs* losing her main gaff early, and the *Grayling* and *Steele* dropping out, the race came down to the *Belden* and the *Rowe*. Ignoring the Race Committee's rules requiring only one vessel at a time through the narrow turn off of Davis Ledge, *Belden* squeezed by the *Rowe* and never looked back. With the crew in water up to their waists, she crossed the finish line twelve minutes ahead of the *Nannie C.* The *Jacobs* and *Joseph Rowe* limped across next, followed by the *Lottie S. Haskins*, to win the small-vessel class.

Gloucester was beside itself. *Belden*'s victory fresh from a hard run from the Banks showcased the fishermen's special talents far better than any single event ever had before. It took a special breed to do their jobs, then come home and win a race, all within less than twenty-four hours. Even for those who had not participated in the race, there was a vicarious thrill in listening to the fo'c'sle stories and knowing that men like Maurice Whalen and his crew were brother fishermen.

Interestingly, even for members of the Eastern Yacht Club, such yarning was appealing. Charles H. W. Foster noted in the introduction to his reminiscences about the Eastern that "spinning yarns among sailors is, to them, the diversion that reading a novel or detective story is to those on shore." Writing some forty years after the fact, he still advised members that if they wanted "to have a real story . . . try to find some old fellow who took part in the race."

He then recalled with some fondness Tom McManus's version of the affair. McManus was aboard one of the racers, standing on the companionway steps with his hands on the hatch coaming. As the vessel came around the leeward stake boat, she jibed all standing. McManus's fingers were in the water, and by his calculation, "another quarter inch, and she would have filled and sunk." Although Foster could not use McManus's own words to describe the experience, he assured his readers that McManus's "language was picturesque, and certainly stirred the life blood of his listeners." Moreover, in typical fisherman fashion, each recital of that particular happening became more startling.[11]

Yachtsmen did their own yarning. Hovey and Forbes had a ball, and no doubt shared their excitement with their friends at Marblehead. Hovey especially had enjoyed himself. Despite the wild sea, he had delighted in acting as the gracious host, plying those guests who were not seasick with food and drink throughout the day.[12]

Of course, not all yachtsmen found themselves in synch with the fishermen, and when they were not, they were simply dismissed. Such was the case with Henry Clark Rouse. In 1899, Rouse, a Cleveland railroad magnate, moved into the Ramparts, his newly completed summer home on Eastern Point.[13] A stickler for flag protocol, he insisted that colors be flown from 8:00 a.m. to sunset from the water tower, boathouse, and pier flagstaffs, and aboard each boat in his mini-fleet, which included two sloops, a launch, and a brigantine. If the locals could overlook his penchant for yachting niceties, they probably found it hard to ignore the fact that Rouse traveled to and from Cleveland in a personal railroad car. Here was a man with all the outward affluence of new money.

In late August 1899, before he had even been in Gloucester a season, Commodore Rouse proposed to reestablish the fishermen's race as an annual Gloucester event run over the same course as the 1892 affair. He set the date for September 9, and he offered $250 for first place and $100 for second, provided that there were at least ten entrants. With no ties to the Gloucester waterfront, and all the trappings of yachting pretense, Rouse had no credibility with his intended audience.

Titles, flag etiquette, and private railroad cars impressed no one, especially if the fishing was good, the notice was short, and the prize money was inadequate. Whatever the reason, the race generated no interest on the wharves, and Rouse was forced to try to ingratiate himself to Gloucester with publicized gifts of $100 to the Fishermen's and Seamen's Widows' and Orphans' Aid Society and $25 to the Gloucester Fishermen's Institute.

Two years later, Thomas W. Lawson learned a similar lesson when he tried to sponsor a race off Boston Harbor.[14] A stock speculator and part-time yachtsman, Lawson commissioned B. B. Crowninshield to design the sloop *Independence* to challenge for defense of the America's Cup. Figuring to thumb his nose at the yachting fraternity that had rejected him (only the Hull-Massachusetts Bay Yacht Club allowed him to join, and the New York Yacht Club barred him), Lawson no doubt thought that his boat would be chosen to defend the Cup, for he organized the fishermen's race for October 1, after the America's Cup series would be over.

When the race was announced, waterfront speculation ran rampant.[15] The prospects for a big race seemed ideal. By October 1, most of the fleet would be home. With the best schooners in port, there would be a chance for a real brouhaha, and if the weather cooperated, as it had in 1892, who knew what would happen. Estimates that *at least* forty vessels would race were bandied about with an air of certainty.

Unfortunately, Lawson's *Independence* turned out to be a dog. Badly beaten in the America's Cup trials, it was reported that in her last race her hull twisted so much that the deck lifted with every wave. No doubt disappointed, Lawson remained determined to prove himself a sportsman to be reckoned with. Returning to Boston in late August, he abruptly changed the date of the fishermen's race to Labor Day.

If he had hoped to assuage his bruised ego by taking charge in this way, he obviously knew little about fishermen. With the majority of the fleet out fishing, there was little chance of getting them home on such short notice. Since a vessel carried no shortwave radio, once she cleared the harbor, she was on her own until she made port again. Even if a vessel could be reached, there was no incentive to come back early if the fishing was good. As one old-timer recalled, "You'd come [in] when you thought you could make out," and not before.[16] The decision was exclusively the skipper's. Moreover, with the crew paid on shares, a shortened trip just meant lower wages. To come back to participate in a race would have been crazy, not to mention cause for a good deal of discontent in the fo'c'sle.

Even so, some owners tried to get their boats home in time. Benjamin A. Smith telegraphed up and down the East Coast hoping to intercept the D. B. Smith and Company's *Priscilla Smith*. An avid yachtsman, Smith was always game for a sporting challenge, and he could not bear to miss the chance for a good race.

In the end, Smith got lucky. On September 2, the *Priscilla Smith* entered the harbor just as the race was scheduled to begin. With hardly a breeze stirring, the judges postponed the contest for a day. Smith was ecstatic. He went out to meet the *Smith* and had her towed to the wharf. There was no time to haul her out, but he ordered a new main and topsails bent on and the hold emptied of fish. Whether or not she had returned because of Smith's telegrams is not clear, though it seems likely that she just happened to be inward bound at the time. Similar telegrams by the owners of the *Richard Wainwright* produced no result.

Of course, not everyone was as enthusiastic about racing as Ben Smith. The Gardner and Parsons's schooner *Independence* arrived home at about the same time as the *Priscilla Smith*.[17] Named for Lawson's sloop, she was one of two new boats that, according to the *Gloucester Times*, was "built partly with the idea of racing for the big prize." Although her owners had the same chance to enter her in the contest that Smith did, they preferred to content themselves with the knowledge that, on her maiden voyage, *Independence* brought home the largest salt fare of the season, 375,000 pounds of cod worth $9,353, or between $195 and $241 a share. Such practicalities, even for a vessel ostensibly built in part to race, pointed out the real priorities of the fisheries. Gardner and Parsons could have had the *Independence* towed and new sails bent on, but why should they cut into the profits of a big trip?

The race itself was fun, but hardly lived up to original expectations. Only eight boats, in three categories, competed: the *Benjamin F. Phillips, Navahoe,* and *Priscilla Smith* in Class A (vessels greater than eighty tons); *Manomet* and *Mattakeesett* in Class B (boats between forty and eighty tons); and *Dixie, Rose Standish,* and *Massasoit* in Class C (schooners less than forty tons).

The weather was not much help either. With the exception of a brief twelve-knot gust, the wind never blew stronger than nine knots all day. That the fishermen were disappointed is putting it mildly. Talk around Fishermen's Corner the next day probably mirrored the reports in the local press: "A fishermen's race without lots of wind, although pretty enough to look at perhaps is . . . robbed of one of its principal attractions. Yesterday's race was exciting more because of the closeness of the contest and evenness of the boats than from any other reason."

Even so, the 1901 affair met at least one of the fundamental purposes of any fishermen's race. It was an excuse to spend a day messing around with boats. Captain Marty Welch of the *Navahoe* had help sailing from several of his friends, in particular skippers John G. Mehlman, B. Frank Rayson, Richard P. O'Reilly, Henry Brown, Herman R. Joyce, and William Blynn. Others aboard for the ride included E. Archer Bradley and Sylvanus Smith, Jr., co-owners with Welch of the *Navahoe;* James R. Jeffery of the *Cape Anne Breeze;* A. L. Millett of the *Gloucester Times;* and a whole host of other waterfront notables too numerous to mention. The other contestants were equally awash with guests, including Ben Smith, who was not going to miss his chance to be in the race.

The only glitch in the proceedings was a flap between *Manomet* and *Mattakeesett* over rules that disqualified the former and kept the latter from claiming any prize money. In a bit of logic that only a yachtsman could understand, Captain Robbins of the *Mattakeesett* rowed over to the judges' boat after his schooner crossed the finish line six minutes behind the *Manomet.* Contending that his rival was on the wrong side of the line at the start, he demanded that she be disqualified. The judges, from Lawson's Hull-Massachusetts Bay Yacht Club concurred, noting that they had asked *Manomet* to return at the time but she had failed to comply.

Unlike members of the Eastern, the judges obviously failed to understand fishermen's etiquette. Judges were for show, not to disqualify legitimate entries. George Goddard had learned that in the 1886 race. No one had disqualified Maurice Whalen for illegally squeezing past the *Joseph Rowe* off Davis Ledge in 1892. Of course, Rube Cameron of the *Rowe* had not been petty enough to make a big deal of it either.

Indeed, Robbins's protest was a clear violation of the fishermen's ethic, and Captains Turner and Price of the *Manomet* were quick to point that out. They vehemently denounced the whole affair, saying that they had violated no rules and heard no recall order from the judges. They were incredulous that "the skipper and crew of a vessel that had been squarely beaten should want to take advantage of a mere technicality, especially since both vessels belonged to the same owners." Nor did Robbins's protest make much sense in light of the rule prohibiting a boat from collecting a prize unless it beat another outright. Even with *Manomet* disqualified, *Mattakeesett*'s crew gained nothing. As one newspaper concluded when it was announced that the Hull-Massachusetts Bay Yacht Club's racing rules would apply to the 1901 event, "It would be a good deal better not to bother the skippers with rules of any yacht club, but simply tell them that the rules of the road at sea will govern the contest, and there would be not a bit of trouble."

Still, the images most took away from the race were distinctly in keeping with the fishermen's mystique. The *Priscilla Smith,* newly home from seven weeks of fishing, sailed up to Boston for the race with anchors on her bows and her crew scraping barnacles off her bottom with long poles. To everyone's satisfaction, she managed a decent showing, finishing seven minutes behind the highly touted *Benjamin F. Phillips.*

Five years later, in the fall of 1906, Sir Thomas Lipton, the perennial America's Cup hopeful, visited Boston, where officials convinced him to offer a cup for the fishermen's race scheduled for Old Home Week, a series of activities set for August 1907.[18] After a tour of the fleet at T Wharf, he readily agreed.

With Tom McManus in charge of a committee to organize the race, at least $2,500 in prize money was raised, not including the value of the Lipton Cup, which was appraised at $5,000. Vessels in the first class (those greater than 85 feet on the waterline) stood to earn $650 for first place (plus the cup), $450 for second, and $200 for third. The first three across the finish line in the second class (boats smaller than 85 feet) would win $600, $400, and $200, respectively. These prizes were not bad for a day's work, and enough of an incentive, or so it was thought, to attract a significant field. Certainly all indications were that it would be a good race.

Just days before the event, 27 schooners were registered, 16 in Class A, 11 in Class B, representing some of the fastest boats and hardest driving skippers in the fleet. Among the large vessels were Marty Welch's *Lucania,* Charlie Harty's newly built *Clintonia,* Wallace Parsons's *Ingomar,* Manuel Costa's *Jesse Costa,* Marion Perry's *Rose Dorothea,* and Crowley Santos's *Mary C. Santos.* Class B entrants included William Thomas's *Helen B. Thomas,* William Price's *Manomet,* Manuel Domingoes's *Belbina Domingoes,* Matthew Greer's *Mattakeesett,* and Joe Mesquita's *Frances P. Mesquita.*[19] Although no one expected that all twenty-seven contestants would race, the general consensus was that at least fifteen would come to the starting line. What was not counted on was how good the fishing was that summer.

On race day, August 1, there were only five racers—in Class A, *Rose Dorothea*, *Jesse Costa*, and *Joseph W. Parker*, under Captain Valentine O'Neill; in Class B, *Frances P. Mesquita* and *Helen B. Thomas*. Three of the schooners were captained by Portuguese skippers, making the race a distinctly "Portygee affair." Still, that did nothing to dampen enthusiasm along the waterfront, especially since the large-vessel class pitted two of Provincetown's biggest rivals—Manuel Costa and Marion Perry—against each other.

It was an exciting race in both divisions. Every vessel except the *Thomas*, which did not hoist her foretopsail, carried a full press of canvas from start to finish. After a nip and tuck battle on the first half of the course, *Rose Dorothea*'s foretopmast snapped as she turned for home. The *Costa*'s crew cheered, convinced that they had won. However, with the wind freshening, the loss of *Dorothea*'s foretopsail and jib topsail actually made her point higher as she sailed close-hauled for the finish line.

Had Captain Costa been a yachtsman with some sense of racing strategy, he would likely have doused his jib topsail and luffed out on the *Dorothea*. However, he was not. As a fishing skipper, sail carrying was a matter of pride, a mark of hard driving. The logic was simple—the deeper a boat buried her lee rail, the more obvious was the evidence of her speed. Although he would never admit it, Costa's stubborn adherence to the sail carrier's credo likely cost him the race. Try as he might to get to weather of the *Dorothea*, the wind kept knocking him off to leeward.

In the end, the *Rose Dorothea* crossed the finish line almost three minutes ahead of the *Jesse Costa*, covering the forty-mile course in just over five hours. In the small-boat class, the race had been equally tight. The *Mesquita* overtook the *Thomas* at Eastern Point and beat her home by exactly two minutes.

For anyone who had followed organized fishermen's races since their inception, or who knew anything about fishermen, it should have come as no surprise that so few captains had participated. As *Rudder* magazine so aptly noted:

> To the men who spend their days in the fisheries the racing of their schooners for fun is somewhat of a joke, a lark that they rarely indulge in, for various reasons. The fisheries are co-operative, and loss of time means loss of earnings to the fishermen. That is one reason why they drive their vessels so hard. They are out for a living, and have no time to fool away near the coast.
>
> These conditions make promoting of a fishermen's race, as a sporting feature, rather difficult.

Given this reality, the premise behind the Lipton Cup, and the expectations of some in the yachting community, seemed especially naive. Sir

Thomas donated the Cup as a perpetual challenge trophy, no doubt fully expecting that it would encourage future races. Clearly *Yachting* magazine believed that it would, reporting that *Rose Dorothea* "will be the *first* fishing vessel to have her name inscribed upon the cup." (emphasis added). It went on to state that "Captain Marion Perry . . . has a sort of elephant on his hands at present, as he will have to defend it if challenged by any of the vessels of the fleet."

Had he been a yachtsman, no doubt he would have, but then again, if he had been a yachtsman he would also have jumped at the chance to meet Theodore Roosevelt. As the story came to be told along the wharves, on August 20, 1907, Perry was down at the waterfront, checking some new gear and rigging.[20] A quiet man, he had entered the Boston race reluctantly, succumbing to the urgings of his wife. When she had seen a picture of the Lipton Cup, she had told Perry how lovely it would look in their house. He had explained that he had no intention of racing for such a useless thing. The fishing was too good to waste time on a race, and besides, even if he won, the others who owned shares in the *Rose Dorothea* were entitled to their percentage of the cup. No matter, she had said. He could give the cup to the town as a gesture of his esteem.

Perry shrugged; all this was over his head. He had gone to sea as a boy because he loved the simplicity of the life. One worked hard, wore what he liked, ate well, and fell asleep knowing that he was free. He had never quite understood his wife's longing for nice things and her concern for social gestures, but he loved her, and that was all that really mattered.

Still, it was amazing what a man would put up with for love. It had been bad enough dealing with the hoopla on T Wharf after the race, but the ovation that awaited him on his return to Provincetown had nearly been too much. The streets had been decorated and were packed with screaming citizens. He had been forced to ride with the town's officials in a parade that snaked its way from the waterfront, up to the town, and eventually to his front door, while a full brass band led the way and a group of broom carriers brought up the rear. It had been the longest day of his life.

As he worked on the quiet wharf, he probably thought back on all this and smiled. At least today the community was lavishing its attention on someone who knew how to deal with it. What he did not appreciate was that, as the winner of the Boston Fishermen's Race, he was something of a local celebrity. When Roosevelt met some 350 Gloucestermen who had sailed in to see him, he was introduced around by James Connolly, who happened to mention that Perry was in port. The President insisted on meeting him.

A messenger was dispatched to Perry's house, where he learned that the captain was down at his boat. Lost in thought as he wrestled with a rigging problem, Perry all but ignored the presidential envoy, who conveyed Roosevelt's invitation. Figuring that he had not been heard, the messenger tried again, only this time louder.

Perry bit through his pencil and dropped the papers he was working on. Turning to the man, he said, "All right, all right! Tell the President if he wants to see me, he knows where he can find me!" With that, he went back to his work.

If Perry had hoped that would be the end of it, he was sadly mistaken. The story quickly made the rounds, and by the time he got home his wife was fit to be tied. Roosevelt joked about it that night in a speech to the fishermen at the Odd Fellows Hall, commenting on how the captain had apparently felt it too big a sacrifice to meet with the President of the United States. When the newspapers got hold of the incident, Perry became a sort of folk hero. Indeed, it was reported that Roosevelt had been tickled when his messenger conveyed the captain's reply to his invitation.

Whether or not all the specifics of the story are true is irrelevant. Certainly we know that its basic elements are correct—three weeks after the race, Perry refused an invitation to meet the President, who was in Provincetown to lay the cornerstone for the Pilgrim Monument. To the fishermen who loved to tell the tale, the important thing about the story was how it illustrated the fishing skipper's independence of mind. Like his contemporaries, Perry had little use for the niceties of polite society. He was a simple man who confronted life on his own terms. If the President wanted to see him, it made perfect sense to Perry that Roosevelt should come and find him.

Of course, why he would want to was anyone's guess. For Perry, winning the Lipton Cup had been no big deal. He never understood the crowds on T Wharf and Provincetown making such a fuss, or the politicians' preoccupation with shaking his hand. He had raced to please his wife, no one else. Anyone with any common sense knew that the Boston Race had little to do with the real business of earning a living. If Perry had gotten his way, he would have been out fishing on August 1, like so many of his colleagues, instead of racing for a cup that, as he told his wife, you could not even drink from.

Perry's attitude typified the outlook of most skippers who raced in the United States between 1886 and 1907. They actively weighed the benefits of racing against the costs of a lost or shortened trip, and more often than not opted to go fishing. They also had little regard for the intricacies of politics. If Perry could ignore the President, other skippers had no compunction disregarding the dictates of yachting sponsors when they did not like the terms under which they had been asked to race.

Of course, if something was not fun, why bother with it? Val O'Neill illustrated that point clearly in 1907. With no chance of winning the Lipton Cup Race, he came prepared for a party. With a host of friends aboard, and a band to add life to the festivities, his *James W. Parker* sailed around the course for the sheer joy of it. Finishing a distant third, O'Neill was content to claim his $200 prize for hosting one of the gala events of the fishermen's social season. Of course, the crews of the other competitors did their share of playing as well.

The matter would have ended there until the *Halifax Herald* series, had yachtsmen in Canada not decided to sponsor a race in 1912.[21] A. H. Brittain, the general manager of the Maritime Fish Corporation of Montreal and a member of the Western Nova Scotia Yacht Club, promoted the event and donated a silver cup for the occasion. Details on the race are sketchy, but it seems to have been largely a parochial affair, the race committee consisting of H. B. Short, the Digby branch manager of the Maritime Fish Corporation, Captain Howard Anderson, the company's Digby superintendent, and Commodore O. S. Durham, of the Western Nova Scotia Yacht Club.

Only two boats raced. The *Dorothy M. Smart,* under Captain Harry Ross, was a 90-foot schooner built in 1910 and owned by the Maritime Fish Corporation. Her rival, the *Albert J. Lutz,* under Captain John Apt, was built in 1908 and was of roughly the same size and dimensions as the *Smart.* Owned by a Digby syndicate of which Albert J. Lutz of Moncton, New Brunswick, was the largest owner, both she and the *Smart* were products of the famed Joseph McGill Shipbuilding and Transportation Company Ltd. of Shelburne.

Racing in August off the coast of Digby, under the rules of the Western Nova Scotia Yacht Club, the vessels apparently made a good showing of it. Fairly evenly matched, they carried a full press of sail around the course, burying their lee scuppers as they went. In the end, the *Lutz* won in a closely contested affair.

The race generated enough interest to warrant a rematch between the same two boats the following year. Indeed, the audience for the 1913 event included a fair cross section of Canadian society, from the Duke of Connaught, the Governor General of Canada, who arrived by special train, to hundreds of fishermen, to a goodly number of yachtsmen, some from as far away as New York. The *Lutz* won again, making her "Winner for All Time" of the Brittain Cup.

Racing had come late to Canada, and its impact was limited, perhaps even more so than it had been in the United States. With the majority of Nova Scotia's salt bank fleet on the Grand Banks from the beginning of June to the end of September, the timing of the Brittain Cup Races for August was clearly not designed to attract a decent field of contenders. That only two vessels raced, and that one of them was the property of Brittain's company, suggests something of a vested interest in testing the *Dorothy M. Smart*'s speed in a match race against a specific rival.

Though the *Smart* and the *Albert J. Lutz* were obviously fast and able boats, vessels like them had become obsolete by the end of World War I. Responding to changing and unstable markets, Canadian fishing entrepreneurs were building bigger schooners by 1920. As the decade progressed, innovations in rail and cold storage facilities opened up a market for fresh fish in Canada and ushered in the introduction of auxiliary power and beam trawlers. As it had ten to fifteen years earlier in the United States, such changes marked the beginning of the end of the age of sail on both sides of the U.S.-Canadian border.

4

"Bucking the Inevitable": The View from the United States

IN EARLY 1926, THE *ATLANTIC FISHERMAN*, A TRADE JOURNAL FOR THE NORTH Atlantic fisheries, ran an editorial commenting on the growing controversy over steam trawlers in Nova Scotia. Noting that "our sympathies are naturally with the fishermen and the vessel owners of the fleets affected by the trawler activities," it went on to observe that "somehow we cannot but feel that our good friends, in protesting against the trawler, are bucking the inevitable."[1] Certainly, if the experience of American fishermen some fifteen or twenty years earlier was any indication, there was little doubt about it.

In fact, trawlers were only one of many changes occurring simultaneously during the first twenty years of the century that redefined the fisheries. In some cases, as with auxiliary power, the challenge came from new technology alone. In others, like the introduction of steam trawlers, the technological challenge was exacerbated by new corporate structures that threatened the highly personalized management style that had defined the fisheries for generations. In either case, sailing fishermen, and especially the captains, found their primacy in the industry challenged and, like skilled workers in other industries, both resented and resisted the change.

The process of change began on March 29, 1900, when Sol Jacobs, the so-called "King of the Mackerel Killers," launched the *Helen Miller Gould*.[2] A clipper-bowed schooner of Mel McClain design, the *Gould* was 117 feet long and carried a 150 hp Globe gas engine. Always a hustler, Jacobs saw the possibilities of auxiliary power for making faster trips more often, a guaranteed formula for greater profit.

Having left to go seining on April 12, he brought the *Gould* to New York about two weeks later with 200 barrels of fresh mackerel that sold for 9 to 10 cents a pound. On September 3 he returned to Gloucester with 720 barrels of salt and fresh mackerel. The highliner for 1900, the *Gould* broke all existing records, stocking $40,660 at a share of $863. The following year she was well on her way to duplicating her success, when a fire caused by a gasoline leak gutted her in October 1901. Though lasting less than 18 months, the *Gould*'s career highlighted the advantages of auxiliary power. In short order another McClain auxiliary, the *Victor*, came down the ways.

The first auxiliaries were not without problems. As the *Gould*'s tragic end pointed out, early gasoline engines were unreliable and subject to fire and explosion. Inadequate engine beds that led to misalignment and the failure of thrust bearings and stuffing boxes were another problem. Auxiliaries were also costly. As Howard Chapelle noted, because they attempted to use engines with minimum changes to the sailing hull form, auxiliaries always left a fairly expensive source of power unused.[3]

Still, *Gould* and *Victor* proved themselves successful enough to encourage a search for a more effective design. As things turned out, Tom McManus's knockabout fishing schooners had hulls that were ideally suited to take advantage of both sail and engine power. When equipped with crude oil or diesel motors—which significantly lowered the risk of fire and explosion—these vessels became, in the words of Chapelle, the apex in the long evolution of New England fishing schooners.[4]

By the nineteen-teens, even when they were built without engines, fishing boats were frequently designed with the capacity to add an auxiliary at some future date. In 1921, the *L. A. Dunton* became the last big schooner, not specifically built to race, that was launched without a motor. Two years later, she had an engine installed. By the late 1920s, Gloucester dorymen seldom, if ever, used their sails. In fact, the last documented case of a Gloucester schooner going out under sail alone was the *Philip P. Manta* in August 1932. After polling his crew, Captain Frank Gaspa took her to the channel grounds under canvas rather than wait for her engines to be fixed.[5]

The transition to power aboard the schooners redefined shipboard life for the fishermen in much the same way that it had for sailors aboard merchantmen and naval vessels some two to three generations earlier. Edward Sloan found that, because steamer captains had usually grown up in sailing ships, they were "so fixed in the ways of sail," that they "usually remained hopelessly, and at times belligerently ignorant of steam." As a result, they tended to resent the engineer, who, in controlling the machinery, undermined their independence and ability to be exclusive master of the vessel. As Sloan put it, to the skipper, "steam was alien and so were the men of steam."[6]

Fishing captains were no different. They represented generations of family tradition in the fisheries, and had taken time to learn and perfect their skill. Because their expertise and reputation focused on their ability to carry sail, the use of power deprived them of their sense of pride in possessing a skill and an understanding of their boats that few other men could claim. Like the skippers of auxiliary merchant steamers in the 19th century, fishing captains aboard auxiliary schooners had to acknowledge, even if grudgingly, that they no longer held a monopoly on the knowledge necessary to effectively command their vessel. Now the engineer, with his ability to coax another knot or two from a balky diesel, might mean the difference in a close race to market. Certainly, the captain's ability to keep a full press of sail on mattered little in an era when sail was becoming the auxiliary source of power.

Nor were such feelings limited to the quarterdeck, either aboard navy vessels, merchantmen, or fishing boats. When steam made its debut, the so-called "black gangs" who worked in the engine rooms were not trained as sailors. Engineers usually came from jobs in locomotive shops or on stationary engines ashore. As such, differences in experience and function divided and fragmented steamer crews into "the men of sail and the men of steam."

Aboard the auxiliary fishing schooners, the dynamics were much the same. When asked to recall the names of some of the engineers they served with, most fishermen could not, usually noting that fishermen and engineers did not mix very well. Like their predecessors aboard the merchantmen and navy ships, fishermen and engineers divided themselves by function and experience, and built up resentments as a result.

As one old doryman explained, "There was kinda bad . . . feelings there [because] the engineer . . . never went out in the dory . . . [and] they give him *more* [than equal shares]. Not that it was all that much, but it was a little more. Oh, they worked for it, but . . . the fishermen kinda resented it."[7]

Such feelings resulted from the fact that the introduction of auxiliary power had undermined the age-old schoonermen's credo of "share and share alike." By creating an unofficial job hierarchy, the auxiliaries left the fishermen in the same position that other skilled workers faced when work rules were changed by new technologies. As Charles Sabel points out, technical *prowess*—not *place* in an officially defined hierarchy of jobs—was what counted for the skilled worker. When the value of his work was called into question, the skilled laborer tended to feel threatened and to isolate himself from those "machine tenders" he identified with the source of change.[8]

Still, the changes wrought by the auxiliaries were gradual and in some sense more subtle than the frontal assault posed by the Bay State Fishing Company. If fishermen had been concerned when a group of Boston investors had organized the company in June 1905, their worst fears seemed to be confirmed when it joined the National Fisheries Company scheme the following year. By trying to combine the Boston fish dealers, fix prices, and further encourage beam trawling, National Fisheries seemed the embodiment of the kinds of trusts that Theodore Roosevelt was getting so much attention for breaking up.

Because of Boston's successful challenge of Gloucester's primacy in the fisheries in the late-nineteenth century, the Bay State Fishing Company had been suspect in Gloucester from the outset. Now that it was showing its true colors, fishermen had no problem believing that the company fully intended to break labor's power. That it had happened to workers in other industries experiencing corporate restructuring simply made the threat more real.

Their assumptions about the competency of the crews aboard the steam trawlers also added to their angst about what lay ahead. According to the *Portland Express*, "They [the trawlermen] can come from Mattawamkeag as well as from Orr's Island, and it matters little whether their knowledge of rigging is confined to tying a knot around a cow's neck so it will not slip and choke her to death."[9] It followed in the schoonermen's mind that, because these rubes lacked the independence of spirit instilled through generations of fishing, they would be easily duped by an aggressive management seeking to end the fishermen's autonomy.

That steam trawlers required both skilled fishermen and skilled engine room workers was irrelevant to the argument of the dorymen. The trawlermen were industrial laborers, pure and simple. Whether they worked on a fishing boat or in a textile mill or a steel plant did not much matter. Technology made factory workers easily replaceable. That made the dynamics of wage slavery, for the all-sail fisherman anyway, the same. Certainly that steam trawling paid a wage rather than sharing the profits of a trip was proof enough to the fishermen that the class tensions that defined the experience of industrial towns would soon characterize life on the waterfront. A strike by trawlermen for higher wages and shorter hours in July 1912 simply confirmed this impression as fact. It did not matter that the strike lasted only a week and that the trawlermen won a wage increase of ten dollars a month.[10]

In addition, it was not particularly significant that the beam trawlers were generally safer than dory trawling and had been pushed since the late 1880s by reformers concerned about the appalling loss of life among schoonermen. Even while grudgingly acknowledging the relatively greater safety of the trawlers—"At least you were on deck and could go warm yourself . . . and you didn't have to go away in the night in a fog"—old-timers insisted that life aboard the schooners was generally healthier.[11] It also took a special breed. As one man put it, "there were no machines to handle the work on board. There was a sort of respect and affirmation of what it took to be a fisherman in the old days."[12]

Like skilled workers in the smokestack industries, what the dorymen feared most about the encroachment of technology and industrial values was the loss of this respect and affirmation and, with it, their sense of control over their own lives and destinies. According to Charles Sabel, job security without the accompanying acknowledgment of craft identity meant little to the skilled laborer. In Sabel's words, the craftsman is "a man hesitant to forego . . . [the] fellowship [he feels with his companions] for a place in a world whose values he mistrusts in so far as he understands them."[13]

By distinguishing themselves from the morons from Mattawamkeag whose idea of rigging was tying a knot around a cow's neck, the schooner-men were setting up a sense of their exclusivity from, and superiority to, the trawler crews, just as they were separating themselves from the engineers aboard their own vessels. That such distinctions were largely artificial was be-side the point. Perceptions, not reality, were what mattered.

By 1916, the two seemed indistinguishable. Following the Fisheries Com-mission's decision to allow beam trawling to continue, executives of the Bay State Fishing Company restructured their firm as a diversified fishing and processing company. They chartered the Bay State Fishing Company of Maine with rights to breed, pack, can, and sell all species of fish. The firm merged the fishing operations of the original Bay State Fishing Company with the processing and marketing activities of Boston's most successful wholesale outfits. The goal was clear: corner the market and, insofar as pos-sible, foster a monopoly on the New England fish trade.

In the same year, the Boston Fish Pier Company was formed, acquiring twenty-eight dealerships. By 1917, thirty-seven independent firms had been amalgamated into two. The impact for the Bay State Fishing Company was impressive. In that year it was responsible for landing thirty-six million pounds of fish, approximately one-third of Boston's annual total.[14]

Although such success was responsible for encouraging the spread of the steam trawler, it also contributed to what might be termed the proletarian-ization of the fishermen by the end of the nineteen-teens. The 1912 strike, then the 1915 walkout for union recognition, and finally the 1918 strike for an increase in wages and crew size had been evidence enough for the schoonermen that they had been right about the rise in labor strife on the wharves.[15]

However, in 1919, it became painfully obvious that they too had become victims of monopoly capitalism. With the wartime economic boom over, market demand decreased, causing fish prices to fall to $2^1/_2$ cents a pound. Although the trawlers' tendency toward big harvests no doubt contributed to the problem, their crews, who were paid a monthly wage and a bonus, were not greatly affected. On the other hand, the dorymen, who worked on shares, were.

As a result, the fisherman's union demanded a fixed minimum price for fish, which the wholesalers flatly refused. Seeing no other alternative, the schoonermen struck in July, and by the middle of August a Board of Arbi-tration settled the dispute in favor of the fishermen.[16] Though they had won, the 1919 strike was a tacit acceptance of the changes that the fisher-men had been fighting against since beam trawling began. One doryman noted years later that "The union was set up to cope with the beam trawlers." It was not needed aboard the schooners, because there a fisherman was "on your own."[17] Collective action, then, even if successful, was an admission that the fishermen's independence and autonomy were no longer assured.

Indeed, David Montgomery, a leading labor historian, has argued that unionization constituted the second level of development in the workers' struggle for control of production. In the first, the workers' superior knowledge of the production process gave them functional autonomy on the shop floor. Completely self-directing, they hired, fired, and paid their helpers, without interference from the boss, while maintaining an informal moral code that limited output and upheld work rules against "hogging" work. This dynamic was clearly evidenced aboard the schooner.

In Montgomery's second level of development, union work rules signaled a shift from such spontaneous solidarity to deliberate collective action.[18] Benson Soffer noted that one of the chief functions of unions for these men was to establish clear rules that would decrease competition between them.[19] Thus unionization was less an expression of strength than an effort to preserve established norms from the encroachments of management.

Anyone who understood the routine aboard a steam trawler knew what the dorymen feared. Every morning the skipper was required to check in with headquarters by radio. The quantity of fish he had aboard, how many sets he had made, his location, weather conditions, other vessels fishing in the vicinity, and anything else that might help the company know exactly what was going on with all its vessels was reported. The data was then tabulated and evaluated, and skippers were ordered to stay out or head in, depending on gluts or scarcities in the market.[20]

It took no skill, no expertise, no ability to "think like a cod fish" to be a trawler captain. If the schooner captain was a self-starter, if he was independent, and if he knew his business intimately because he had worked his way up from the fo'c'sle, it seemed that the only thing that a trawler skipper had to know was how to take orders. His status aboard ship came not so much from a hard-earned reputation as from an officially prescribed job hierarchy in which he was the relative equivalent of a shop floor foreman or middle level manager.

As if all that were not bad enough, by the end of World War I, many schooners had had their spars cut or unshipped and were being turned into motorized draggers or trawlers. By 1926, reports on the latest draggers had displaced any mention of the dory schooners in the *Atlantic Fisherman*. A story featuring the *Pauline M. Boland* was typical. A dragger, she was, like her sisters, referred to as a "schooner." Characterized as "one of the best and most efficiently equipped" boats of her kind, *Boland* was a study in functionality.[21]

Her trawl winch was located between the pilothouse and mainmast, with all the hoist and pump controls handy to the winch man, whose platform just forward of the pilothouse put him within easy speaking distance of the skipper. A well-laid-out engine room made everything accessible while allowing plenty of room to move around. The cooling system regulated engine temperature for maximum efficiency and minimal fuel consumption.

As for crew comfort, she had "a real honest-to-gosh toilet just as you have at home." There was progress for you. The *Atlantic Fisherman* pointed out, "Some better than the old lee rail, boys!" Still, for someone brought up with sail, such things meant little. James Connolly, who prowled the wharves of Gloucester in the mid-1920s, gave form and substance to the feelings of many of the older fishing skippers when he wrote:

> Let a vessel's name be mentioned twenty years ago on Fisherman's Corner, and the question at once was, what length of main boom? What hoist of mainsail had she? Today they ask, what horsepower has she? . . .
> [N]obody gets excited over the doings of vessels which carry an engine in that space where a pot-bellied red hot cabin stove and locker and bunk and lazaretto space would have been of old. . . . The best engine ever built is still an engine, a machine. . . .[22]

Still, as Connolly rightly observed, "to linger sighing over the industrial current of the times is a waste of time perhaps—that current being no more to be turned back than the flood tide." Certainly, the *Boland* was part of the rapid redefinition of the New England fisheries after World War I.[23] The change began in 1920 when the *Mary* was built as a pure dragger. Until then, vessels involved in dragging had been small and had engaged in fishing for flounder and other bottom fish.

At 81 feet long and 54 tons, the *Mary* was the first dragger with a crude-oil engine modeled on the big steam trawlers. As a prototype, she had her share of problems. Still, built for $22,000 (before upgrades and repairs), she proved her worth on her first trip, stocking $3,200 for 32,000 pounds. Her second trip netted $4,600 for 37,000 pounds of black backs taken in just fifty-five hours of fishing.

More significantly, from every equipment failure, changes were made that ultimately perfected dragging technology. By mid-1921, new draggers were being built based on the lessons learned from *Mary*. With sail spread reduced, bowsprits eliminated, and a pilothouse added, these vessels were pure power draggers. Built primarily for inshore work, and for harvesting the various and sundry sorts of flatfish, these boats sometimes ventured into deeper water where they took the occasional haddock or cod.

Costing anywhere from $15,000 to $20,000 to build, draggers represented a good investment, and an affordable one for the ambitious fisherman wanting to own his own boat. Although the average skipper could not afford to buy a share of a quarter-of-a-million-dollar steam trawler—even if the Bay State Fishing Company had provided such an option—draggers operated on the traditional shares system. That meant that, at the very least, a captain could become part owner of his boat.

In 1924, Captain Dan Mullins of New Bedford built the first so-called "baby trawler," the *Mary R. Mullins*. With the efficacy of offshore dragging proven, Mullins reasoned that a bigger boat could fish off Georges Bank both winter and summer and turn a decent profit. Seventy-seven tons, 84 feet long, and sporting a 100-hp C-O engine, the *Mary R. Mullins* could ice down 90,000 pounds of fish.

Her success encouraged others to build even bigger vessels. The John Chisolm Fisheries Company refitted *Bettina* with a 180-hp engine for trawling. Busalacchi Brothers had the *Nina B* built at 122 tons with a 240-hp motor, and O'Hara Brothers launched *Colleen* at 65 tons with a 230-hp engine. At somewhere in the neighborhood of $70,000 to build, these boats were significantly more expensive than the inshore draggers, but they were still remarkably affordable, given the costs of the steam trawlers.

This, of course, was the key to their proliferation. Owners of these boats operated their vessels out of Boston and went after haddock, cod, and other species usually pursued by the dorymen and steamers. Their strategy was simple. Because the baby trawlers were cheaper to build and operate and could fish in all kinds of weather, proportionately they could catch as much as the steamers for less overall cost. This made them competitive and, some believed, qualified them as the likely successor to the steam trawlers.

At 82 feet overall, with a 100-hp diesel and a carrying capacity of 75,000 pounds, the *Pauline M. Boland* represented an intermediate type of vessel known as the offshore dragger. By 1926 it had proven itself, in the words of the *Atlantic Fisherman*, "the most certain type of all." These vessels could fish in deep water and, when it was too rough, make the most of their time inshore. This flexibility seemed especially beneficial in light of the condition of the flounder supply by the mid-1920s. The Nantucket fishing grounds showed serious signs of overfishing, with experts predicting that, at present rates, there would be no fish in a few years. This was despite the fact that flounder fishing had been seriously pursued for only about fifteen years, and intensively for only five or six.

With predictions that she would be able to fish alongside the steam trawlers "most any time," *Boland* promised to be a moneymaker for her crew, skipper, and owner alike, all for only $35,000 built and fitted for sea. That figure was pretty cheap when one considers that in 1912 it had cost between $25,000 and $30,000 to launch the average auxiliary schooner.[24]

By the winter of 1925–26, there were at least one hundred vessels using trawling gear in New England waters. Sixty percent of the 130-plus million pounds of fish landed at Boston Pier were trawler fish, and that does not even take into account the more than five million pounds shipped from Nantucket, or the equally significant poundage landed at Fulton Market, T Wharf, Portland, and elsewhere.[25]

Even old sailing masters like Clayt Morrissey and Marty Welch acknowledged the inevitable encroachment of the future. Morrissey had been the skipper of *Walrus*, the first beam trawler ever owned at Gloucester. Welch captained the steamer *Thelma* through most of the 1920s.

The waterfront was changing, as the formation of the Gloucester Fishing

Where once a forest of masts had dominated Gloucester's waterfront, the two-masted schooner was an oddity in the 1920s. Many old schooners were converted to draggers by having their rigs cut down and powerful diesel engines installed. Increasingly, though, fishing boats were being built as draggers and trawlers from the start. This photograph provides a view of the Atlantic Supply Company Wharf, with the city of Gloucester rising up the hill from the waterfront in the background. Notice the draggers moored to the left of the picture. (Photograph courtesy of Mystic Seaport Museum, Willits D. Ansel Collection, Mystic, Connecticut)

Masters' Producers Association proved in 1926.[26] The Master Mariners' Association had for years been the only organization representing Gloucester's fishing skippers. However, by the mid-1920s, it was growing out of touch with the new realities. Dominated by old schooner captains who congregated down at the rooms on Main Street to reminisce, play cards, and shoot pool, its members seemed too preoccupied with promoting international fishermen's races to address the real issues of an industry in transition.

Under the leadership of Captains John Dahlmer, Len Firth, Howard Tobey, Harry Clatterberg, Gerry Shoares, Marty Welch, and John Matheson, the Fishing Masters' Producers Association was to be an organization of "active producing skippers" established for "mutual protection." The last two were members in good standing of the Master Mariners' Association and were actively involved in the racing scene, but they were also full-time fishermen who realized that collective action was essential if long-standing grievances against market practices in New York and Boston were ever to be resolved. Unlike its forebear, the Fishing Masters' Producers Association was designed to "function solely along business lines, with the social side tabooed." Membership was strictly limited to "fishing vessel masters who are actually engaged in fishing," although the founders entertained the possibility of admitting vessel owners at some later date.

As outlined in its bylaws, the association's goals were broad-based and were designed to advance the cause of those men "who originate the product that sets a-going the whole machinery of the fishing industry," a cause that many sympathetic to the movement felt had been ignored for too long. Among its objectives, the association sought to encourage new and modern methods, carry on educational work in developing a code of ethics to promote public confidence, and familiarize consumers with the part producers played in the industry.

The Fishing Masters' Producers Association's emphasis on business principles reflected a conscious effort to deal methodically with new challenges confronting the fisheries, and the fishing captains in particular. In forming a new organization, Gloucester's skippers were tacitly accepting the fact that the 19th-century precepts undergirding the old Master Mariners' Association had little bearing on their economic concerns in the 1920s. The modern fishing skipper needed to acknowledge a broader horizon, to not only be open to new techniques, but to encourage their development. He even had to be sensitive to public relations issues, no less than did the admen who hawked the growing number of products that an image-conscious and consumer-oriented society seemed unable to do without.

Whatever else they were, the 1920s were a time of conspicuous consumption, when image was often more important than substance. It was the era of the *Great Gatsby,* the flapper, speakeasies, and Madison Avenue. Business ideals governed the age, with Calvin Coolidge sounding the bellwether for the nation with his now famous observation that "the business of America is business." To survive in such a decade, the fishing industry, and the fishing captain, had to adapt, to be flexible. Indeed, the change was so fundamental, so broad-based, that not to adapt was to court certain extinction.

This point was driven home painfully during the Great Depression for those firms and skippers who continued dory fishing. With some seven million people unemployed in 1931, the U.S. Department of Labor's Immigration Bureau prohibited the seasonal movement of alien fishermen into the United States unless they could show an unrelinquished domicile in the country. The order was devastating for the schooners. Thomas J. Carroll, president and general manager of Gorton-Pew, observed:

> We have three vessels to go handlining. Two of them have shipped crews, but the other one has been in for three weeks and has been unable to sign a single man. The situation does not apply to all kinds of fishing,

but only to handlining. Skilled fishermen are required on a handliner, and even with experienced crews the boats have not been earning any money. An inexperienced crew would mean a "broker."

The problem, according to Carroll, was that "the life of the handline fisherman is a hard one, and . . . it is impossible to get enough American young men to man these vessels." He went on to note that a number of sons of American fishermen were employed in Gorton-Pew's loft, but "would not go fishing for twice the amount we are paying them."[27]

The shortage of American-born dorymen was not new. Since the mid-19th century, skilled immigrants had found work in the American fisheries, replacing native-born men who eschewed the dangers of the sea for the safety and security of land jobs. As long as immigration continued, there was no problem in finding crews to go dory fishing. By the 1920s, though, dory trawling was already an aging profession. A former fisherman on the *L. A. Dunton,* who shipped aboard that boat in 1924, recalled that, at 23, he was the youngest man in the crew. Most of his shipmates were well over 35 years old.[28]

As Americans had done in the previous century, many of the Portuguese immigrants who had come over as fishermen prohibited their sons from following them into the fisheries. According to one son of a Portuguese skipper:

> Pretty near every [Portuguese] fisherman, whether captain or crew, if possible, didn't want to see their sons go fishing, back in the dory trawling days. It was really rough, rough, a lot of men were lost. They'd put out in their dories and they didn't know if they were coming back or not. Fathers didn't want to have their sons go through such a hard life. That's why not many of the sons followed their fathers [into fishing]. They went into other fields.[29]

As the draggers and trawlers crowded the schooners out of the market, assimilation made the schooners completely dependent on skilled labor available almost exclusively from the Canadian Maritime Provinces. With that door slammed shut, there was a diminishing pool of labor on which to draw when the Portuguese and "white washed Yankees" from Nova Scotia retired or died. Although Sicilians allowed their children to enter the trade, and in many cases encouraged it, their interest in the shore fisheries and in the growing dragger fleet did nothing to redress the labor shortage among the schoonermen.[30]

For the dory trawlers to survive the Depression, companies like Gorton-Pew had to request special waivers to employ seasonal fishermen. To receive the waiver, the firm was required to file a bond stating that the men it employed would return home at the end of the fishing season and not accept any other employment in the United States. By the early 1930s, there was clearly no future in the dory fishery.

Old-timers hung on doggedly simply because they knew no other lifestyle, their crews supplemented by youngsters out of school in the summer months and looking for adventure. Many of the boys who went fishing had frequented the wharves for as long as they could remember, and, as a result, had developed something of a love affair with the old schooners. They had come to know the dorymen and relished the prospect of working side by side with them as equals. Besides, for these young men, life aboard a schooner was fun. The work was hard and the pay was low in comparison to what they could get dragging, but they were not going fishing for the money. It was a lark. As one recalled:

> [T]here were big fleets out of Nova Scotia and in nighttime you'd go aboard their boats. They'd come aboard yours, and they'd tell stories and do a little dancin' . . . some boats they'd let you have a drink. . . .
> A breeze would come up and four or five American vessels would start to run [for port] and the Canadian legion would immediately put the word out over the central telephone exchange, "Dance Tonight." . . . You really did have a lot of fun [then], and you had the time for it.[31]

Whether it was fun or not, some of the young guys stayed on beyond the summer, preferring the freedom of fishing to the rigors of high school. Even these, however, realized that they were just marking time until they could find a real job, or a site aboard a dragger. Sometimes, the decision was made for them, as in the case of one Gloucester teen who was fired from the *Marjorie Parker* because the skipper did not want the young man on his conscience. "You're seventeen years old," the boy was told. "I'll get you a site with my brother," who captained the trawler *Lark* out of Boston.[32]

That simple act encapsulated a fundamental truth that had, in a few short years, transformed the waterfront—schooners were for old men whose better days were behind them, or youngsters looking for a little fun. In the Canadian Maritimes, that reality began to manifest itself at the end of World War I, nearly twenty years after the *Helen Miller Gould* ushered in the era of change in the United States. Interestingly, the response of fishermen on both sides of the border was almost identical, and for good reason. As skilled workers, they saw the threat of the corporation and technology for what it was—a clear assault on their job security and skill-based sense of self and, in many cases, on the community patterns that reinforced them.

5

"Bucking the Inevitable": The View from Canada

In COUNSELING NOVA SCOTIAN FISHERMEN ABOUT THE INEVITABILITY OF BEAM trawling, the *Atlantic Fisherman* opined that "The labor-saving machine is omnipotent. If it disrupts established trade practices, such practices must give way to a new."[1] The words were eerily reminiscent of the 1914 U.S. Bureau of Fisheries report that accurately predicted that "the unregulated use of otter trawls will inevitably result in the practical displacement of the less efficient line fishery. . . ."[2]

Even though the Bureau of Fisheries' and the *Atlantic Fisherman*'s positions were understandable in light of the realities of industrialization, the underlying truth that defined both positions meant little to men confronted with the prospects of losing a way of life that had defined their families and communities for generations. Like their American counterparts, Canadian fishermen believed that the success of the industry rested on the cooperation of labor and capital. As one report from Lunenburg, Nova Scotia, put it:

> The fisheries of Nova Scotia . . . have skilled seamen who cooperate with each other and with firms of long standing who are scattered over the rural parts of Nova Scotia. The beam trawler implies corporation control. Its appearance in number means that the skilled fishermen who are able might secure jobs as coal heavers for a monthly salary or leave the country and seek an opportunity in other lands.[3]

As early as 1912, Lunenburgers showed more than a passing interest in the fight against beam trawlers.[4] Nova Scotia had already outlawed trawling within the three-mile limit, and many in the province were pushing the Canadian Government to prohibit offshore otter trawling as well. No doubt a lot of Lunenburgers took heart in Captain F. G. Robinson's assertion to them that the Gloucester fishermen would wage an all-out fight to stop the beam trawler in American waters.

Watching the American struggle, Lunenburgers probably realized that the way the United States dealt with the issue would ultimately and eventually impact them. How could it not, with beam trawlers already operating in

74

Canadian waters and on the Banks? Surely, the U.S. Bureau of Fisheries' decision to allow beam trawling in areas where it was already being practiced could only be taken as a bad omen for men who advocated a total ban on the new vessels.

For the Lunenburgers, the threat of technology was exacerbated by the fact that interests from outside the community were behind the introduction of the trawlers. That many of them were from Halifax only heightened their suspicions. Just as Gloucesterman viewed Boston initiatives with a jaundiced eye, Lunenburgers were always wary of changes coming from Halifax.

However, the issue concerned not just Halifax or the threat of new methods. Trawlers were ushering in new market conditions with which Lunenburg was ill-equipped to deal.[5] Since 1911, firms from the Canso–Mulgrave–Port Hawksbury area, Halifax, and Lockport had successfully introduced trawlers to provide a regular supply of fresh fish for growing Canadian and international markets.

The implications for the salt fishery—Lunenburg's bread and butter—were obvious. At the turn of the century, Lunenburg County had more than 140 fishing schooners. By 1925, the number had dropped to fewer than 100. Throughout the 1920s, significant numbers of both men and boats left the fisheries to pursue more lucrative activities. The career of choice for many was rum-running. During the winter of 1922–1923 alone, at least twenty-four schooners were sold into that line of work.

Of course, that was not the only option. Many Lunenburg men moved south to the United States looking for work. By the early 1920s, the out-migration was so great that Lunenburg had to turn to Newfoundland to remedy the resulting labor shortage of skilled men. So dependent was Lunenburg on Newfoundland fishermen that, in 1928, two of her schooners laid up in Burin, Newfoundland, for the winter for the convenience of their crews, who all hailed from that area.

Even when Lunenburgers became involved with trawlers in 1919, they had to rely on Halifax and other ports to market their catches because of a lack of cold storage facilities. In that year, three trawlers were built for Lunenburg interests, but none used Lunenburg as its home port. One of them, the *Jutland*, landed 200,000 pounds of salt fish at Halifax on her first trip. The *Promotion* worked out of Liverpool, plying the fresh fish trade.

In 1926, Lunenburg Sea Products, Ltd., built a cold storage plant that paved the way for the introduction of fresh fishing at Lunenburg. Two years later, the diesel-powered *Geraldine S.* became the first dragger in the Lunenburg fleet. She remained an anomaly for a time because conservative business attitudes and high initial capital costs for draggers encouraged local businessmen to try and save the salt fishery. Among other strategies, vessels were sent fishing off Greenland, and the length of the fishing season was increased.

Such efforts did not forestall the inevitable, however. As in the United States, even if trawlers and draggers had not been introduced, auxiliary-powered schooners would have redefined both markets and the way fishing was done. By the winter of 1926–1927, a small fleet of auxiliaries was landing fresh fish at the Lunenburg Sea Products facility on a weekly basis.

The pace necessitated by the new fishery alienated many salt bankers. A fourth-generation fisherman recalled that his great-grandfather had been a shore fisherman, and his dad and granddad had gone in schooners to Labrador, the Magdalen Islands, the Gulf of St. Lawrence, and the Grand Banks. He himself had begun dory trawling at age thirteen. Despite this long heritage, he quit the business and came ashore to build dories in 1936. After two years of fresh fishing, he had had enough of seven-day fishing trips.[6]

Gone were the days of no fishing on Sunday, of relaxing, socializing, and reverence. As one old-timer recalled that era:

> After you cleaned up an' ate breakfast you might take a nap. An' when Sunday afternoon come . . . you used to get together an', there were fellers that would sing an' some of 'em used to have accordions an' violins an' we'd have a sing-song. . . .
>
> An' the fellers what couldn't sing, why they enjoyed it maybe more so than the fellers that was singin'.
>
> So we'd have singin' and we'd have grace. . . . An' the cook, he used to soak out salt meat . . . fresh, an' then he'd roast it for Sunday dinner . . . an' he'd make a big cake an' put a lot o' frostin' on it—it was some good.
>
> But today it ain't like that. It's just an endless chain—goes right around. These fellers on the draggers here think they're doin' good fishin' on Sunday, but they're not. They're losin' on the other end.[7]

And therein lay the flaw in the *Atlantic Fisherman*'s observation that when new labor practices proved their efficiency, the old must "give way to a new." For these fishermen, there was a whole lot more at stake than economic efficiency. Control over their work environment and pace of work was a fringe benefit that no union contract or reconstituted work schedule could guarantee. A few extra dollars from Sunday work might be nice, but it had to be weighed seriously against the freedom one had to give up to get it. For many salt bank fishermen, the trade-off was no bargain at all.

By the mid-1920s, Lunenburgers' worst fears were being realized. Unless something was done, and done fast, dorymen would be as obsolete in Canada as they were becoming in the United States.[8] In 1928, under pressure from the fishermen, the government appointed a commission to study the condition of the fisheries in the Maritime Provinces, and to suggest solutions for the benefit of both the fishermen and the industry.

After hearing repeated claims that there was overwhelming evidence to show that beam trawling was damaging to the fishermen and the future development of Nova Scotia's fisheries, a majority of the commission recommended its prohibition from Canadian waters. With the chairman of the committee filing a minority report favoring the new technology, the Canadian government struck a compromise. Trawlers would be allowed to work during the winter months but would be restricted during the rest of the year.

Far more limiting than the American solution, the government plan rankled trawler interests. In Halifax, an association of trawler-owning corporations was organized to push for the opening of Nova Scotian ports to beam trawlers, and thereby extend their access to the fishing banks offshore.

At a meeting held in the early summer of 1929 at Halifax, representatives of Lunenburg Sea Products, Ltd., Lockport Co., Ltd., I. A. Robertson, H. R. L. Bill, Swan Brothers, Shelburne Fisheries, Ltd., and Austin E. Nickerson, Ltd., unanimously passed a resolution calling for the free landing of fish caught by Canadian-built boats, or by vessels owned either by Canadian citizens or by corporations in which majority stock was held by Canadians. All other landings would be subject to a one-cent-per-pound duty. The resolution was forwarded to the subcommittee of the Fisheries Commission of the House of Commons, and telegrams outlining the position of the fish producers and packers were sent to the Nova Scotian representatives in the federal Parliament.

The logic of the proposal, while conciliatory to the fishermen, appealed to patriotism and a sense of fair play. Ralph P. Bell, president of the Lockport Co., and spokesman for the organization, pointed out that while "We are inalterably opposed to the continuance of the free landing of fish in Canadian ports by foreign craft[,] [w]e are likewise opposed to building up trawler fleets to the detriment of the shore fishermen." Agreeing that abolition of the trawler would mean greater prosperity for Nova Scotia's shore fisheries, Bell went on to observe that the corporations he represented could not support a policy that in any way restricted the development and improvement of fishing methods.

He was also quick to remind reporters that many of those who now ran the companies he spoke for were "men who worked their way up from the bottom of the ladder commencing as fishermen without a cent, in the old day of oars and sail." In the considered opinion of these men who had "run the gamut of the industry," restricting free landing to Canadian-built vessels was not only "Canadian in spirit," but it would prevent excessive trawler development by doubling or tripling the investment required to bring cheap, secondhand, foreign-built boats under Canadian registry.

Such a solution was also equitable, Bell argued. Even if a foreign person or company opted to engage in trawling offshore, the relative costs created by the duty would allow the individual fisherman to compete successfully, although his boat and equipment were built and supplied locally. Moreover, proposals under consideration in Ottawa limiting the number of trawlers to firms already operating such vessels unduly restricted access to the new technology at a time when it was controlled largely by American interests. The Halifax group's proposal, it was contended, would stimulate the building of Canadian boats and provide profitable employment "for the sons of fishermen in the Province." The industry should be left "free and untrammeled to experiment, develop, or advance along any new or modern method," Bell asserted. "But see that such development—if it must take place—does so on a relatively fair basis."

Such arguments did little to convince Lunenburg's fishermen. On August 13, 1929, P. J. A. Cardin, the minister of marine and fisheries, Colonel J. L. Ralston, the minister of defense, and W. A. Found, the deputy minister of fisheries, traveled to Lunenburg to investigate conditions. They stayed at the home of J. J. Kinley, president of Lunenburg's Board of Trade. That evening, the ministers entertained a large number of citizens who wished to voice concerns about the problems facing the Lunenburg fisheries.

At a meeting the next morning at the courthouse, more testimony was taken. Although a wide range of topics was discussed, the recurring theme was the "beam trawler menace." Indeed, Mr. Kinley set the tone for the meeting when, after introducing the visiting dignitaries to the crowd, he pointed out his desire that they be made aware of how beam trawlers were interfering with Lunenburg fishermen on the Banks, causing great financial loss, and sometimes loss of life.

Although a W. H. Smith spoke in favor of the Halifax group's proposal, most of what the ministers heard condemned the new technology. From Riverport, to West Dublin, to Liverpool, wherever they traveled in Lunenburg County that day, the story was much the same: the beam trawler posed a serious threat to the Nova Scotian fisheries and must be stopped. As a result of such inquiry, an amendment was made to the Fisheries Act in 1929 that required any otter trawler fishing from a Canadian port to have a license from the minister of marine and fisheries. Additionally, it authorized the governor-in-council to fix regulations under which licenses would be granted.

On October 30, 1929, by order-in-council, the issuance of licenses to boats built after November 1, 1929, was limited to vessels built in Canada. For existing fishing vessels that were not Canadian built, temporary licenses good through April 1, 1932, would be issued. License fees were set at one cent per pound of fish landed for non-Canadian boats and $2/_3$ cents for Canadian craft.

This latter proviso was quick to draw fire from several Halifax firms operating trawlers. Contending that the license was actually a tax, they argued that it could not legally be imposed by order-in-council. As such, they refused to pay until the matter was properly adjudicated. One Halifax company owed $61,000 in back taxes by the fall of 1930. After repeated efforts to collect, E. N. Rhodes, the minister of fisheries, turned the matter over to the Justice Department for prosecution. When the company challenged the action on grounds of constitutionality, Rhodes asked that the firm's attorney submit a stated case that would then be presented to the Supreme Court of Canada.

Approximately four months later, in February 1931, the matter was being argued before the Exchequer Court. The National Fish Company of Halifax owed some $20,000 in licensing fees for three trawlers dating back to the first three months that the license requirement was in effect. Arguing that the federal government had no authority to impose taxes by order-in-council, company attorneys defended their client's nonpayment as perfectly legal. The case was adjourned for a month at the request of the crown to allow further study of company records and figures.

Interestingly, although the government's decisions exasperated the trawler interests, they did little to mollify the fishermen's agitation against beam trawling. In the first months of 1930, the Lunenburg Board of Trade passed a resolution calling for nothing short of the elimination of the steam trawler. Pointing to the destruction done to gear and property by these vessels, Lunenburgers noted that trawlers had shown indifferent results and had failed to pay dividends even remotely close to that yielded by the fishing schooners.

Opinion on the wharves was unanimous and focused on three main points: (1) proportionately, schooners could catch as many fish of a better quality without destroying the grounds or smaller fish; (2) with the advent of auxiliary power, dory trawlers could profitably engage in winter fishing; and (3) the introduction of cold storage facilities allowed Nova Scotian fishermen to amply supply the Canadian market.

Yet, the issue ran deeper than simple economics. Lunenburgers could not ignore the potential threat to long-established community patterns if the trawler became entrenched. As the local correspondent for the *Atlantic Fisherman* put it, the fleet not only employed two thousand men directly, but was responsible for "building a community of self-respecting, progressive and happy citizens."

It is true that these people did not have much monetarily. Life in Lunenburg and the surrounding county was hard.[6] Every spring the vessels set sail for the Banks after the men had gotten their crops planted. Gone upwards of three months, they left their womenfolk to tend gardens, feed animals, and raise the children until they got back—if they got back. Each season brought news of schooners lost in gales or of dorymen gone missing.

The money earned by fishing helped supplement the family's income, or, perhaps more accurately, farming supplemented the money earned aboard the schooners. In either case, there was never a lot of cash on hand. One lived from hand to mouth, at little more than a subsistence level.

Still, for all that, these people were happy, they were proud, and they were

independent. One old-timer, remarking on all the newfangled opportunities available some forty years later, told an interviewer, "In them days people was poorer . . . but they was happier." Another man observed that, although life was simple, "it was just happy. You was a millionaire."

Nostalgia may play tricks on the imagination, but there was no denying
the realities of life in the tiny villages scattered throughout Lunenburg
County. Forced by isolation to be nearly self-sufficient, families were close-
knit and neighbors cooperated. They had to for survival, but there was more
to the situation than that.

Kinship patterns went back generations. Everyone knew one another, and
one's identity came from being so-and-so's son or daughter, or so-and-so's
grandchild. The community became part of an extended family network
where everyone was related by tradition and necessity, if not by blood. Such
ties bred mutual respect if not always mutual affection, and certainly fostered a sense of interdependence. People knew that they could count on
their neighbors. When a family needed wood for the winter, the men organized a sawing party and went out to the woods while the women stayed
at home quilting. At night, dances at the store or fish shed were common.

Whatever the source of their values, Lunenburgers were sure of one
thing: those values would not survive the introduction of beam trawlers. If
loyalty, trust, and cooperation were hallmarks of a man's character, it was
easy to see how corporate rules would undermine and destroy long-standing personal relationships. Indeed, Lunenburgers prided themselves on a
tradition of mutual respect and understanding between labor and capital, a
tradition they feared would be swept away if the companies behind the beam
trawler got their way. For them, an outright ban on the new technology was
the only viable answer.

As the Depression deepened, the urgency of this solution increased. In
the early spring of 1931, the Lunenburg Board of Trade sponsored a con-
ference attended by representatives of fishermen and fishing interests from
throughout Nova Scotia. A resolution calling for "the abolition of the steam
or otter trawlers on the grounds that the trawler is ruining the fishing business in Nova Scotia" was passed by acclamation. An executive committee was
appointed and sent to Ottawa with explicit instructions to lobby the government, the Nova Scotia members of Parliament, and the Maritime and
Fisheries Commission.

Their argument was simple and direct: eliminate the trawler by prohibiting these vessels from landing fish or taking on supplies at any Canadian
port. With rampant unemployment, job security for some twenty-thousand
Nova Scotian fishermen was both an economic and political imperative. The
delegates contended that, at a time when governments everywhere were
"making a supreme effort to find employment for people," the fishermen's

proposal constituted "a concrete suggestion to help the Government out of some of its present difficulties."

Independent of the unemployment issue, it was argued that the trawlers were an anathema to conservation, and interfered with or destroyed the line fishermen's gear. Challenging the trawler operators' contention that, since other nations used these vessels on the Banks, it was an international problem, the Lunenburgers countered with a question: "Why [are] foreign steam trawlers . . . on the banks so far from their base?" The answer, they said, was obvious. "[T]hey have depleted the fisheries at home and must now go further afield." If Canadians wanted to save their fishing grounds, they needed to make it difficult for foreign vessels by closing their ports to the new method of fishing.

Nor, reasoned the fishermen, was it true that market forces necessitated the use of trawlers to guarantee a continuous supply of fresh fish for the Canadian consumer. In a by now familiar argument, they noted that auxiliary power made the schoonermen perfectly capable of meeting that demand and more.

As straightforward as the Lunenburgers' logic may have seemed, lawmakers could find no easy way to balance such assertions against the equally compelling perspective of the trawler interests. By the end of 1931, the fishermen were frustrated. At the annual convention of the United Maritime Fishermen held at Halifax, there was sharp criticism of the government for its beam trawler policy. Formed a little over a year earlier in June 1930, the United Maritime Fishermen represented some two hundred local fishermen's unions organized by Rev. M. M. Coady in Nova Scotia, Prince Edward Island, New Brunswick, and the Magdalen Islands.

The culmination of more than nine months of work by Coady, the United Maritime Fishermen brought together representatives of 3,314 fishermen, departmental officers, fisheries supervisors, and inspectors to promote cooperation within the industry, further the interests of fishermen and fish workers, secure "just legislation," settle disputes between members, and "promote social intercourse, a higher standard of community life and the study of economic and social questions bearing on our interests as fishermen and citizens." Assured of the Department of Fisheries' cooperation, the organization was committed to moving the industry "in line with modern success in the best sense of the word."

What that meant was obviously open to interpretation, especially when it came to the beam trawler, but for the United Maritime Fishermen the issue was clear. Had they had any doubts, the delegates to the 1931 convention were certainly convinced by what they saw on the wharves in Halifax. One vessel landed 350,000 pounds of fresh fish, but when it was culled, only about 100,000 pounds was actually marketable. The remaining 200,000 pounds was so small or mutilated that it had to be sold to fish meal plants. Talking with the trawlermen, the delegates were appalled to learn that another 175,000 pounds was brought aboard but pitched over the side because of size or damage before the vessel made port.

In the face of such evidence, the convention unanimously voted to adopt a resolution condemning the "indifference" of the government to "the repeated demands of the United Maritime Fishermen for complete and immediate abolition of the trawler." Many at the convention were incredulous that the Department of Fisheries could take such a "very decided stand . . . in favor of the trawler interests." Pointing to the "obvious" depletion of the fish supply and the destruction of spawning grounds, the fishermen found it impossible to understand how any middle course was serving either their interests or the long-term well-being of the Canadian fisheries.

The struggle against the trawler had taken on a moral imperative for the fishermen. In their view, they were involved in a life-or-death struggle for their very way of life. As such, the stakes were too high to settle for anything short of total victory. If the evidence from the United States was any indication, efforts at government compromise only served the corporate interests promoting trawling. The fishermen concluded that, to have any chance at all, they had to force Ottawa to unequivocally accept their point of view.

Of course, such a change was not possible. The *Atlantic Fisherman* had been right in 1926, when it pointed out the futility of "bucking the inevitable." As their American counterparts had back in 1919, Lunenburg dorymen found themselves victims of corporate interests and economic realities beyond their control. As the Depression dragged on and markets became glutted with fish (in no small part the result of the trawlers' efficiency), prices bottomed out. Making a living from the sea—hard enough even in the best of times in Lunenburg—became nearly impossible by 1937. With discontent in the fo'c'sles growing, many crews became restless and refused to ship to the Banks. Talk around town and in the county turned to unionization.

For the most part, the skippers sided with the men. In December 1937, Captain Angus Walters, the feisty master of the famed racer *Bluenose,* was elected president of the Lunenburg Station of the Fishermen's Federation of Nova Scotia. Never one to bite his tongue, Walters promptly supported the fo'c'sle men's demand for a ¼-cent-per-pound increase in the price of haddock. His rationale was blunt and to the point:

> The dealers say they can't afford to pay more for fish. I ask them did not fish bring them wealth? Dealers always argue that it was a poor year. I ask them how they can [afford to] buy up vessels and draggers at the cost of hundreds of thousands of dollars? I'd like to ask some of them who complain most loudly how much money their fathers left them—money that was made by the sweat of the men who sailed to the Banks?[10]

The dealers, led primarily by the Maritime Fish Corporation and General Seafoods of Halifax, refused to concede a price increase or to recognize the fishermen's union. Walters and his organization of Master Mariners had had enough. They refused to sail until the fishermen's demands were met.

Securing the support of the Halifax Fish Handlers and Fish Cutters Union, the Lunenburgers were able to tie up the dragging fleet and to shut down Maritime Fish Corporation's and General Seafoods' main plants. After three weeks of on-again, off-again negotiations, Angus L. MacDonald, premier of Nova Scotia, arbitrated a temporary settlement that got the schooners out to sea, and the fish handlers and cutters back to work, on January 19, 1938.[11]

Like the 1919 American strike, the fishermen's victory came at a high cost. The Lunenburg tie-up was the first labor strife in that community since the fisheries had begun. With it, the Lunenburgers' worst fears were realized. Impersonal business dealings, threats, and class strife had replaced labor-management cooperation, personal integrity, and a sense of mutual responsibility and respect. It was a bitter pill to swallow for people whose values were grounded in generations of a close-knit community.

There was no wonder that the fishermen remained critical of the government for its apparent bias in favor of the trawler companies. In the spring of 1938, when three beam trawlers sought to renew their licenses to land fresh fish in Nova Scotia, the dorymen objected vehemently. Echoing the arguments they had raised in the first years of the decade, they charged J. E. Michaud, the minister of fisheries, with ignoring their interests. Continuing to contend that they could adequately supply the fresh fish market, they refused to acknowledge the economic realities that had forced them to strike only months before.

There was no small irony that Lunenburgers made their stand in the same year that fishing schooners raced for the *Halifax Herald* Trophy for the last time. The races and protests may have allowed the dorymen to feel that they were still relevant, but both were largely symbolic acts. The races had long since stopped being working-class sport, and, like protests by skilled workers in other industries, fishermen's concerns ultimately fell on the deaf ears of a society that believed that progress was inevitable.

6

"Bona Fide Fishing Vessels": The Early Races for the *Halifax Herald* Trophy, 1920–1921

In early June 1921, news reached Gloucester that the *Esperanto* had foundered off Sable Island. Initial shock quickly turned to spirited debate. On Fishermen's Corner, up in the Master Mariners' Hall, at the Board of Trade rooms, and down on the wharves, men argued over the practicality of mounting a salvage operation.[1] From a purely dollars-and-cents point of view, such an expedition was foolish. *Esperanto* was fifteen years old and well past her prime. Only a few months earlier, Gorton-Pew had put her up for sale, reasoning that it was to their advantage to get rid of some of their schooners while market prices were still fairly high.[2] Logistically, raising her from the sands off Sable Island would be difficult, if not impossible. Over two hundred vessels had come to grief in those waters, and not one had ever successfully been salvaged.

However, this was the *Esperanto*. Seven months ago, she had sailed into Gloucester Harbor triumphant, winning the *Halifax Herald* Trophy by sweeping the Canadian *Delawana* in two straight races. Who could forget the euphoria that spread through Gloucester's streets that November day? The celebrations seemed to go on forever, and there was more than a little pride in knowing that she had won the series not only for Gloucester, but for America. If the *Esperanto* could be raised, there would be time to repair her and fit her out for the elimination races in the fall.

Such reasoning clearly ignored the impracticality of saving an old, damaged boat, and the significant cost of outfitting an expedition to salvage and bring her home, but it resonated well with several of the city's leading citizens. R. Russell Smith of Gorton-Pew and J. Norman Abbott helped underwrite a large portion of the costs of the expedition, while Mayor Percy W. Wheeler, ex-mayor Charles D. Brown, and a handful of business and community leaders organized a committee to oversee the operation.

In mid-June the beam trawler *Fabia* left Gloucester with a crew of salvagers headed by A. B. Saliger and chief diver Jack Gardiner, who'd supervised the underwater operations on several Hamburg-American liners that had been scuttled by their German crews in the recent war. Talk along the waterfront held that if anyone could bring the *Esperanto* back, these men could.

Over the next four weeks, rough seas, heavy swells, dense fogs, and unusually strong tides made life aboard the *Fabia* miserable. All told, there were less than forty-eight hours of decent weather during the whole voyage. Even so, the crew managed to raise *Esperanto* six times, twice lifting her whole length. Each time, though, the elements or the equipment betrayed their efforts. On July 17, the *Fabia* returned to Gloucester with a tired and frustrated crew determined to try again.

The next evening a meeting was held at the Board of Trade offices to kick off a drive for additional funds to mount a second expedition. By the twenty-third the *Fabia* had been refitted with heavier wires and stood ready to return to Sable Island. That morning, however, a cable reached Gloucester reporting that *Esperanto* was breaking up. According to the telegram, her spars and deck planks had washed ashore and her seams had opened so badly that there were places in the hull where a knife could be stuck without difficulty. Apparently, she had several large tears on her port side, and her false keel had been pretty much torn off.

Despite this, Gloucester refused to give up on the salvage mission, and preparations to sail continued apace. Later that day, though, even the most die-hard advocate of salvage had to admit defeat. Additional communications with Sable Island confirmed the initial reports. Waterfront denizens grudgingly acknowledged that, with her hull opening up, she would have been "a difficult job to handle," but without spars it was pointless to even try.

As with most things surrounding international fishermen's racing, the motives for the salvage enterprise were a strange mix of politics, community pride, patriotism, and working class consciousness. In this case, in particular, the latter was an especially strong motivator among the skippers, in large part because of *Esperanto*'s history and the challenge posed by specially built schooners like *Mayflower* and *Bluenose*.

Esperanto was a dying breed—a sail-powered salt banker in an era of auxiliary engines and fresh fishing. Designed by Tom McManus, she had a great pedigree.[3] She had been built by Tarr and James and had first been skippered by Charlie Harty. When she had slipped down the ways in 1906, few failed to notice that the smooth sweet lines of her underbody promised to make her a fast sailer. That is what people expected from a vessel designed for Charlie Harty, who had commanded such greyhounds as *Grayling* and *Fredonia*.

With her slightly curved bow, long bowsprit, and moderate run, *Esperanto* was easy on the eyes, while her solid oak construction gave her the strength to weather life on the Banks. In short, she was a typical Gloucesterman, well suited to her task, and before long she had slipped into the workaday routine of earning a living.

This contrasted sharply with *Mayflower*. At $52,000 initial cost, she hardly seemed to be the kind of vessel that would, in the words of the Deed of Gift for the *Halifax Herald* Trophy, encourage the building of "the best possible type of craft in pursuit of the industry," at least not in any significant number to reverse the trend away from sail. Moreover, fishing companies were not investing in all-sail schooners anymore, and building super-expensive racers was not likely to induce them to do so in the future. If *Mayflower* was any indication, only costly hybrid schooners stood a chance of winning the *Halifax Herald* Trophy, and only syndicates organized by well-meaning yachtsmen were interested in building them.

There was something disconcerting about this to the schoonermen, and more than a few of them openly railed against construction of "racers" on general principle. That *Mayflower* was a Boston boat only hardened their opposition. Many Gloucester residents felt that the international races were intended solely for Gloucester and Nova Scotia vessels, and, as such, *Mayflower* represented an unwelcome intrusion. Besides, although Gloucester had some quick boats, few believed that an older, more traditionally built fishing schooner could beat the Starling Burgess-designed *Mayflower*.[4]

Even while she was being framed up, talk around the waterfront had it that, if *Mayflower* raced, there would be no Gloucester entry to challenge her. There were those who believed that it would be better not to race than to have Gloucester's reputation besmirched by losing to a Boston boat that had been sponsored by yachtsmen. To some, *Mayflower* represented just another effort by Boston interests to undermine Gloucester's primacy in the fisheries, a trend begun at the end of the nineteenth century and most dramatically evidenced by the Bay State Fishing Company.

Still, the vilification of *Mayflower* had little to do with her merits as a fishing schooner, or the fact that she was a Boston boat built by yachtsmen. These were surface issues and focused much of the energy and emotion of the debate over her eligibility, but they belied an underlying and more fundamental reality. The people of Gloucester had made her a symbol of what was wrong with the fishing industry, and once that happened, reason went out the window.

Indeed, with Gloucester acutely sensitive to the fact that the viability of sail was all but over, the definition of what constituted a legitimate all-sail fishing schooner became extremely important. *Esperanto* represented an ideal, a standard against which all the supposed inadequacies of *Mayflower* could be measured.

More than anything else, the issue was timing. Had *Mayflower* been built at an earlier time, she would have generated enthusiastic discussion along the waterfront, and even a good deal of healthy speculation about how she would stack up in a head-to-head race against the fleet's fastest schooners.

No one would have grumbled that she was a freak, and if an opportunity to race had availed itself, it would have been welcomed with open arms and a lot of side bets.

Certainly that was what had happened thirty-two years earlier with *Fredonia*. Built by Boston yachtsman J. Malcolm Forbes to race the pilot boat *Hesper*, she had been designed by Starling Burgess's father, Edward. Even though she was launched flying the Eastern Yacht Club ensign, and began life as a yacht before Charlie Harty took her fishing, no one questioned her credentials as a fishing schooner. It was a far cry from the hoopla that followed waterfront speculation that *Mayflower* would be sold as a yacht after the 1921 international races.

In fact, viewed in historical context, neither the glorification of *Esperanto* nor the objections to *Mayflower* made sense. Those who argued that she was an expensive racer built only to indulge the whim of wealthy yachtsmen ignored the fact that the same remark could have been made about the venerated *Fredonia*. Indeed, it would be fair to argue that, by any objective standard, J. Malcolm Forbes was considerably more self-indulgent than Fred L. Pigeon, the prime mover behind the *Mayflower* project. As the *Atlantic Fisherman* rightly pointed out, America's chances of holding on to the international trophy, if it depended on a boat from the old fleet, were slim at best. By building *Mayflower*, Pigeon created a schooner on a par with *Bluenose* and *Canadia,* and kept the United States competitive.

Nor were the yachtsmen who headed up the Schooner *Mayflower* Associates strangers to the fishermen. Men like Charles F. Adams and C. H. W. Foster, who sat on the Board of Directors, were members of the Eastern Yacht Club from way back. Not only had they been friends of J. Malcolm Forbes, but they had taken an active interest in earlier fishermen's races.

If that were not enough, Captain J. Henry Larkin's reputation should have been. A tall, quiet man, he had been a skipper since 1901, and had commanded some of the best schooners in the fleet. Consistently a highliner, Larkin was well liked and widely respected in fishing circles all along the North Atlantic seaboard. As the captain of the *Mayflower,* and a member of her syndicate's Board of Directors, Larkin should have brought the same air of legitimacy to the project that Charlie Harty had to the *Fredonia* enterprise. He did not because *Mayflower*'s detractors tended to disregard or downplay anything that did not support or reinforce their prejudices.

Such shortsightedness made their other criticisms equally groundless. Pointing to her martingale, upswept laminated spreaders, scientific design, and three thousand extra trunnels, many naysayers argued that her radical design disqualified her as a legitimate fishing schooner. What they ignored was the fact that boats like *Fredonia* and *Carrie E. Phillips* revolutionized fishing vessel design in their day by departing from the norm in equally unconventional ways. The *Phillips,* for example, introduced steel wire shrouds, quarterlifts on the main boom, and bowsprit shroud spreaders, among other things.

Some of the "experts" on the wharves noted that *Mayflower* lacked the carrying capacity of a real fishing boat. Considering that one of *Esperanto's* biggest loads was 300,000 pounds of herring under hatches with an additional 200 barrels on deck, *Mayflower* measured up quite well. She could stow 400,000 pounds given her original hold arrangement, and an additional 200,000 pounds if the space reserved for her engines was used. Everett B. James, the man who built the *Mayflower,* claimed that she could carry more fish than any other American boat with the possible exception of *Catherine,* the biggest knockabout schooner out of Gloucester, built in 1915. Most importantly, when she put into Gloucester on July 14, 1921, from her maiden voyage, *Mayflower* landed well over 200,000 pounds of salt fish, an impressive number by any standard. Still, that was irrelevant to her critics.

As a self-conscious effort by the *Halifax Herald* to prove that the "age of sail is not ended," the International Races had taken on special meaning for the people of Gloucester. That was an interesting development when one considers that, in 1920, they had nearly not happened. William Dennis and his associates evolved the idea seemingly by happenstance after the success of the Halifax Fishermen's Carnival. The terms of the Deed of Gift were not even made public until after the first International Races. Gloucester almost failed to field a challenger. In short, there was nothing particularly special about the event when it started, nothing to distinguish it from earlier fishermen's races save for its international flavor.

That a short year later the event was almost sacrosanct in Gloucester speaks volumes. In an age of auxiliary power and trawlers, the chance for a legitimate race under sail was too good to pass up. Unlike earlier races that Boston boats had won—for example, the 1886, 1888, and 1901 contests—there was simply more at stake for the Gloucestermen now. Granted, the public interest in the *Halifax Herald* affairs was far greater than that for any of these others, and national honor was an issue. However, these things *followed* the first races, they did not precede them.

Gloucester's commitment to making the international series an annual event, on the other hand, developed concurrently with the first contests. Besides, it is unlikely that popular interest and nationalism by themselves would have sufficiently motivated the fishermen. After all, public opinion had never carried much weight with them before. One need only recall Marion Perry's snub of Theodore Roosevelt in 1907, or the hoopla over *Hesper* that nearly scuttled the first race in 1886, to realize the truth of that fact.

For the fishermen and for Gloucester, the *Halifax Herald* Races were personal. They were a way to hold on to some past glory, a glory firmly rooted in the age of sail. Given this, it is no wonder that many Gloucesterites felt that the international series should be open only to Gloucester and Nova Scotian vessels, and that *Esperanto* should be raised to defend the city's honor.

Indeed, the way *Esperanto* had won the first *Halifax Herald* series added to her mystique.[5] She had sailed into Gloucester Harbor in October 1920, after spending ten weeks on the Grand Banks salt fishing. Her hull was crusted with salt, marine growth showed below her waterline, and her paint was all but worn off. Her patched mainsail was four years old and showed all the signs of abuse that came with four seasons on the Banks. Because there were no all-sail vessels in port when Gloucester was asked to field a vessel to race the *Delawana,* the American Racing Committee had been in a pickle before the *Esperanto* sailed in.

As the story goes, her first skipper, Charlie Harty, was a member of the Racing Committee, and he sat staring out to sea while his colleagues argued. He caught sight of an old schooner entering the harbor and within a few minutes recognized her as the boat he had commanded some fourteen years earlier.

"There's our vessel," he shouted. "It's the *Esperanto,* she could run and she could reach and she could go to windward when I had her. Get her in trim and she'll sail again."

No one argued. Harty's reputation as the "greatest man to trim and sail a vessel out o' Gloucester" made him an indisputable authority. Besides, there was no choice—it was *Esperanto* or nothing.

Benjamin Smith of Gorton-Pew, which owned *Esperanto,* readily assented to the choice, and promised to help underwrite the cost of getting her ready to race. Smith was a yachtsman and had long taken an interest in fishermen's races. Back in 1901, he had sent telegrams up and down the East Coast to find the *Priscilla Smith* in time to race in the affair that Tom Lawson had sponsored. He could hardly pass up the chance to participate in an international contest against Canada's best.

Some 250,000 pounds of salt fish were emptied from *Esperanto*'s hold, and work began to get her in shape. She was hauled out on the Marine Railway, her underbody was scrubbed clean, and a fresh coat of paint was applied. When she slid back into the water, few would have recognized her for the tired heap that had sailed into port a few days earlier. Her hull was painted a shiny black with a yellow stripe just below the scuppers running her full length. Inboard, her bulwarks were white and blue. The only remnant of her old self was the newly patched four-year-old mainsail she had come home with.

On October 25, Gloucester turned out in force to see her off. As *Esperanto* was towed out past the old Halibut Wharf, the hundreds of people lining the waterfront let out a cheer. Sirens wailed and school bells rang from shore, while on the water small boats escorted *Esperanto* out past Eastern

Point. One fourteen-year-old, who had skipped school like so many of his classmates, recalled years later that she made a handsome sight as she sailed out of the harbor that day, "in her new paint, and with Mikey Hall, her mast headsman, at the mast head!"[6] Thirteen days later, she was back as the undisputed "Queen of the Fleet."

The 1920 races had lived up to the ideal envisioned by Tom McManus when he initiated the first fishermen's race back in 1886. For McManus, the races were to be simple, allowing only time for skippers to haul their schooners, clean and paint their bottoms, race, and be back fishing with a minimum of "expense and unnecessary delay." *Esperanto* had pretty much done just that. There was something refreshing in the straightforward, unpretentious nature of the fishermen's races that contrasted favorably with the rules and technicalities that complicated America's Cup competition. It captured the popular imagination in both Canada and the United States and led *Yachting* magazine to declare that "this championship race appears destined to become a classic."

However, such optimism was misplaced in light of the changes redefining the fisheries. It had been nothing more than sheer luck that *Esperanto* had sailed into Gloucester when she did. With the American Race Committee despairing of finding an entry, serendipity brought them the right boat, but even then, only because Charlie Harty had the keen eyes to see beneath *Esperanto*'s facade and recognize a champion.

If any one of the variables had changed, the results might have been radically different. If Charlie Harty had not been on the committee, or if *Esperanto* had stayed out fishing a few days longer, it is conceivable that the first international series might not have happened, or if it had, it might have involved an American auxiliary with her engine removed. In either case, the elements of excitement that characterized the 1920 races, that made them a throwback to an earlier time and so captured the popular imagination, would never have been.

Indeed, by 1921, when Gloucester launched its futile effort to raise *Esperanto*, it was clear that it would be impossible to ever recapture the spirit of the first series. Certainly the idea of racing envisioned by McManus went down with *Esperanto*. As specially built schooners like *Mayflower, Bluenose,* and *Canadia* captured headlines in 1921, the notion of taking a boat fresh from the Banks, sprucing her up, and letting her race was becoming passé.

Although this bothered the Gloucestermen, they were keenly aware that the racing schooners were likely the last hurrah for the age of sail. According to Dana Story, son of famed Essex shipbuilder A. D. Story, extremely large turnouts for launchings were commonplace in the last days of sail. "As [launchings] began to be less frequent, the word would spread seemingly everywhere and people would come from miles around to witness the event." It was as though they "began to realize that what they were watching was the last of an era."[7]

Thus, despite their ambivalence about her, it seemed that all of Gloucester and Essex turned out to watch *Mayflower* take the plunge on April 12, 1921.[8] In a scene reminiscent of the nineteenth-century launchings of such speedsters as *Fredonia,* some eight thousand people crowded into the little village, making the narrow causeway leading into Essex impassable. One observer characterized the festive atmosphere as a cross between a town meeting and a firemen's muster, with dignitaries, fishing captains, and townsfolk chatting amiably while youngsters scrambled for the best view of the preparations going on in the James Yard.

Ultimately, such enthusiasm for what Charlie Harty characterized as "the finest vessel ever built!" could do nothing to check the politics behind Gloucester's efforts to disqualify the *Mayflower.* Wilmot Reed, secretary of the Gloucester-based American Race Committee, met a delegation from the International Race Committee as it arrived to inspect the *Mayflower* and attend her launching. In the brouhaha that ensued, some heated words were exchanged between Reed and representatives of the *Mayflower* syndicate before the Boston men hustled the Canadians into a cab and took them to the Parker House.

After the fact-finding group returned to Halifax, H. R. Silver, chairman of the International Committee, told the press:

> My information is that there is no material difference in the construction of this boat [*Mayflower*] as compared with other United States fishing vessels. Whether she will be eligible as a defender of the international trophy at the races this year is entirely in the hands of the committee in charge of the United States elimination race . . . just as the Canadian committee will decide what vessels shall enter for the elimination race at Halifax.

The pronouncement had little impact on the Gloucester committee. In May the Canadians were apprised that *Mayflower* did not have a proper anchor cable aboard, and that she had taken her time getting to the Banks. She left Boston on April 28—two days before the Deed of Gift deadline for eligibility—and stopped off at Gloucester, Shelburne, Canso, Souris, Prince Edward Island, and the Magdalen Islands on the way.

When the *Halifax Herald* wondered out loud about such doings, the *Mayflower* Associates challenged *Bluenose* to a race the next January and charged Gloucester with instigating the controversy. According to the Bostonians, Gloucester just could not abide the thought of a Boston boat defending the trophy. Although the Gloucester committee denied the charges, they were quick to point out that it was a fact that the Deed of Gift specified that "any vessel competing must have actually sailed from her last port of departure for the fishing banks not later than April thirtieth." The inference was obvious because *Mayflower* had failed to do so.

By June, the Gloucester people were getting desperate. Forgoing subtlety, Wilmot Reed reportedly told the *Halifax Herald* that "If the Canadians put up a sufficiently loud protest to the American Committee . . . the Yankee racer *Mayflower* will be disqualified from entering the contest." That Reed's remarks came as the expedition to raise *Esperanto* was being organized seems hardly coincidence. Indeed, it could be argued that *Esperanto*'s sinking could not have happened at a better time for the Gloucester committee. It put into stark relief the difference between real working boats like *Esperanto* and specially built racers like *Mayflower*. If *Esperanto* could be raised and entered in the fall elimination races, Gloucester could make an eloquent statement about what fishermen's races were supposed to be, certainly far more eloquent than all the petty carping that had surrounded *Mayflower* since she had been framed up.

Clearly, there was something appealing—maybe even poetic—in resurrecting *Esperanto* to challenge *Mayflower*. Consciously or not, Gloucester was trying to hold on to a traditional and time-honored part of its culture. At the very least, it hoped to thwart another Boston assault on its heritage. The logic was sound. Everyone knew that what had made the 1920 races so successful was the romanticism of real working boats competing in the McManus tradition. The New York press had said as much back in March when it bemoaned what it saw as a conscious effort to pervert the original intentions of the international races. There was no doubt that Gloucester was banking on some of this feeling when it sought to raise *Esperanto*. As the *Atlantic Fisherman* so astutely noted:

> If the expedition is successful the *Esperanto* will be entered in the elimination races in the fall. There is little question but that public sentiment would be strongly behind her as to render still more difficult the task of the American committee in making an impartial decision on the status of *Mayflower*.

Though the effort to raise *Esperanto* failed, on September 15 the Gloucester committee got its wish when the International Trustees abruptly banned *Mayflower*. Because she had been the only entrant, the American Race Committee had had no choice but to name her to defend the Trophy. Now that the Canadians had acted, the Gloucester Committee wasted no time in disqualifying her, declaring the next day that she would not be allowed to race. Given Wilmot Reed's comments back in June, one can only imagine how relieved the Gloucester folks were to have a legitimate reason to ban the *Mayflower*.

Why the Canadians had barred her was not initially clear. Since no reason was given for the action, rumors ran rampant. Early speculation had it that the trustees felt that her rig violated the spirit of the Deed of Gift, which called for contestants to use their regular working sails in the races. Allegedly *Mayflower*'s rig was oversized for a boat of her dimensions, and her crew supposedly freely admitted that it would be cut down when she went fishing.

That this was so much nonsense would have been obvious to anyone who had bothered to compare *Mayflower*'s sail plan with *Bluenose*'s. They were, for all intents and purposes, identical.[9] *Bluenose*'s total sail area was slightly larger than *Mayflower*'s, 10,937 square feet to 10,785 square feet. Although *Mayflower*'s mainsail and foresail were a bit bigger than *Bluenose*'s, (4,270 to 4,100 square feet, and 1,832 to 1,640 square feet, respectively), the Lunenburger's fore and main gaff topsails, her staysail, jumbo, and jib topsail more than made up the difference. *Mayflower*'s mainmast was some seven feet higher than *Bluenose*'s, and her foremast measured 83 feet to *Bluenose*'s 73 feet. The latter's fore-topmast, however, was more than six feet taller than the Boston schooner's, although their main-topmasts were about equal, with *Bluenose* having a slight advantage.

The unofficial rationale for the trustees' decision, articulated much later, was that *Mayflower* was a yacht, and as such violated both the letter and spirit of the Deed of Gift. Pointing to the term "schooner-yacht" on her sail plan, and noting that a commercial fishing company did not own her, supporters of the trustees contended that she was constructed only to defend the cup. Edgar Kelly of the *Halifax Herald* was quoted as saying, "The action of the slick Yankee yacht fanciers is 'not cricket.'"[10]

Cricket or not, there was more than a little hypocrisy in this argument. Shortly after *Esperanto* had cleared Halifax Harbor with the International Trophy in her hold, William Dennis had named a committee of interested ship owners and others to find a challenger that was big enough to work the Banks and "at the same time fast enough to beat anything Gloucester can produce." They had approached William J. Roue, a Halifax ginger ale manufacturer and amateur naval architect, to design *Bluenose*.[11]

As to "yacht fanciers" putting their noses where they did not belong, Roue had gotten his commission because he was a member of the Royal Nova Scotia Yacht Squadron, and he had known many of the men who came to make up the International Committee. Indeed, he spent most of his Saturday afternoons racing aboard R. A. Corbett's sloop *Windward*. Corbett, along with Dennis and H. R. Sloer, had helped conceive the idea of an international series. Designing fast boats for several members of the squadron, Roue's reputation had been established well before the Halifax Race Committee asked him to design *Bluenose*, or named him as a trustee of the *Halifax Herald* Trophy.

Most Canadians believed that *Bluenose* was a wonder schooner. A crewman was heard to remark after one race, "The wood is still growing for the vessel that can beat her." Here she is seen showing her winning form in one of the international races. (Photograph courtesy of Mystic Seaport Museum, Rosenfeld Collection, Mystic, Connecticut)

Although it would be hard to refute the fact that Fred Pigeon and his friends at the South Boston Yacht Club (where he and his brother Roy were members) and the Eastern were largely responsible for *Mayflower*, it is equally difficult to ignore *Bluenose's* yachting connections. Indeed, a rumor was current in Lunenburg for quite a while that, for all intents and purposes, she was a yacht financed largely by Halifax yachtsmen. Though Dennis dismissed the charges, claiming that fully 80% of her cost was financed by subscribers from Lunenburg County "involved in the fisheries,"[12] he could not deny that it was unusual for a fishing schooner to have brass trim, sail covers, electric lights, and an electric signal bell system, not to mention a brass bed for the skipper.

In the name of national pride, such inconsistencies were easy to ignore. Winning back the *Halifax Herald* Trophy had become a national priority in Canada. It was certainly no coincidence that the Duke of Devonshire, Canada's Governor-General, made a special trip from Ottawa to drive the first bolt in *Bluenose*'s keel at a specially held ceremony marking the beginning of construction at Lunenburg's Smith and Rhuland yard.

It would probably be fair to say that the International Trustees were convinced that the only American boat with a chance of beating *Bluenose* was *Mayflower*, so they acted accordingly. Stories circulated that *Bluenose* captain Angus Walters had stated unequivocally that he would not race if *Mayflower* were the defender. These rumors, along with Gloucester's refusal to field a challenger, led some to believe that the International Trustees banned *Mayflower* because she was built "so close to the limit" that other contenders were frightened off.

Although this interpretation has some validity when one considers Gloucester's response, it is not entirely clear what impact Walters's alleged statement had, or if indeed he made such a statement at all. Reports coming out of Lunenburg in June 1921 observed that when *Bluenose* arrived on May 30 with her first trip of fish, Walters had become "quite provoked" when he heard comments suggesting that *Mayflower* should be disqualified because she would probably beat *Bluenose*. He and other Lunenburg skippers pointed out that *Bluenose* was every bit as good as *Mayflower*, and folks should wait until after the race to declare which was the better boat.

The sad thing was that the entire flap over *Mayflower* obscured the fact that she, and *Bluenose* for that matter, met the spirit of the Deed of Gift. If they were departures from the norm, that was what the *Halifax Herald* Races were supposed to encourage—"development of the most practical and serviceable type of fishing schooner." The only ones who seemed to recognize that fact at the time, however, were the members of the Boston Chamber of Commerce, and that was because they had an agenda.

When the trustees summarily disqualified *Mayflower* on September 15, 1921, the chamber's Maritime Committee appointed a special task force to investigate the situation. The resulting resolution argued that:

> Whereas several public spirited citizens of Boston interested in promoting the fishing industry of New England have built a model fishing schooner with the idea of evolving an economical and workable vessel which shall not need auxiliary power [and is] strong and sturdy;
> And whereas this vessel . . . has engaged in salt fishing the past season and is now fresh fishing and will continue in this occupation through the coming winter;
> Be it therefore resolved that the Maritime Association of the Boston Chamber of Commerce declares *Mayflower* to be a genuine fishing vessel built to promote the fishing industry. . . .

The resolution went on to ask the International Trustees to reverse their decision and let *Mayflower* race.

Of course they did not, but perhaps there was some consolation in knowing that *Mayflower* was not their only victim. Shortly after the 1920 Canadian elimination races, Captain Joseph Conrad approached Amos Pentz, Shelburne's mayor and one of Canada's best known vessel designers, about building a new boat that could compete in the *Halifax Herald* Races.[13] The two decided that the craft should be thoroughly Canadian—from material, to craftsmanship, to crew—to typify the best that Canada had to offer.

Construction began in December 1920, at the famed McGill Shipbuilding and Transportation Company of Shelburne. Except for the keelsons, clamps, and large spars, which were Douglas fir, every piece of wood that went into *Canadia* was grown in Shelburne County. She was, as the Shelburne folks proudly called her, a "home product."

A semi-knockabout design, *Canadia* represented no distinct departure from most of the Canadian schooners of that day, except for her waterline length. Over half built when a copy of the revised Deed of Gift was given to her owners, she was 116 feet at the waterline, four feet over the maximum specified. Conrad and Pentz protested that she was built in good faith when they thought that 125 feet was to be the maximum waterline length allowed. The trustees ruled that, although she could compete in the elimination races, if she won she would be disqualified from competing for the International Trophy.

They decided the same thing about Lunenburg's *Independence*, which, interestingly enough, had competed in the 1920 elimination race before the Deed of Gift was drafted.[14] That the 1920 elimination race was not an elimination race until the sponsors of the Fishermen's Carnival Regatta decided to challenge Gloucester probably had something to do with it. Now that the international series was a big event, however, the trustees were being scrupulous about enforcing their rules to the letter.

The result was a ridiculous situation that left many fishermen scratching their heads. If either *Independence* or *Canadia* won the 1921 eliminations, they would be barred from representing Canada in the races for the cup. Instead, the Halifax Race Committee would pick the schooner that made the best showing from among the eligible vessels that competed. This would not be a very satisfying result for men who believed that boats should race on their own bottoms, vessel for vessel, just as on the Banks. As the situation turned out, *Bluenose* won both elimination races, saving the trustees the embarrassment of applying their convoluted rules.

Meanwhile, in Gloucester, the American Race Committee scrambled to organize a qualifying race. With nearly everyone caught up in the enthusiasm of an old-fashioned fishermen's regatta, it seems ironic that no one noticed that there was something a bit counterfeit about the whole matter. If the original intent of fishermen's races had been to allow "any and every vessel designed and built for fishing purposes" to race, as Tom McManus put it, the vagaries of the politics that barred *Mayflower* guaranteed that, despite

Gloucester's best efforts to the contrary, the traditional focus of these contests was lost. In fact, Gloucester's agitation against *Mayflower* sabotaged the very purity of the races that it was, rhetorically at least, designed to preserve.

An earlier generation of fishermen would likely have been turned off by the politics and gone fishing. In 1921, though, the stakes were too high. Patriotism and community pride motivated the nonfishermen on the American Race Committee to seek victory at any cost.

That attitude created an opportunity for the skippers to showcase their skills to an international audience at a time when those skills were becoming irrelevant. Under such circumstances, the definition of what constituted a "bona fide fishing schooner" took on new importance. Just as they had found it necessary to distinguish themselves from the trawlermen and the engineers aboard the auxiliaries, sailing skippers were using their vessels to highlight their differences from those outside their culture—specifically the yachtsmen. Indeed, they had no choice. If the races became glorified yachting regattas, yet another means of holding onto their heritage would be lost.

Moreover, with nothing equivalent to *Mayflower* in the fleet, what choice did they have but to exalt the virtue of what vessels they had? Not surprisingly, when the elimination race was held on October 12, much was made of the fact that the five contestants were all bona fide fishermen. At nineteen years old, the *Philip P. Manta* out of Provincetown was the oldest, but not by much. *Arthur James* had been built in 1905. She had seen sixteen seining seasons and four collisions, the most recent in 1916 off Castle Island, where she sank in fifty feet of water after being run down by a steamer.

Elsie was eleven years old, and only months before had returned to Gloucester after two years in Lunenburg with Gorton-Pew's Canadian affiliate. The *Elsie G. Silva* was a fair-sized knockabout, the last of her kind built in Gloucester in 1915. Reputed to be one of the fastest boats in the Portuguese fleet, she had once sailed from Graves Light to Eastern Point in one hour and ten minutes. The *Ralph Brown*, an equally respected schooner, rounded out the field.[15]

With Marty Welch at the helm, *Elsie* defeated the other vessels handily, *Ralph Brown* coming in second, followed by *Arthur James*, *Elsie G. Silva*, and *Philip P. Manta*, in that order. Within days, *Elsie* was hauled out and a new coat of copper paint applied to her bottom. When she left Gloucester, she received nearly as much fanfare as *Esperanto* had the year before.

To no one's surprise, *Bluenose* beat her, two races to none. Even in defeat, several Gloucester skippers told reporters that they were glad that *Mayflower* had not raced. It was better for *Elsie* to lose, they reasoned, than to have had *Mayflower* win and have the Canadians question her legitimacy. Such statements highlighted the attitudes that had governed Gloucester's behavior throughout the controversy. Before *Mayflower* had been disqualified, no one from Gloucester had wanted any part of the series, and many had believed that it was a matter of pride not to participate in an event that perverted the purpose and intent of the fishermen's races. By the same logic, it was preferable to go down to defeat with a legitimate fishing schooner than to win with a yachtsman's freak.[16]

So strong was the debate over what constituted a "real" fishing schooner that it generated some discussion about changing the Deed of Gift after the 1921 series. In particular, there was talk of limiting the competition to vessels that had fished for at least two years. Some even proposed that the restriction be set at three or five years. If the latter were adopted, *Bluenose, Canadia,* and *Mayflower* would automatically be disqualified. If the limit were set at two years, *Bluenose* could still compete, but no new American boat could be built to challenge.

Setting minimum age limits appealed to the sentimentality that old workhorses like *Elsie* generated in America and Canada. There were even those in Nova Scotia who felt that *Bluenose* should not have been selected to represent Canada. They argued that because *Elsie* had labored for more than ten years on the Banks, an older Nova Scotian vessel should have been chosen. Although nothing came of these ideas, they reflected a nagging concern on both sides of the border that international racing was at risk of losing its unique appeal as working-class sport and degenerating into a contentious free-for-all.

Still, such feelings had little place in an atmosphere where national and community pride put great stake in winning the *Halifax Herald* Trophy. As the events of 1921 demonstrated, there were too many competing interests for the international series to ever be what it had been in 1920. With technology quickly making vessels like *Elsie*—and the men who sailed them—obsolete, it was inevitable that the Gloucestermen would soon accept the virtues of racing schooners, and in the process lose control of the very races in which they were supposed to star.

7

Forgetting Principle: Nationalism, Civic Pride, and the Quest for the Trophy, 1922

WHEN IT BECAME OBVIOUS THAT NOTHING IN THE GLOUCESTER FLEET COULD touch *Bluenose,* several fishing captains and businessmen met for dinner in a Halifax hotel to discuss the possibility of building a new schooner.[1] Jeff and Billy Thomas, two of Gloucester's highline skippers, Kenneth Ferguson of Gloucester National Bank, United Sail Loft's Marion Cooney, the owner of Fulham Fish Company, and the enigmatic Ben Pine attended the initial meeting and committed $25,000 to the project. On October 25, 1921, they told the press that they planned to organize a company and promised to raise whatever additional funds were necessary to field a contender. In a spirit reminiscent of the Canadians' efforts to build *Bluenose,* the entire city of Gloucester seemed to rally behind these men, forgetting that only days before, so much had been made of *Elsie*'s virtues as a bona fide fishing schooner. The only thing that mattered now was constructing a boat that could beat *Bluenose.*

When considered in context, the apparent flip-flop made sense. Because *Esperanto* had affirmed Gloucester's self-image as home to the finest fishing fleet in the world, there had been no incentive to build a racing schooner after the 1920 series, and probably every reason not to. Indeed, the city's opposition to *Mayflower* had in part grown from such thinking. *Bluenose,* however, had proven that building a racing schooner was the only way to win the *Halifax Herald* Trophy. Protests that it was better to lose with *Elsie* than to win with *Mayflower* notwithstanding, Gloucestermen were too proud to accept defeat lying down. If building a racer was what it took to be competitive and to reestablish their primacy within the North Atlantic fleet, so be it.

At the heart of the enterprise was Ben Pine, a self-made man who began his career as a junk collector. A Newfoundlander by birth, he came to Gloucester in 1893 at age ten determined to make it big. He spent his youth in a dory buying and selling junk around Gloucester Harbor, with an occasional fishing trip to the Banks to supplement his income. By 1905, he had gone into business with Joseph Langsford. The firm of Langsford and Pine

acquired twelve medium-sized vessels, mostly schooners, that fished for mackerel in the spring, swordfish in the summer, and mackerel and herring in the fall.[2]

Well-established by 1921, Pine had a reputation as a tightfisted, hard-headed businessman, except among some of Gloucester's youth. They found him an easy mark. He paid local kids one to two cents for old bottles, which he stored in the back of his office. According to one former Gloucester resident, youngsters would "go around and . . . help themselves to a few bottles . . . [then] sell them [back] to him again."[3]

With adult business associates, however, he was less gullible. He seldom paid cash for outstanding debts when he could settle a bill by bartering material in his yard for services rendered. If employees did not live up to his expectations, he fired them without ceremony. To those he liked, however, he could be a mentor. One skipper recalled that "he was like a father to me."[4] Still, even with partners, he was always the shrewd wheeler-dealer, looking for ways to work the angles. As one man explained it:

[H]e'd go 50/50 on the ownership of a vessel . . . [When] the season was over [and] the vessel had to buy new dories or new gear . . . Piney said, "Well, look, I'll buy the dories. I'll buy the trawl gear." That sort of thing.

[A]fter three years or so when, maybe the co-owner . . . wanted to get out of it . . . how much of the vessel [was] left that he [still] owned? And this is where Piney always took 'em, because the only way they could sell out their shares . . . was . . . for a rather small part of the vessel, after he deducted the cost of dories and gear and all that stuff. They found they had no value left.[5]

For all this, Pine was something of a romantic. Like others in Gloucester, he had an affinity for the beauty of the schooners and a pride in his adopted city's place in the fishing industry. Though he had never really been a fisherman save for the few trips he had made as a boy, Pine liked the company of the skippers who had built Gloucester's reputation. In fact, he may have even envied them their stature. It might be fair to say that he was a frustrated captain and saw the *Halifax Herald* Races as a way to fulfill a fantasy. At the very least, his civic pride and sense of sportsmanship played into his desire to get involved in racing.

Pine had borrowed the *Philip P. Manta* from her Boston namesake so that he would have a boat to captain in the 1921 elimination race. Though the

(Opposite) Ben Pine had spent little time as a fisherman, but like many in Gloucester, he became enamoured with the romance of the all-sail fishing fleet. As a leader in Gloucester's effort to field a winning racer, Pine helped define the public's image of what a fishing skipper was like, even though he'd never captained a schooner on the Banks. (Photograph courtesy of Mystic Seaport Museum, Rosenfeld Collection, Mystic, Connecticut)

schooner was old and finished last, Pine showed a real talent for handling his vessel. The experience must have invigorated him, and being named to *Elsie's* crew only served to fuel his racing fever.

When he got back to Gloucester, he contacted his friend Manta, who promptly joined the syndicate to build a Gloucester racer. Other local men followed suit, including Captain Robert Wharton of the *Fabia,* and Pine's business associates Captain James Mason, Charles A. Steele, and J. Norman Abbott (these last three would soon join Pine in forming the Atlantic Supply Company). Captain Charles C. Colson, George E. Roberts, Herbert W. Wennerberg, Alexander McDonald, Carmello Capillo, and Charles F. Fuller rounded out the original subscribers. The group called itself the Manta Club, with every member, except Jeff Thomas, owning a sixteenth of the boat. As skipper, Thomas received a 3/16ths share.

In light of all the noise Gloucester had made over *Mayflower,* it was ironic that the group chose Starling Burgess to design their schooner, and even more ironic that his plans called for a scaled-down version of the *Mayflower.* The new boat, named *Puritan,* after Edward Burgess's first America's Cup defender, was slightly smaller than *Mayflower,* with high, slack bilges like the Boston boat but none of her "radical" elements.[6]

Amid all the excitement over *Puritan,* Clayt Morrissey's new schooner got little initial attention from either the press or the public.[7] In retrospect, that seems almost symbolic. As the races became the province of civic and business leaders like Ben Pine, it was inevitable that their efforts would receive the lion's share of attention. Indeed, it is significant that Morrissey turned out to be the last bona fide fishing captain to skipper an American contender for the *Halifax Herald* Trophy. Because it took racers to be competitive in the international series, and syndicates to organize the capital to build them, skippers who wanted to participate had to go out of their way to solicit sponsors, or be lucky enough to be connected with monied interests who wanted to be involved with the races. Jeff Thomas and Henry Larkin fell into the latter category, Morrissey into the first.

To build a new vessel, Morrissey sought out the financial support of Frank C. Pearce of the local fisheries firm of the same name, Arthur D. Story whose yard built his boat, and East Point summer residents F. Wilder Pollard and Jonathan Raymond. The first two arrangements were not unusual because fishing companies often underwrote part of the cost of building vessels for "worthy" captains, and A. D. Story frequently took shares in vessels he built to guarantee that he made some money from the boats he sold. The connection between Morrissey, Pollard, and Raymond was a bit more unusual, although even this relationship made sense, given the traditional interest of many East Pointers in the fisheries and in fitting into the Gloucester community.

The Manta Club launched *Puritan* in the spring of 1922, with every expectation that she had what it took to beat the highly touted *Bluenose*. Unfortunately, she ran aground off Sable Island before she had the chance to prove herself. According to Captain Jeff Thomas's son, she was so fast that she had outrun her crew's ability to chart her location when she met with disaster. The truth is, like many fishing captains, Thomas's navigating wasn't his strong suit. (Photograph courtesy of Mystic Seaport Museum, L. Francis Herreshoff Collection, Mystic, Connecticut)

What is intriguing is how Morrissey's schooner got her name. Until March 1922, few suspected that she would be called the *Henry Ford*. The official reason for the choice was that Mrs. Morrissey so admired the Detroit automaker that she wrote him asking for permission to name the craft after him. Rumor had it, though, that the Morrisseys were hoping that such an honor would move Ford to contribute funding for the vessel. Unfortunately, it did not. Ford wrote back, agreeing to lend his name to the boat and saying that he would follow her career carefully.

If the rumor was true, it points up just how far afield fishermen had to go to build vessels that were competitive. If it was not, there is still something significant in the fact that Eastern Point capital was involved in building the *Ford*. When people like Pollard and Raymond invested in a schooner, they did so to be part of the racing scene. They did not care if the *Ford* proved to be a highliner. That was not why they had spent their money.

Given this, Gloucester's original objection to the racers was well founded. In the old days, when fishing companies built boats for their captains, they did so to turn a profit. Even when headed by avid yachtsmen like Gorton-

The *Henry Ford* got off to an inauspicious start. As she was being brought to Gloucester to be fitted out, she broke free of the tug that was towing her and ran aground.
Fortunately, she survived the incident and went on to become the 1922 American
challenger for the *Halifax Herald* Trophy. Here she is shown in the final stages of construction at the Arthur D. Story Yard in Essex, Massachusetts. (Photograph courtesy
of Mystic Seaport Museum, John P. Samuels Collection, Mystic, Connecticut)

Pew's Ben Smith, the firm's chief expectation was to make money fishing.
By contrast, the racing schooner investor was in it simply for the sport. Even
the Manta Club, with its ties to the industry, was organized only to build a
winning boat. *Puritan's* profitability on the Banks was a secondary concern
at best.

   None of this mattered to Morrissey, Thomas, or Larkin. They were fishermen, and a high-quality schooner meant that they could pretty much
guarantee a successful season. What difference did it make who put up the
money to build it? Besides, it gave them the chance to be on center stage in
an exciting public spectacle. Under such circumstances, it was easy enough
to forgo any qualms about the evils of "racers."

   Still, it was becoming increasingly obvious for whom the races were being
run. When *Puritan* sank off Sable Island on June 23, 1922, Ben Pine hardly
flinched.[8] Within days of Jeff Thomas's return to Gloucester, he chartered

the *Elizabeth Howard* from her New York owner and began refitting her for fishing so that she could qualify for the elimination races.[9] Built in Boothbay, Maine, in 1916, the *Howard* was a big Tom McManus–designed knockabout.[10] Spending most of her life as a fish carrier out of New York City, she had sailed from nearly every Atlantic port and spent time in the Mediterranean. This fast and weatherly boat's owner, William Willard Howard, had offered her to the American Committee a year earlier. Writing to the *Gloucester Times* in the summer of 1921, he had said that, despite her registry, his vessel would be a "fit representative of Gloucester" in the elimination races against *Mayflower.*

No one had taken him up on his offer, but Pine must have remembered it. He and Marion Cooney became managing operators of *Howard* in July 1922. Newspapers reported that Pine was outfitting the *Howard* for Thomas to go fishing for halibut. However, that never happened. Instead, she was sent fishing under Captain Albert Pico.

According to Thomas's son, shortly after the *Puritan* disaster, his father came home from a meeting with the Manta Club, madder than a wet hornet. "I'm all through with racing," he declared. "Don't want no part of it." His son always believed that Pine was behind his father's decision, and, given Pine's disposition, he was likely right.[11] As if to confirm the point, before the American trials, Pine decided to skipper the *Howard* in the race himself.

By August, the American Committee had accepted five entries for the trials: *Mayflower, Elizabeth Howard, Henry Ford, Yankee,* and *L. A. Dunton.* The *Yankee* had been built in August 1921 for Boston Captain Mike Brophy, and had proven to be an erratic performer.[12] *Dunton* was the most traditional vessel of the lot and, since her launching the year before, had shown herself to be a capable fisherman but a poor sailer. Why her captain, Felix Hogan, even bothered to enter the 1922 races is unclear, especially because his son reported that he really was not interested in competing. The best explanation was probably that one of the vessel's stockholders, sailmaker Louis A. Dunton of Boothbay, offered Hogan a free suit of sails if he would race. It was the same offer he had used to get the schooner named for himself a year earlier.[13]

If Pine's and Dunton's actions left any question about who was calling the shots, the continuing controversy over *Mayflower* removed any doubt.[14] The *Mayflower* Associates made application in 1922 to allow their vessel to enter the elimination race, noting that she had proven herself a real fisherman. Following a winter of fishing, she was highliner of Boston's schooner fleet, her last trip of 116,000 pounds setting a record for the year. Despite the logic of the case, the Halifax Trustees dragged their feet deciding on her eligibility, prompting the *Mayflower* Associates to charge that the Canadians had "an understanding with the Gloucester 'bunch.'" When the American Committee announced that it would insist on *Mayflower's* eligibility if she won the elimination series, officials of the *Mayflower* Associates recanted their charges. As things turned out, the committee's resolve was short-lived.

The International Trustees upheld their ban, arguing that because the Deed of Gift was intended to encourage development of vessels in *both* the American and Canadian fisheries, it was unfair to race a Yankee fresh fisherman against a Canadian salt banker. Because boats engaged in fresh fishing were built for speed, Canadian boats would be placed at an unnecessary disadvantage if they were forced to race schooners like *Mayflower.* That such a rationale excluded pretty much every vessel in the American fleet, and that *Mayflower* had been salt fishing, seemed beside the point.

The American Committee met for six hours to discuss their response and issued a letter proposing that the International Races be suspended for a year, pending a revision of the rules that would allow American and Canadian boats to compete equally. In place of the *Halifax Herald* series, a free-for-all race of the fastest American and Canadian vessels was suggested for 1922, with an appropriate cup and purse to be offered. Despite the letter, preparations for the races continued apace, and committee members acknowledged that if the trustees rejected the American idea, they would go on with the races anyway. Quite simply, too much was at stake for them not to proceed.

On October 12, four schooners came to the line in what was to be the first race of a best-two-out-of-three event.[15] *Henry Ford* won easily. In the second race, *Howard* and *Yankee* made a race of it for the first leg, then Clayt Morrissey's schooner forged ahead and never looked back.

Two days after the race, Ben Pine announced that he and his associates had given orders for construction of "a new *Puritan*" to be built over the coming winter. He hoped that she would qualify for both the city's 300th Anniversary Race and the International Races in 1923. The proposed vessel would be a bit smaller than *Puritan,* but it was hoped that it would be every bit as fast. Pine told reporters that he was convinced that *Puritan* could have "taken the measure of anything afloat today," and he wanted his own craft "for next year."[16]

In so doing, Pine took the next step in pushing the fishing skippers to the sidelines of international racing. Caught up in the excitement of competition, there was no way that he was going to let anyone else race his new beauty in either event. He had come too close to winning the American trials in a borrowed boat to forgo the thrill of skippering his own schooner in future contests.

On the evening of Friday, October 20, 1922, less than twenty-four hours before the international series was set to begin, Clayt Morrissey was told that his schooner's sails were too big.[17] He stayed up all night supervising their cutting but still managed to beat *Bluenose* the next day, or so he and his crew thought. Unfortunately, they had not counted on the Sailing Committee. Ignoring a postponement signal, the captains had decided to race. With the schooners within spitting distance of each other as they approached the line, Angus Walters had yelled, "What say Clayt, Let's have a race. I'm going to race if I have to sail alone." It was the sort of contest that happened on the way to and from the Banks all the time. One vessel would saunter up alongside another, some words would be exchanged, and then they would be off under a full press of sail.

As far as the fishermen were concerned, the race was official. When the Sailing Committee dispatched a boat to get Morrissey to turn around, one of the crew shouted, "Tell the judges to go back to Halifax." After the race, Captain Walters declared, "Whatever anybody says, it was a race and the best boat won." The Sailing Committee disagreed, ruling the contest "no race." According to the Committee, both vessels had committed a false start, and Ford's mainsail was still too big. Apparently the official measurer had made a mistake. Clayt Morrissey's response to the controversy was simple and direct: "I'm going fishing Monday."

Twenty years earlier, he would have. Yet, matters were not so simple anymore. The Halifax Herald Races had become more than a fishermen's race. Morrissey carried the honor of the United States on his shoulders. He found that out when Secretary of the Navy Edwin Denby, President Harding's official representative to the series, told Ford's crew that it was a matter of patriotism.

"Never let it be said," Denby entreated, "[that] the men of Clark's Harbor, the Pubnico's, and Barrington, helped to trail Old Glory in the dust."

So, on Monday, October 23, they raced again. Again, with recut mainsail and all, the Henry Ford won. That should have been the end of it, Morrissey reasoned. He had won twice, Captain Walters having announced his willingness to honor the results of the first race. As he made preparations to get his boat ready for fishing, Morrissey dismissed inquiries from the press about whether he worried about losing the prize money. "It has cost me and my men enough already so that the matter of a few thousand dollars does not count against the principle involved," he said.

However, the powers that be were not through with him yet. Jonathan Raymond, one of the Ford's owners, invited Morrissey and his crew to a late-night dinner at his estate, the Ramparts, located in the affluent Eastern Point section of Gloucester.[18] About 11 P.M., after much talk and some illicit hooch, Morrissey asked his men what they thought. They voted unanimously to continue racing.

Rumors flew around Gloucester about what had transpired at the Ramparts. Some of the crew chatted about all the money that had been bet on the races, while others said, "everything was explained to us at the dinner. Now we're going out and fight and win!"

The *Henry Ford* buries her lee rail during the 1922 international series. It was photographs like this one that captured public imagination and fueled the romanticism
surrounding the fishermen's races. (Photograph courtesy of Mystic Seaport Museum, Rosenfeld Collection, Mystic, Connecticut)

Morrissey's first mate, John Matheson, told the press, "We have changed
our attitude to meet public demand and so that the contest may be recognized officially."

By Wednesday morning, October 25, Morrissey's mind was filled with con-
flicting emotions and impulses as he paced the deck of his schooner. "Come

ashore, Clayton," his wife pleaded. "Let someone [else] sail her. You're sick, I'm sick, and my boy is sick to the point of death. Let's get rid of this miserable business."[19]

The captain was torn. A devoted family man, Morrissey had sacrificed a lot in the name of patriotism and community pride. Little had he dreamed when the *Ford* was launched back in April how complicated life would become. Back then, he had anticipated her completion with what one contemporary called "a boy's enthusiasm."[20] Now he regretted ever having raced her.

Caught up in the hoopla of the last several days, Morrissey came to realize just how ludicrous the situation was. For the life of him he could not understand why sails that had served him well on the Banks suddenly were all wrong for racing. After all, the Deed of Gift stipulated that "the sails used in racing shall be made of the ordinary commercial duck of the same weight and texture as generally used in this class of vessel and shall have been used at least one season in fishing."[21]

For Mrs. Morrissey, the issue was clear. She knew her husband, and these races were not good—for him, for her, or for her family. She begged Clayton to stand by his original decision not to race. As the two huddled together, talking for a long time, tears streaked both their faces. Finally, Morrissey sadly shook his head and escorted her to the rail. Tenderly placing his hand on his wife's shoulder, he told her, "I must go, they've got me."

Morrissey lost that day, and the day after that as well. By the time *Bluenose* sailed for home, public frustration with the series was rampant. Official protests were lodged with the International Race Committee, but few people expected anything to come of them (they were right). Talk around Gloucester strongly supported boycotting the 1923 *Halifax Herald* Races and organizing a race open to schooners from any New England port.

Tom McManus spoke for many when he observed that "the manner in which the races were conducted was so disgusting to . . . the general public . . . that if they are not changed and simplified, so that they will really be contests sailed by fishermen, as fishermen, and not, under yachting rules and yachtsmen management, they are in great danger of losing their public appeal."[22]

Captain George Peeples of the Gloucester Master Mariners, and chair of the International Sailing Committee, echoed those sentiments when he told reporters, "Fishermen should race as they fish, wearing working sails whether large or small, carrying as much or as little ballast as they wish, changing to meet the varying conditions of wind and weather. These things they do everyday while fishing. There is no need for rules to bring fishermen into the races."[23] Even William Dennis blamed conflicts between yachting and fishing interests for the problem. He voiced his hope that yachtsmen would be divorced from future events.

However, in and of itself, yachting involvement was not the problem. While glorifying the working-class character of the races kept the public interested and allowed for finger-pointing when yachting niceties got in the way, it blurred the reality that changing times had made the international series a hybrid event, neither fishermen's regatta nor pure sport.

Clayt Morrissey might have opted to go fishing like many of his predecessors during earlier races, but there were fewer economic incentives to do so. Because they usually were not directly involved in the fisheries for their livelihood, owners of the racing schooners were less interested in a good trip than in winning the *Halifax Herald* Trophy. Had they been interested in the fisheries, they would have invested in the auxiliaries and trawlers, which were undercutting the profitability of all-sail vessels.

To complicate the problem, early races had been little more than diversions for the fishermen. With the popularization of sports in the 1920s, the general public tended to characterize the fishermen as sportsmen, a fallacy that communities like Gloucester would never have accepted when the events were local. Even for those who may not have understood the fishermen's perception, patriotism and community pride would have been irrelevant because the races were parochial, one-shot deals.

Fishermen now found themselves in a peculiar position. Propelled onto the international stage by circumstances beyond their control, they were expected to act like the other sports heroes of the period. Unfortunately, to do so occasionally meant giving up their fiercely held independence. No doubt that was a large part of what Morrissey felt when he told his wife, "they've got me." For its part, the public sympathized with his plight and was quick to blame the yachtsmen. They extolled the virtues of the fishermen's way, but only because Morrissey had conformed to the popular definition of a working-class sports hero. Had he acted on instinct and gone fishing, he would have been as vilified as the yachting crowd.

Quite simply, the races had created an appealing fantasy based on middle-class perceptions of an earlier, more heroic time. The spirit that emboldened the pioneers seemed to still be alive among the hardworking fishermen of Gloucester. Indeed, standing tall, with broad shoulders and a long narrow face, Morrissey was the incarnation of the tough, no-nonsense, commonsense folks that had made the country great.

(Opposite) Captain Clayt Morrissey, left, with Tom McManus, aboard the *Henry Ford* in 1922. The McManus-designed *Ford* won two races during the 1922 international series, even with a mainsail mangled from the cutting demanded by the official measurer. That she could still lose the series because the judges ruled the first race a no contest led McManus to seriously question the viability of future races unless they conformed to "fishermen's rules." (Photograph courtesy of Mystic Seaport Museum, Rosenfeld Collection, Mystic, Connecticut)

That was a nice-enough sentiment, and one that certainly added to the tourist appeal of the races, but it was hardly consistent with the life experiences of fishermen who took the heroism that landlubbers extolled as nothing more than a job requirement. In three short years, racing had been transformed from a working-class sport into a well-orchestrated public spectacle. Thus, the success of Secretary of the Navy Denby's appeal to patriotism and first mate John Matheson's acknowledgment that the *Ford*'s crew had to "meet public demand so that the contest may be recognized officially."

As the races became the domain of men like Ben Pine, the fishing skippers were marginalized. Given the values of the mainstream society that the races were meant to attract, that was inevitable. Put bluntly, the fishermen's culture had to be sanitized for public consumption. Still, the feistiness of that culture could not be completely eradicated, guaranteeing that the races would feature a certain edginess and spice centered on the differences between yachtsmen's etiquette and the fishermen's way.

The class conflict implicit in that division gave voice to the real conflict that was transforming the waterfront. It also allowed the public to champion the fishermen's cause without having to address or understand its real meaning. The result, not unexpectedly, was that the issues confronting fishermen were ignored, simplified, and ultimately turned into popular entertainment.

8

Boosterism, Sentimentality, and Working-Class Sport: Racing Between 1923 and 1929

STILL REELING FROM THE 1922 FIASCO, ORGANIZERS OF GLOUCESTER'S 300TH Anniversary Regatta made it clear that they were planning a "genuine fishermen's race," along the lines of the 1892 "Race It Blew."[1] In an oft-repeated refrain in the months preceding the contest, much was made of the fact that the event was open to any fishing vessel from any port, with no rules "as to sail, ballast or anything else in particular." With the race set for August 27, 1923, preparations through the summer generated widespread public enthusiasm in Massachusetts. There was a feeling on the streets of Gloucester that the city had something to prove, that after all the histrionics of the previous fall, Gloucester was going to show Halifax how to put on a real fishermen's race.

A popular subscription raised $1000 for a new mainsail for *Henry Ford* to replace the one maimed by the official measurer in 1922. In a spirit reminiscent of earlier waterfront celebrations, average citizens and affluent residents of Eastern Point worked together on committees and contributed money for prizes and the associated costs of putting on a race. The Race Committee solicited Sir Thomas Lipton, the perennial America's Cup challenger, to donate a trophy for the contest. He graciously agreed, and a beautiful cup arrived from London at the end of May.

A little more than a week before the event, the O'Hara Brothers, fish dealers from Boston, launched their aptly named *Shamrock* at A. D. Story's. More than six thousand people packed the tiny village of Essex. According to one account, a person could have crossed the street by stepping from one car hood to the next without touching the ground. Though obviously untried, the O'Hara schooner was the sentimental favorite among many racing enthusiasts. Because she was named for Sir Thomas Lipton's America's Cup challengers, it seemed somehow that it would be fitting if she could win his cup. Marty Welch being her skipper only added to her popularity.

Clayt Morrissey entered the *Henry Ford* the day after he arrived home from the Banks. Ben Pine's new boat *Columbia* had been in a collision with a French trawler and was temporarily laid up at St. Pierre, so he opted to skipper *Elizabeth Howard* again.

From left to right, Captain Marty Welch of *Shamrock;* Jack O'Hara, of O'Hara Brothers; Sir Thomas Lipton, who donated a cup for the 1923 Gloucester Anniversary Race; and Gloucester Mayor William J. McInnis. Long a highliner in Gloucester, Welch was famous in racing circles for his captaining of *Esperanto* and *Elsie* in the first two international series. Like so many of the skippers who had grown up in sail, Welch was showing the signs of age by 1923. (Photograph courtesy of Mystic Seaport Museum, Rosenfeld Collection, Mystic, Connecticut)

With the field set, talk around Gloucester turned to the prospects for the race. The captains were popular men in town, and each had his partisans. Everywhere one went, the arguments were the same. Sure, the *Shamrock* was not broken in yet, but Marty Welch was a sail carrier. Who could forget his masterful handling of *Esperanto* and *Elsie* in the 1920 and 1921 international series?

That may be true, others retorted, but the *Ford* should have won the international series last year. If she could take *Bluenose,* it was a sure bet that she could beat this field. Of course, there were those who believed that Ben Pine could not be counted out. He had more than proven himself a talented racing skipper. By race day, the anticipation was palpable.

Unfortunately, Monday, August 27, dawned foggy and calm. Because no race was possible, and the Race Committee did not want to detract from the other anniversary events, the regatta was rescheduled for the thirtieth. As

The 1923 Anniversary Race gave Gloucester a chance to shine. Event organizers found just the right mix of boosterism, hype, and old-fashioned small town charm to make the event a success despite uncooperative weather. Here, crowds gather around the Gloucester National Bank to catch a glimpse of some of the notables gathered for photographs. (Photograph courtesy of Mystic Seaport Museum, Rosenfeld Collection, Mystic, Connecticut)

thousands of disappointed citizens milled about the streets, the strains of distant music were heard from the direction of Blynman's Bridge.

The Fifth Infantry Band marched into town accompanying Sir Thomas Lipton and Boston Mayor John F. Fitzgerald. The procession ended at Post Office Square, where Mayor William McInnis welcomed the guests to the city. To the cheers of the assembled crowd, Lipton exchanged greetings with the politicians, then headed down to the wharf for a photo opportunity aboard *Shamrock*.

From there, it was off to the Gloucester National Bank to take pictures of Lipton, the three skippers, and the trophy. The amiable Lipton was a real favorite among the fishermen, and there was sincere disappointment when he said that he could not stay until Thursday to watch the race.

As things turned out, he did not miss much. After an initial postponement to await a breeze, the schooners got off at 10:30 A.M. Six hours later,

Those lining up to have their picture taken in front of the Gloucester National Bank included, from left to right, Mayor Mahoney of Lawrence, Massachusetts; Jack O'Hara, owner of the *Shamrock;* J. F. Fitzgerald, former mayor of Gloucester; Gloucester Mayor William J. McInnis; Sir Thomas Lipton; Captain Clayt Morrissey of the *Henry Ford;* Captain Marty Welch of the *Shamrock;* Tom McManus, designer of the *Ford;* and Mr. Ferguson, chair of the 1923 Anniversary Race Committee. (Photograph courtesy of Mystic Seaport Museum, Rosenfeld Collection, Mystic, Connecticut)

Ford was ahead but so far from the finish that the committee called things off until the next day.

Conditions on Friday morning hardly seemed better. A thick haze nearly blanketed the horizon as a light southerly wind barely moved the racers over a glasslike sea. After what seemed like an interminable delay, the race finally got underway. It was a close contest until the schooners rounded the third mark. As *Shamrock* dropped far behind, it came down to a stern chase, with *Howard* closing fast on the *Ford.* Pine and Morrissey organized their crews along the weather rail and trimmed their sails so that everything aboard both vessels was drawing perfectly. The spray flying over their bows, *Howard* and *Ford* buried their scuppers, exposing a significant portion of their glistening undersides to the crowds on the spectator boats. When it was over,

Clayt Morrissey and his family, aboard the *Ford*, following his victory in the 1923 Anniversary Race. What a difference a few months can make. During the 1922 international series, Clayt and his wife had stood in the same place and she had begged her husband to let someone else race the *Ford*. Pictured with Morrissey, from left to right, are his daughter Anthusa, his mother, and his wife. (Photograph courtesy of Mystic Seaport Museum, Rosenfeld Collection, Mystic, Connecticut)

Morrissey had won, but it had been close. *Howard* came across the line only fifty seconds behind the *Ford*.

The race had been a fitting end to the Anniversary Week and seemed a nice segue to the international series. With a fifty-second time difference over a thirty-one mile course, folks were still talking about it when *Columbia* arrived home two weeks later. Pine's partisans were adamant. What could he do in the elimination race on October 12 when he was at the wheel of his new racer if he had been able to give Morrissey a run for his money with the *Howard*? Others felt that Morrissey was a man to be reckoned with, and that the *Henry Ford* had proven herself plenty fast over the last year. The consensus was that either vessel or skipper would do Gloucester proud against *Bluenose*. *Ford* had already beaten the Lunenburger twice, and with mangled sails at that. The only reason the cup was not in Gloucester right now, most reasoned, was because of the shenanigans of the Sailing Committee.

Amazingly, all the ill feeling that had surrounded the international series the previous fall seemed to disappear in the excitement generated by the Anniversary Race. Perhaps the fact that the race was local and harkened back to an earlier, simpler time rekindled the belief that real fishermen's races were still possible. Perhaps Gloucester was just too heavily invested in trying to guarantee the success of international racing. Whatever the reason, the city was taken aback when the International Trustees sent word that they needed copies of plans for any likely American challenger to make sure that the U.S. contender conformed to new rules governing displacement, spar size, and freeboard.[2]

The American Race Committee was incensed. They wired back that they expected a "vessel-for-vessel" contest, with no special rules. They went on to state that whoever the American defender was must be accepted "as is." When news of the trustees' request became public, the growing excitement over the fall racing season turned to frustration.

As the wrangling dragged on, Clayt Morrissey realized that he had seen it all before, and, frankly, he wanted no part of it. *Ford* left to go fishing and probably would not be back in time for the elimination race. *Elizabeth Howard* likewise headed for the Banks. *Columbia* remained tied to the dock, still sporting some of the scars of her recent collision. Pine was not sure what to do. If the Canadians disqualified her, he would send her fishing. However, if he sent her fishing before word came from Halifax and *Columbia* was ruled eligible, she would be out to sea during the elimination race.

The Gloucester press, with more than a little self-righteous congratulations, noted how smoothly the Anniversary Race had gone without an obsessive attention to rules. There was even talk that the *Halifax Herald* contest be discontinued and Gloucester hold real races open to any vessel and crew "engaged in or identified with the fishing industry."

After an abortive attempt to send a group to Halifax to discuss the trustees' demands—apparently a mutually convenient time could not be arranged—telegrams flew back and forth, until the Americans, in exasperation, issued an ultimatum. If the Canadians persisted in a strict adherence to the letter of the revised Deed of Gift, then Gloucester would not participate in the competition.

Halifax wired back that only *Columbia*'s plans needed to be sent. The Race Committee complied with the request, but told reporters that if Pine's boat was disqualified—she was technically in violation of the freeboard rule by five inches—there would be no race. The committee also would not allow any "sail cutting" or other "radical alterations" to any contestant just to comply with the whims of the trustees.

By this time, it was early October, and the prevailing feeling throughout Gloucester was that there would be no international series. There was certainly no way that the elimination could take place on October 12 with *Ford* and *Howard* gone and *Columbia* still in need of repairs. Then on October 4, the Race Committee got word that Halifax had OK'd *Columbia* despite "a slight difference in free board which [the] Trustees are willing to concede." The telegram went on to suggest October 20 as the first race day.

Ben Pine was ecstatic, and on Monday, October 8, he had *Columbia* hauled out. Her unusually painted light grey topsides were repainted the more traditional black, she was thoroughly scrubbed below the waterline, and hull repairs were completed. By the time she was back in the water a couple of days later, *Elizabeth Howard* had returned, and Pine got her ready to race as well.

It seemed unlikely that Clayt Morrissey would be home in time for the elimination race, but public sentiment was strong that the *Ford* should be given a chance to qualify as the challenger. Sensitive to that feeling, the Race Committee wired the trustees asking for a delay in the international competition until October 27. The Canadians agreed. Now Gloucester crossed its fingers and waited, hoping *Ford* would show up off Eastern Point in time to race.[3]

On Wednesday, October 17, the Race Committee met and decided that if the *Ford* was not back "before another 24 hours expired," *Columbia* would be declared the challenger. As if to heighten the drama, at noon the following day *Henry Ford* sailed into port with more than 200,000 pounds of fish. Fresh from the Banks, she carried no topmasts, and her hull showed the signs of a season of fishing.

No sooner had she tied up than people on the wharf anxiously began asking if *Ford* would race. Tired and in need of a haircut and shave, Morrissey trekked up to Main Street, where members of the Race Committee accosted him as he reclined in a barber's chair at his favorite shop. After some discussion, he told them he would rather not race. It was his opinion that *Columbia* should be certified as the American contender and the matter be put to rest.

Not satisfied with that answer, the Race Committee held a meeting at eight that evening to try to persuade Morrissey to reconsider. As a large crowd gathered outside the Master Mariners' Hall, discussion inside dragged on for nearly two hours. At about ten o'clock, riggers Harry Christiansen and George Roberts opened the doors and announced that Morrissey was going to race. Repeating the dynamics of 1922, events once again demonstrated that racing was no longer for the fishermen but a matter of good public relations, and once again Clayt Morrissey was the victim.

The event was set for Sunday the 21st, with a field of *Elizabeth Howard*, captained by Harry Gillie, *Columbia* under Ben Pine, and Morrissey aboard *Henry Ford*. Excitement over the event was heightened by the race against time. *Ford* had to unload a hold full of fish, not to mention her dories and trawl gear, and had to have her top hamper rerigged. *Howard* needed one of her topmasts stepped as well, while *Columbia* had to have her ballast adjusted for trim, a new main boom slung, and her main and main topsails bent on. Morrissey and his crew volunteered to help unload the fish, and Frank C. Pearce, who had bought her catch and was part owner of the *Ford,* offered his lumpers overtime pay to finish the job. By Friday night, the hold was empty and most of the fishing gear was ashore. On Saturday, all the contenders were ready.

The buildup to the race provided the kind of excitement that Gloucester seemed to thrive on. Morrissey's last-minute arrival had elements of Maurice Whalen getting into port just thirteen hours before the 1892 "Race It Blew." The frenzied preparations to have *Ford* ready resembled the herculean efforts that put *Esperanto* into racing trim in 1920. All the elements of a good yarn were in place. Unfortunately, the weather did not cooperate, and *Henry Ford* did not defy the odds to win.

Time ran out with *Columbia* well ahead of the field but still six and a half miles from the finish line. The Race Committee unanimously named *Columbia* the U.S. challenger. Many felt that the results of the elimination race were never in doubt. According to one reporter, the only reason that it was staged at all was to allow Pine an opportunity to test *Columbia* under racing conditions and "to prove to a critical public that there was no intention to ignore or freeze out the *Ford.*"

As far as Morrissey was concerned, they need not have bothered. Despite newspaper copy about the determined fight soon to be waged by the brave men of Gloucester in their effort to recapture the *Halifax Herald* Trophy, Morrissey declined to join the eleven skippers who crewed aboard *Columbia* when she left for Halifax. As a fisherman, he had better things to do, like get the *Ford* ready for the winter season. The way events worked themselves out, he was probably glad that this time he had trusted his instincts and gone fishing.

No sooner had *Columbia* cleared the breakwater in Gloucester Harbor than she struck bottom and had to turn back. Minor repairs and a gale delayed her departure until Thursday, October 25, forcing the Canadians to agree to postpone the start of the international series until the 29th.[4]

During the first race, *Columbia* and *Bluenose* got into a luffing contest off of Bell Shoal. With *Bluenose* headed for the rocks, her pilot ordered the helmsman, Albert Himmelman, to bear off. Himmelman yelled back, "Bear away and we strike him!"

"Strike him or strike the rocks," was the reply. The pilot's advice suited Walters's strategy just fine. He ordered the staysail doused and winged out the foresail. *Columbia* was blanketed. Now *Bluenose* closed in on the Gloucesterman, the two boats within spitting distance of each other.

Bluenose's main boom raked *Columbia*'s deck, touched her port main shrouds, then moved forward and got caught up on her forestays. *Columbia*'s

sheer pole was torn away before the boom finally unshipped itself and skid-
ded ahead six or eight feet. The Canadians scrambled to shove it aft and get
it back on the saddle. As they did, the boom fouled *Columbia's* jib stay and
dragged her along for about a minute. With *Columbia* completely blanketed,
Bluenose swept past and worked herself clear.

The Lunenburger surged in front, leaving the American dead in the water, her sails temporarily refusing to fill. Pine recovered quickly, though, and
began the stern chase. By the time it was over, *Bluenose* had crossed the finish line one minute and twenty seconds ahead of *Columbia.*

The Americans were annoyed by Walter's flagrant foul, believing that,
had it not happened, *Columbia* would have won. The Canadians felt that
Pine's refusal to give *Bluenose* sea room had caused the collision, and Walters had done the only thing he could to avoid piling up on the rocks. In
keeping with the spirit of playing by fishermen's rules, however, neither skipper filed a protest, so the results were official. Deciding that the situation
had been too close for comfort, the Sailing Committee issued special rules
governing the remainder of the 1923 series, the most important being that
all navigation buoys had to be passed to seaward.

After the next race was called off because of no wind, the schooners tried
again on Thursday, November 1. In a close contest, with a twenty-five-knot
wind out of the northeast, the vessels made a dramatic show as they worked
their way around the course. *Columbia's* long narrow prow split each on-
coming wave like a knife, sending tons of green spray into the air on either
side, a hissing foam running back past her lee scuppers. Meanwhile,
Bluenose's high full bow pounded through the onrushing sea, sending froth
cascading to leeward in a blinding shower of white water.

When it was over, *Bluenose* had won by two minutes and forty-five seconds.
It had been a hard-fought contest in a hard-fought series under real fishermen's conditions. Unlike the 1921 and 1922 events, the rules and bickering
had not gotten in the way of the racing. Even while the collision in the first
contest had generated shoreside debate, it had not created nearly the
amount of heat that other controversies had in years past. Ben Pine did not
even choose to challenge the results or claim a foul.

Just as such feelings were being given voice, news broke that Pine was
lodging a protest, charging that *Bluenose* had violated the special rules by
sailing inshore of the Lighthouse Bank Buoy. The Sailing Committee met
for several hours that evening to consider the matter. When questioned
about what happened, Walters admitted that he had sailed on the wrong
side of the buoy, but explained that he had not seen it in time to pass to seaward. The committee decided to disqualify *Bluenose* and award the race to
Columbia, tying the series at one apiece. They then scheduled the deciding
race for Saturday, November 3, to give the Lunenburgers time to repair the
topmast damaged during the race.

Walters was furious. As Clayt Morrissey had a year earlier, he declared his intention not to race. As far as he was concerned, *Bluenose* had won the series outright, and there was no need for a third contest. When told that such a decision would lead the Sailing Committee to award the series to *Columbia,* the feisty captain relented just a little. He said he would race again, but only if the committee declared Thursday's event a "no contest." With no likelihood of that happening, Walters got his crew ready to leave for Lunenburg.

A. H. Zwicker, president of the Schooner *Bluenose* Company, Ltd., began organizing a substitute crew to race if Walters and his men remained adamant. Premier Armstrong of Nova Scotia met privately with Walters, asking him to abide by the Sailing Committee's decision. In what turned out to be a poor choice of words, he added, "After all, it's only sport." Walters shot back that, although it was "only sport," it was a "working sport," and if the premier doubted it, he should join the *Bluenose* crew.[5]

At 1:30 P.M. on Saturday, November 3, *Bluenose* cleared Halifax Harbor for home. Ben Pine refused to sail over the course alone to claim the cup by default. The International Trustees declared the 1923 series suspended with no winner, and held the prize money and trophy in trust. Walters's actions had been a throwback to an earlier time, when fishing captains broached no challenges to their authority, either on or off their vessels. If something was wrong, it was wrong, no matter how many fellows in suits tried to convince one otherwise. No skipper worth his salt did anything he did not want to do, especially if it was not in his best interest, and he certainly did not bow to demands and pressures from shore-bound businessmen or politicians.

Indeed, Walters's retort to Premier Armstrong seemed oddly reminiscent of Marion Perry's answer to Theodore Roosevelt's messenger back in 1907. "If he wants to see me, he knows where to find me!" Perry had said. If you doubt that it is "working sport," Walters declared, "join the *Bluenose* crew." The implication of both statements was that polite society could play on the fishermen's terms, or not at all.

There is little doubt that Morrissey had wanted to make the same statement a year earlier. That he did not may reflect the symbolic importance that the races had taken on in Gloucester. With the entire community caught up in the throes of racing fever, the key financial backers of the *Ford* putting pressure on him to race, and even the Secretary of the Navy making it a matter of patriotism, Morrissey found it impossible to resist the pressures to continue despite his better judgment. Although Walters underwent similar pressure, technology in Canada had not yet turned racing into a last hurrah for fishing under sail. Because it was still a matter of "working sport," it was subject to fishermen's rules, and Walters was just the cantankerous son-of-a-gun to stand up and say so.

By the original standard that led to organized fishermen's regattas, where racing was to be done on the fishermen's terms, boat for boat, with a minimum of rules, he was right. The public appeal of the 1920 series had rested on this simplicity. The protests against "yachting influences," and the persistent demands to return the *Halifax Herald* Races to the control of the fishermen, likewise reflected the assumption that this event was unique because it was "working sport."

Yet, the public perception of what "working sport" meant was grounded in an overly simplistic and romanticized view of the fishermen. As *Rudder* magazine aptly noted:

> The Fishermen's Race has always attracted a great deal of attention from the public, who led by newspaper reports feel that the event is the only one in which the traditions of North-American seamanship are upheld. The sentimentalists and romanticists, gaining their entire knowledge of ships and seamen from the rather hectic novels of the fishing-fleet, pound the arms of their easy chairs and tell the world that the fishermen are the real curly-headed boys when it comes to boat-handling. . . .
>
> [T]he Fishermen's Race as staged over a short, alongshore course, brings out nothing but a fairly high-grade example of sail handling and helmsmanship. The Struggle with the Elements so dear to the heart of the fictionist, is absent. As a test of seaworthiness, and proof that the fishing-schooner is superior to all other types of sailing vessels, the race is a huge joke.[6]

Still, people wanted to believe that Marty Welch, Clayt Morrissey, and Angus Walters were like Disko Troop, Rudyard Kipling's hero in *Captains Courageous*. The 1920s was a decade of hero worship, and many of those heroes were sports figures. Athletes were lionized as bigger than life characters by sportswriters and radio broadcasters. With pluck and determination, they overcame often overwhelming odds to succeed, both on and off the field.[7]

Babe Ruth, perhaps the most famous sports figure of the era, had grown up on the mean streets of Baltimore's waterfront district.[8] Supposedly orphaned at an early age—though this has proven to be a myth—George Herman Ruth spent his formative years in and out of St. Mary's Industrial School for Boys, where his talent for baseball earned him a position with the minor league Baltimore Orioles. By 1920 he had gone from the minors, to a successful pitching career with the Red Sox, to home-run king of the Yankees. His visits to children in hospitals and promises to hit them homers were the things of legend, not to mention great newspaper copy.

In more ways than one, Ruth seemed to embody the American Dream, but he was not the only one. Jack Dempsey, the Heavyweight Champion of the World, grew up in Manassa, Colorado, a dusty mining community where he was working full-time as a miner by the time he was a teenager. Determined to make something of his life, he began drifting, fighting in back rooms of saloons and gaining experience. By 1918 he was a contender. In 1919 he won the championship. The scrappy "never-say-die" attitude that got him out of Manassa became his trademark, and eventually endeared him to fans. His 1923 defense against Argentine Luis Angel Firpo at the New York Polo Grounds was typical. Knocked out of the ring and landing on a typewriter in the press row, Dempsey crawled back into the ring and won the match by a knockout.[9]

Dempsey and Ruth were working-class heroes. They embodied the spirit of rugged individualism that for most citizens epitomized the American character. Indeed, it was this part of their stories that gave newsmen fodder for their bylines, captured the public imagination, and fed its idolatry.

This same phenomenon surrounded the popular enthusiasm over the fishermen's races. It had fueled William Dennis's rationale for the international series in the first place, and had been behind Calvin Coolidge's characterization of *Esperanto*'s victory in 1920 as a "Triumph for Americanism." Fishermen represented a dying breed of men, who, like the American cowboy, were strong, stoic, and virtuous because of their stubborn adherence to a moral code grounded in an earlier, simpler time. In an age of excess like the 1920s, there was something strangely comforting in knowing that such men existed.

Public image was one thing. However, fishermen did not race for popular amusement. They were not professional athletes like Ruth and Dempsey, and never pretended to be. Although they no doubt reveled in the public attention, and were not adverse to seeing themselves characterized as heroes—certainly such images often fit with their sense of self—they raced because it was supposed to be fun. When it was not fun, or when they felt themselves unfairly treated, they saw no reason to carry on just in the name of good sportsmanship. That was not their way. As Angus Walters rightly told Premier Armstrong, racing was not just sport to the fishermen.

Unfortunately, the public was conditioned to expect its heroes to persevere despite the odds, to give their all to win, and if, like Dempsey, they got knocked out of the ring, to crawl back into it. The game was the thing. That Walters refused to play by these rules made him persona non grata in many quarters. Newspapers editorialized endlessly about his appalling lack of good form, and lamented the likely damage to the goodwill and sportsmanship that the *Halifax Herald* series had engendered since its inception. It was easy to forget the fact that such words had not been relevant to the International Races since 1920.

Sportswriters in particular were taken aback by Walters's truculence. Believing their own rhetoric, they condemned his "obvious" unwillingness to play fair. Even in private, they were incredulous that he seemed so willing to flaunt social convention and to act the part of the petulant child. Leonard

Fowle, yachting editor for the *Boston Globe,* wrote to his son from Halifax announcing:

> All racing off for 1923, and no winner in the international fishermen's match. This a result of the action of Capt. Angus Walters and his all captain crew from Lunenburg, who when Thursday['s] race was awarded to the *Columbia* on a protest refused to race any more.
>
> Rather poor sports, and cry babies, who when they were beaten at their own game would not play any more.[10]

Subsequent actions by Walters and the other *Bluenose* owners did nothing to alter this opinion. The shareholders of the Schooner *Bluenose* Company retained counsel and voted to authorize Walters to take whatever legal steps he deemed "fit and proper to protect or enforce the rights of the schooner *Bluenose,* her master, crew, and owners" to the trophy and prize money. If that meant taking the case to the Canadian Supreme Court, company sources said, that was what they would do.

Although such behavior may have been unseemly to the general public, it was in keeping with Angus Walters's combative style and personality, and, indeed, his upbringing.[11] Walters was a product of the hardscrabble life of a Lunenburg fishing family. His dad, Elias, was one of the town's highliners, and he fully expected his sons to follow in his footsteps. Tough and taciturn, Elias was a strict disciplinarian. He never coddled Angus, knowing full well that, the sooner a fisherman learned that life was rough and unforgiving, the better. Like most of the boys in Lunenburg, Angus spent every spare moment hanging around the sail loft on Pelham Street, listening to yarns and daydreaming about skippering a schooner on the Banks.

At age thirteen, he shipped aboard his father's vessel as a throater. Elias showed his son no special treatment, expecting him to pull his weight like everyone else in the crew. If Angus was going to be a captain someday, he had to know every aspect of the business, and the best place to learn was in the fo'c'sle.

Being a good skipper was more than seamanship and navigating and having a sixth sense about where the fish were, although that was all part of it. A good captain had to be as rough-and-tumble as the men he commanded, sometimes more so. After all, a salt banker was no place for the fainthearted, nor were the waterfront saloons where skippers sometimes had to recruit their crews.

Success and survival depended on a captain's ability to command respect from hard-bitten men who could curse and drink with the best of them. Elias was such a man. He drove his men hard and took no guff aboard his vessel, but he also knew the limits of his crew and boat. More importantly, he could catch fish, and few of his trips ever came back brokers.

By the time Angus got his first command, he was clearly his father's son. Over time, he built a reputation as a taskmaster, but, despite his gruff demeanor, dorymen scrambled to crew for him because he was a moneymaker. Walters was stubborn and driven. A physically small man, he was capable of intimidating men significantly larger than himself with nothing more than an icy stare or a profusion of well-chosen epithets. Recalled one old Lunenburger:

> Once Angus made up his mind to do something and he knew he was right the old Devil himself couldn't change his mind.
> Cap'n Angus had a tongue as sharp as a shark's tooth. If the Old Boy himself couldn't change Angus's mind once he was satisfied he was on the right track, neither could anything keep him off deck when things weren't just right.

A former crew member observed that Walters never smiled when he came on deck in the morning. His eyes quickly took in every detail, and heaven help the men on watch if anything was out of line.

Though such qualities made for an effective skipper, they failed to conform to the idealized public image of one. Angus Walters was the genuine article, but the *Halifax Herald* Races were not designed for him, or for men like him. By 1923, fishermen on the American side had become secondary to the interests of men like Ben Pine who were living vicariously into the popular image of the fishermen. It is particularly telling that "Captain" Pine, the sportsman, was more socially acceptable than a real fishing skipper who thumbed his nose at the niceties of accepted convention.

Regardless of clamoring to the contrary, the public did not really want a genuine fishermen's race if it involved genuine fishermen, especially when the romantic alternative was so much more appealing. Middle-class citizens and yachtsmen wanted to be able to imagine themselves aboard a fishing schooner running before a howling gale, and that required characters they could identify with. Walters was hardly sympathetic enough for such a role.

Of course, the vessels had their own romantic appeal and fed the illusion. Yachtsmen across the country were inspired by the International Fishermen's Races to build new vessels to fishermen specifications. Indeed, some of them were so caught up in the mystique of the Gloucestermen that they insisted that their boats conform in every particular to the real thing.

In the fall of 1922, for example, two fishing schooners were built at Essex as pleasure craft. The one at the James Yard was a 139-foot knockabout de-

(Opposite) Captain Angus Walters was an abrasive, tough-as-nails competitor. Caring little for the niceties of sportsmanship, he approached racing as he did everything else in life. His upbringing had taught him that whatever a man had in life he had to fight for. (Photograph courtesy of Mystic Seaport Museum, Rosenfeld Collection, Mystic, Connecticut)

signed by William H. Hand, Jr. The other, at Story's, came from the board
of Starling Burgess and Frank C. Paine and was built for San Francisco lum-
ber magnate L. A. Norris. Norris stayed in Gloucester to oversee the construction of his yacht, and he reportedly visited rigger George Roberts in his
shop to attend to details.

"I suppose that you are doing an especially fine job on the rigging for the
Mariner," Norris began.

"No," Roberts replied, "I can't say that we are. It'll be about the same as
we make for the regular fishermen."

"By golly, I'm glad to hear it," the lumberman said with a smile. "I don't
want anything about the *Mariner* different from the regular Gloucester
schooner."[12]

Such reasoning apparently even led some yachtsmen to subscribe to the
Atlantic Fisherman, or at least to buy enough issues of the October 1923 edition to justify a couple of advertisers specifically targeting them in their ads.
How strange it must have been to thumb through the pages of a journal ded-
icated to "the men who actually fish for a living" and come across an adver-
tisement from W. M. Frost announcing: "Boats-Yachts. Frost's Boats built on
the lines of the famous Jonesport models from our own design. Speed and
workmanship guaranteed on all classes of boats"; or from sailmaker Louis J.
Larsen of New York: "Fine Yacht Sails for Cruising or Racing"; and on the
line below, in smaller print, "Fishermen's Sails."[13]

All this contributed to the air of unreality that had come to surround the
Halifax Herald Races since 1921, and, in many ways, that defined the 1920s
as a whole. Indeed, the pettiness of the controversies that characterized the
international series seemed to reflect a larger banality that was coming to
shape much of popular culture and entertainment in the so-called Jazz Age.

People in the 1920s were looking for heroes and clamoring to be entertained. They valued rules and traditions, as the upsurge in church atten-
dance during the decade suggests, yet they glorified criminals and fell for
every stunt, fad, or craze that came along. Society was becoming urbane,
consumerism was a shared value, and old-fashioned community patterns
were being replaced by a mass culture promoted by Madison Avenue hype.
Society was in transition, and as such it reflected the confusing and often
contradictory patterns that accompany change.[14]

The international fishermen's series was a product of the times, and of
the same public relations and marketing techniques that made baseball, the
Model T, and Rudolph Valentino into national icons. It appealed to the real-
life Jay Gatsbys who searched for meaning and personal fulfillment in yachting regattas and country clubs.

Like F. Scott Fitzgerald's hero, it also symbolized the lost innocence of a
time that simultaneously embraced change and feared its ramifications. Although the fishermen's races were a reassuring affirmation that real-life he-

roes and grass-roots values still existed, the boosterism that turned them into media events on both sides of the U.S.-Canadian border guaranteed that they would always be something less than the genuine article.

In words that could easily have been penned to describe Gloucester's ambivalence toward the *Halifax Herald* Races, Fitzgerald wrote that Gatsby believed in

. . . the orgiastic future that year by year recedes before us. It eluded us then, but that's no matter—tomorrow we will run faster, stretch out our arms farther. . . . And one fine morning—

So we beat on, boats against the current, borne back ceaselessly into the past.[15]

Despite themselves, Gloucesterites wanted to be part of the glory and public attention that accompanied the international fishermen's series, even going so far as to forget the aggravation of the experience from year to year. How else does one explain that, by 1923, folks who had been ready to organize their own races a year earlier, were anxiously pressuring Clayt Morrissey to race in the elimination event to guarantee a good show.

Like local business and community leaders everywhere in the 1920s, members of Gloucester's Race Committee were enthusiastic supporters of civic pride, progress, and promotion, but unlike many of their small-town compatriots elsewhere, they did not have to look far for an angle. The *Halifax Herald* competition was tailor-made to showcase Gloucester's advantages and her products.

Still, traditional values were strong enough in Gloucester to quickly frustrate fishermen and civic leaders alike when they confronted the tomfoolery of international racing. Some like Clayt Morrissey simply refused to play anymore. Others reveled in the simple pleasures of homespun events like Anniversary Week, and took joy in pointing out how poorly the *Halifax Herald* Races measured up.

Through it all, though, there was the confusion and self-contradiction that characterized the era. On the one hand, international competition and the building of racing schooners smacked of the promotional schemes that defined so much of the commercial and social life of the 1920s. Yet, on the other, they represented a harking back to a simpler period that time and technology was changing forever, but that neither Gloucester nor society as a whole was quite ready to relinquish.

Over the next three years, this point was made repeatedly, as Gloucester futilely attempted to organize an international series.[16] Despite the Trustees' decision to suspend competition for a year after the 1923 mess, the American Race Committee telegraphed Halifax just to make sure in September 1924. When the Canadians responded that there was no enthusiasm

for a race that year, Ben Pine issued a challenge to Angus Walters for a special contest between *Columbia* and *Bluenose,* if money for a purse could be
raised. Nothing came of it.

The next year the *Columbia* Associates decided to get their schooner ready
to race, and informed the Race Committee that she would be at their dis-
posal, should they choose to challenge for the *Halifax Herald* Trophy. On October 3, 1925, the committee voted unanimously to do just that.

The Canadian answer was lukewarm. After a week's delay in responding,
the trustees said that the earliest date for a series would be between November 5 and 15. Because of a shortage of funds, they proposed a combination elimination and championship event. Neither the dates nor the for-
mat suited the Americans, so they passed.

It seemed to many that the days of racing were over. As if to drive that
message home, *Columbia* was sold at auction on January 16, 1926, to satisfy
$10,400 in liens against her. In a little less than three years of fishing, the
schooner had not been able to pay for herself. Indeed, she had spent all of
1925 tied up at Booth's Wharf in Gloucester. Her builder, A. D. Story, bought
her for $10,100 to satisfy a $10,000 mortgage on which he had foreclosed
earlier.[17]

Still, Ben Pine remained undaunted. He sought out new partners,
formed a new corporation, and bought *Columbia* back in March, assuming
all of her outstanding bills. Pine invited any stockholder in the old *Columbia*
Associates, Inc., the syndicate that built the schooner, to join the new corporation. However, there was little incentive beyond sentimentality and
sportsmanship for any of them to do so.

There was something symbolic in the fact that the January 1926 issue of
the *Atlantic Fisherman* had only two articles on dory schooners, and one of
them highlighted the details of the *Columbia* sale. More significantly, the
news was relegated to the back pages in the "Fishing Ship News" section,
given equal play with the fact that Captain Carl Olsen had bought a half interest in the schooner *Progress.* A few years earlier, any information about
one of the racing schooners would have been front-page news in the *Atlantic
Fisherman,* and certainly as significant an item as the auction of the American champion would have received several pages of detailed reporting. Instead, the January 1926 issue featured part one of a two-part series on "Trawling and Dragging in New England Waters."

The March edition devoted four paragraphs to the resale of *Columbia* to
Ben Pine and his associates, again in the "Fishing Ship News" section, right
above an article on a record catch made by the Gloucester trawler *Fabia.*
Gone only four days, Captain Bob Wharton's boat landed 240,000 pounds
of fish at the Boston Fish Pier.

The juxtaposition of the *Fabia* and *Columbia* stories served as an unspoken commentary on the changing realities of the fisheries. According to the

Columbia had been built to win the *Halifax Herald* Trophy, but when racing was suspended after the 1923 series, Ben Pine found that she was something of a white elephant. Beautiful to look at, she never paid for herself as a fisherman. (Photograph courtesy of Mystic Seaport Museum, Rosenfeld Collection, Mystic, Connecticut)

Atlantic Fisherman, the repurchase of *Columbia* was "actuated chiefly by public spirit and a desire to retain the ownership of the crack schooner in Gloucester." If a fishing vessel's reputation came from her ability to make money on the Banks, it was a sad epithet that *Columbia* had been fishing so little in three years, and that the only folks who wanted to own her were mostly motivated by "public spirit."

There was small wonder, then, that when rumors began circulating in late July 1926 that the Canadians were going to hold an elimination race and revive international competition, Pine and his colleagues were ecstatic. On July 27, the *Boston Globe* reported that Vice Commodore Gerald Ford of the New Rochelle Yacht Club had just returned from Nova Scotia, where preparations were underway to hold races for the *Halifax Herald* Trophy. Ford declared that it was very "probable" that a fishermen's regatta would be sailed in American waters in the fall. A few days later, the report was confirmed when the International Trustees wired the American Committee, announcing their plans to hold an elimination event, with the winner to travel south to Gloucester.

Ben Pine and the Americans did not have to be asked twice. The American Race Committee quickly voted to challenge the Canadians for the cup. In anticipation of a positive reply, work began immediately to get *Columbia* ready to race. When H. R. Silver answered on behalf of the Trustees that a series after October 12 suited the Nova Scotians, the Gloucester committee was elated. Two years of frustration erupted into a new round of racing fever. The pettiness and petulance of earlier competitions faded into memory, replaced by an almost naive sense of anticipation that somehow, this year, things would be different.

For Pine and his colleagues, the possibility of an international event was especially exciting. It had been only about four months since they had bought *Columbia* back from A. D. Story, promising to assume responsibility for all her debts. If *Columbia* could race and win, the first-prize purse would go a long way toward satisfying the liens against their schooner.

Just as racing enthusiasm was taking hold of Gloucester, a storm swept over the Banks, casting a debilitating pall over Nova Scotia. The so-called "August Breeze," according to old-timers from Lunenburg, marked the beginning of the end of dory fishing in Canada. With six schooners and at least one hundred men lost, it became harder to find men to crew aboard the schooners until, in the words of one fisherman, "they was all gone."[18]

Reeling from the loss, the Canadians suggested that, out of respect for the dead, the races should be postponed or canceled. In what can only be characterized as an extremely insensitive response, Wilmot Reed of the American Race Committee told the press on September 1 that, although Gloucester regretted the recent loss of life, "We are now and have been ready since the Spring of 1925 to compete with the Canadian Schooners." To reinforce the point, the next day Ben Pine issued a challenge to *Bluenose* to race for a purse of between $700 and $1000. Others in Gloucester were rumored to be willing to raise up to $5000 for such a match race.

So intense was the desire for a contest that the talk around Gloucester was that it did not really matter whether the Canadians took the challenge or not. Speculation focused on the possibility of a *Columbia-Ford-Mayflower* matchup—a real fishermen's race with a minimum of rules and a maximum of competition. The feeling was that Gloucester knew how to organize a regatta without any of the hassles that had become synonymous with international competition, so who needed the Canadians anyway?

On Wednesday, September 8, Clayt Morrissey went over to the Atlantic Supply Company to talk to Ben Pine about a face-off between *Henry Ford* and *Columbia*. In a bit of good-natured posturing, he told Pine that he thought *Ford* was a superior vessel, and he welcomed the chance to prove it. Pine responded in kind, and Gloucester had herself a race.

Community leaders were invited to join a host of subcommittees to handle everything from publicity to fund-raising. By the end of the week, Pine and Morrissey agreed that the first race would be on October 2, and that if their boats were the only entrants, it would be a best two-out-of-three affair. With the contest open to any "legitimate fishing vessel from any American port," provisions were made for a three-out-of-five series if other schooners participated. Of course, the event would be sailed according to fishermen's rules.[19]

To make things interesting, a special invitation was issued to the *Mayflower* Associates. Not surprisingly, in light of all the bad blood that had existed between the Race Committee and the Associates since 1921, the Boston group issued a tart reply: "[I]f anyone wants to race the *Mayflower*, they'll have to buy her." Meanwhile, John O'Hara, who had been responsible for *Shamrock's* participation in the 1923 Anniversary Race, enthusiastically entered his firm's schooner *Gossoon*. O'Hara and her captain, Larry Norris, were excited by their boat's prospects.

Hoping to broaden the event's appeal, the Race Committee invited *Bluenose* and *Haligonian* to participate. The latter had been built a year earlier for a group of Halifax yachtsmen headed by H. L. Montague. They had hired William Roue to design a vessel that could beat his *Bluenose*, but after a season of fishing she had fetched up on shore in the Strait of Canso and been hogged, postponing any face-off with the Lunenburger indefinitely. Perhaps because of this, Montague jumped at the chance to race off Gloucester, accepting the invitation immediately. Angus Walters, meanwhile, remained his usual contentious self. He told the press that he would think about racing the Americans when he was paid the money owed him from the last international series. Moreover, he had no intention of competing in non-Canadian waters.

With the field apparently set, *Haligonian's* owners began to equivocate. Word reached Gloucester that the Halifax boat had suffered some damage during the season and probably would not be able to race. A bit later, Montague wired the Americans that, although his schooner might be repaired in time to compete, the cost of getting her prepared would probably be prohibitive. The Race Committee did not hesitate. Because *Ford* and *Columbia* were getting $1000 to cover expenses, the committee would extend the same courtesy to *Haligonian*. With the addition of the $1000 promised by the Government of Nova Scotia, it seemed that any reasonable obstacle to the Canadians' participation had been eliminated.

Of course, nothing was ever easy when it involved international competition, even on a scaled-down level. *Haligonian's* owners now reported that she had blown out her sails and could not possibly afford to replace them. Wilmot Reed telephoned Halifax directly and not only offered to supply Montague with a new set of sails, but guaranteed *Haligonian* a place on the ways in Gloucester if she could not be hauled out quickly at home. Even such largesse failed to get a firm commitment from the Canadians, who, after being denied a delay of the race, simply withdrew. In the meantime, *Gossoon* had dropped out as well.

The work done by the Race Committee and its affiliated subgroups proved to be a masterful blend of community values and self-promotion. Realizing the popular appeal of fishermen's races as sport, the committee changed the race dates from October 2 through 4 to October 11 through 13, so as not to conflict with the World Series. Reporters from New York booked reservations at local hotels while tourists from all over began to pour into Gloucester to be part of the prerace excitement.

Against this backdrop of savvy public relations, more traditional community patterns defined the day-to-day preparations for the contests. Donations from the affluent residents of Eastern Point and Bass Rocks poured into the Race Committee, as they had for such events in the past. George F. Fuller, a retired Worcester manufacturer who summered in Bass Rocks, offered five cups for five successive races, in hopes of encouraging future contests. A heavy investor in *Columbia*, Fuller gave his trophy as a token of his "goodwill and affection" for Gloucester. For his trouble, he was named to *Columbia*'s crew. Not to be outdone, local businessman Frank E. Davis donated a trophy to be awarded annually to the "fastest sailing fishing schooner in the North Atlantic."

Meanwhile, speculation about the contenders generated lively debate throughout the city. *Ford* defenders pointed out that she had won the Anniversary Race in 1923. *Columbia* partisans just snickered and reminded the others that their boat had walked away from *Ford* in the elimination race that same year. *Ford* was just back from the Banks and was not in racing trim then, came the response. This year would be different because both vessels had been on the ways and were ready to compete.

As for the skippers, everyone agreed that Clayt Morrissey was a real sail carrier and could match tactics with the best of them. However, Ben Pine knew how to handle a fishing schooner as well, especially inshore, where these races were taking place. Betting was hot and heavy, but as race day approached, it was still even money. The scene recalled an earlier time when, as James Connolly had observed, one could be fooled into thinking "that the main interests of [Gloucester's] people . . . were the building and racing home of fast fishing schooners."

As the boats tuned up for the race, they looked like excursion vessels with their complement of guests, cameramen, and reporters. While Pine and Morrissey studied their vessels' responses to changing wind conditions and different points of sail, the men and women aboard for the ride relaxed and enjoyed the outings. On shore, and aboard the schooners, a party atmosphere permeated the preparations as fishermen, yachtsmen, tourists, and the press mingled freely, swapped stories, and shared a sense of camaraderie reminiscent of a bygone era.

Ben Pine's afterguard during the tryouts reflected the easy blending of people that had characterized community celebrations in the nineteenth century. Commodore Roy Pigeon of the Cottage Park Yacht Club advised Pine about sail trim and tactics, while Captain Norman Ross served as first mate. Pigeon was the brother of Fred Pigeon, the prime mover in the building of *Mayflower*. At fifty-five years of age, Ross had skippered such Gloucester schooners as *Golden Rod, Bay State,* and *Benjamin A. Smith*. Coming to Gloucester as a young man from Guysborourgh, Nova Scotia, he had worked his way up from a hand to one of the highliners in both the halibut and mackerel seining fleets.

Clayt Morrissey sought advice from Jack Mehlman, supposedly one of the North Shore's best yacht handlers. Interestingly, no one commented on these "yachting influences," perhaps because, as a local event, the 1926 contest reflected earlier patterns of yachtsmen involvement in the fishermen's races.

In many ways, the *Ford-Columbia* race was a chance to revel in a bit of nostalgia. There were still a lot of people in Gloucester who remembered when fishermen were sailors, and not, as one man put it, "machinists." While many old-timers readily acknowledged how much easier life was because of engines, they could not help feeling a bit sentimental about the days of sail.

Back then, when one went out in his boat, there was "no noise, smell, nor shimmyin'. You just slid along, breathing in the pure air, sails a bellyin', your bo't heelin' in th' breeze makin' just tug 'nough on th' tiller to keep you interested. . . . [Besides,] it sure was fun to sail a bo't in a smashin' breeze." Few would have quarreled with the old Gloucesterman who told a reporter in the spring of 1926 that the new motorized boats were "all in line with the general progress th' old world has made in th' last quarter century." The unspoken "but' was a wistful musing about the price that had been paid in aesthetics, loss of old skills and traditions, and maybe even a little fun.[20]

The popular appeal of such thoughts helped sell newspapers, and acted as a magnet for tourists hoping to partake in a bit of living history. All in all, it was a win-win situation for Gloucester, which could market itself by playing to the very traditions that modernity was sweeping aside.

The first race on October 11 lived up to all the hype. Hard fought throughout, *Columbia* made the turn for home only thirty seconds ahead of *Ford*. The final leg was a replay of the 1923 Anniversary Race, only this time it was Morrissey who had to come from behind in the last five miles. As Pine had with the *Howard* three years earlier, Morrissey made a valiant effort, but *Columbia* was just too good on the wind. She gradually added to her lead, and crossed sixty-four seconds in front of the *Ford*.

With the next day Columbus Day, the crowds for the rematch were enormous. Spectator boats were packed from stem to stern, and on shore, one could not turn around without tripping over somebody. Excitement was high, but the race was almost secondary. This was an excuse for a party, a community celebration. *Columbia* won going away, and shortly after both vessels were tied up at the dock, the two crews came ashore, mingled together, laughed, joked, and exchanged congratulations and good-natured ribbing.

The Gloucester Cadet Band began to serenade the crowd and, before long, a parade was organized through the streets of town. Pine and Morrissey smiled happily as they walked side by side between boisterous well-wishers, their crews whooping and shouting as they went. Trucks and cars joined the procession and crew members scrambled aboard, while drivers leaned on their horns. It took two hours to meander from the waterfront, up through town, then out to George Fuller's Bass Rocks estate, where the procession finally broke up.

The next night, the City Hall Auditorium was the place to be. After gathering at the Master Mariners' Hall, the crews marched to the auditorium, once again accompanied by the Cadet Band. They entered to thunderous applause, and after feasting on a sumptuous banquet, settled in for the speechifying. Along with the usual self-congratulation and presenting of trophies, George Fuller treated the crowd to some theatrics. When his turn came to present his cup, he announced that he had heard all the talk about how the purse should be split, and he was just the man to do it.

Waving a fistful of bills, he divided the money in half, placing one stack in the trophy and thrusting the other into Clayt Morrissey's hands. After getting Morrissey to present the cup to Pine, Fuller put a big silver bowl on the table, lined it, and poured two hundred fifty silver dollars from a pewter pitcher that he had secreted under the table. He handed the bowl and money to Morrissey as a consolation prize. Wild shouts and applause rocked the building.

The evening was a fitting end to a whirlwind of frenzied preparations. Like the races and other activities during the previous month, the awards banquet had all the flavor and simplicity of a Norman Rockwell painting, right down to the officers of the high school ROTC marching onstage carrying the Davis and Fuller trophies. The touch of Americana made things genuine and no doubt accounted for the success of the whole affair. It also explained the widespread public interest in what was, for all intents and purposes, little more than a local event.

However, therein lay the problem for Ben Pine. He had built *Columbia* to win the *Halifax Herald* Trophy, not a locally sponsored contest. With *Haligonian* and *Bluenose* set to race a two-out-of-three series on October 16 and 18, and if necessary the 19th, Pine telegraphed Halifax right after his Columbus Day victory, challenging the winner for the international title. He even corralled Morrissey to accompany him to Halifax to watch the Canadian contest.

He need not have bothered. *Bluenose* ran away from *Haligonian* in the first race, crossing the finish line some thirty minutes in front of the Halifax schooner. After two "no races" in which *Bluenose* was ahead when time ran out, she won the series on October 20 by more than seven minutes.[21] Captain Walters took her home and made ready for the winter layup in Lunenburg. Pine never got an official answer to his challenge.

The Canadians clearly were not interested, and except for Pine and his associates, including his friends on the American Race Committee, neither was anyone else. Gloucester as a whole might get worked up over the race, but it was a small cadre of sportsmen and community boosters who kept the embers warm. Indeed, if it had not been for Pine, it is unlikely that Morrissey would have stayed involved with racing as long as he did.

Still, Pine was persistent. On September 7, 1927, he met with the Race Committee at the Master Mariners' Hall and got them to issue a challenge to the Canadians. Plans were made for an elimination series in October, and Pine told reporters that if *Columbia* won she would sail to Halifax under Clayt Morrissey with the U.S. and Canadian flags flying. They would wait for ten days and race whether the cup was on the line or not. It was time, Pine declared, for the Canadians to "put up or shut up!"

Unfortunately, all hopes for such a confrontation were swept away by a hurricane that tore through the Banks on August 24. *Columbia* was lost, and with her, the possibility of any racing for the foreseeable future.[22] Indeed, with no vessel to race, Pine's racing ardor temporarily cooled. Through all of 1928, neither he nor the committee made a peep about organizing a contest.

Given the success of the 1926 regatta, however, it was only a matter of time until the idea was revived. When it was, there was little pretense that fishermen's racing was anything more than community boosterism. That fact became readily apparent during preparations for the 1929 races.[23] At a meeting held July 23 at the Master Mariners' Hall, the American Race Committee voted unanimously to change the race course to two laps around an equilateral triangle of five-mile legs. This brought the race closer inshore to allow the public to "see the race from start to finish." Of course, the committee also acknowledged that it was "a very nice thing to acquiesce to the wishes of a large contributor to the race fund."

There certainly were a lot of them. Colonel and Mrs. John W. Prentiss, who had been trying to rehabilitate their reputations with Gloucester's common folk since 1923, donated $1000 to the cause and a $500 cup for the winning skipper. Gertrude and Louis Thebaud, wealthy summer residents from New Jersey, contributed $2500. E. F. Hutton made his schooner yacht available to the Race Committee "for a judges' boat or for such purposes as they desired to use the craft." Local businessman and former mayor Frank E. Davis offered a cup worth $800 to the winner, with the stipulation that any vessel winning the trophy three years in a row would retain permanent possession. Setting a goal of $20,000 for the race fund, the committee had no trouble exceeding the mark. Everyone wanted to contribute, from local businesses to civic groups to yachtsmen.

Following in the tradition of Henry S. Hovey, who donated a cup for the 1892 race, Chandler Hovey gave $1000 to be distributed among the crews. The Hoveys were longtime members of the Eastern Yacht Club and had taken an interest in fishermen's regattas since their inception.

Of course, George Fuller, who had gotten such a kick out of racing aboard *Columbia* in 1926, was a contributor, as were Kellog Birdseye and firms like the Postum Company and General Seafoods Corporation. Not to be outdone, the Elks Lodge kicked in $200, and the Plumbers Union and Permanent Firemen each gave $25. Mayor Parsons promised to allocate a portion of the $3000 allowed the city under Massachusetts law for "advertising purposes" to promote the race. Fuller told Parsons that he would match the city's contribution dollar-for-dollar, to which the Mayor responded, "You better get your pocketbook ready."

The community's commitment to the races was phenomenal, yet understandable. Just the hint of a race had always managed to stir excitement in Gloucester, but in 1929 it was obvious that opportunities for fishermen's regattas under sail were dwindling. The losses of *Columbia* and *Henry Ford* (*Ford* had run aground off Newfoundland in June, 1927) narrowed the field of contenders to a handful of older vessels, the newest of which was built in 1913. The racers included: *Thomas S. Gorton,* which was launched in the summer of 1905 and had seen service in the haddocking, shacking, and Newfoundland herring trades; *Elsie,* of international racing fame; *Mary,* which Ben Pine bought and re-christened *Arthur D. Story;* and *Progress,* the smallest of the lot, at 117 gross tons and 96.7 feet overall.[24]

Like the boats, all the skippers were seasoned veterans. Wallace Parsons, of the *Gorton,* was in his fifties, and was considered a successor to the great Tommie Bohlin. A quiet unassuming man, he was born in Newfoundland and made a name for himself as a Gloucester sail carrier on many a trip home from the Banks in the dead of winter. A consistent money maker, Parsons was popular with dorymen and masters alike.

Norman Ross had command of the *Elsie.* Pushing 60, he too was considered a Bohlin protégé, making his mark as skipper of some of Gloucester's finest schooners. Responding to the decline of working sail in the fishing fleet, Ross brokered his reputation as a boat handler into stints as a yachting captain. He skippered *Zodiac* in a race from New York to Spain, and most recently had been master of the yacht *Ingomar.*

Marty Welch was sixty-four and had long ago established his reputation as a highliner and racer. He had commanded *Esperanto* in the first international series and made a good showing in the second with *Elsie*. Now he was skippering *Progress*, another underdog.

These men were a dying breed. As technology redefined the fisheries, it was becoming harder to find folks with the expertise to handle vessels under sail. Of course, yachtsmen had the know-how, but to have a yachtsman captain a fishing schooner would have been blasphemous. So too would having a fishermen's race that reflected modern realities. As *Rudder* magazine commented, such a contest would feature draggers "pulling along with Diesel engines wide open and perhaps the forestaysail set if the wind slant was favorable."[25]

Obviously such a spectacle would have had little appeal, either to the community or to the general public. Quite simply, it lacked the romanticism inherent in a contest that pitted "iron men and wooden ships" against each other. In that respect, at least, the 1929 races were the genuine article, allowing Gloucester to celebrate its love affair with the schooner fleet and lionize the men who epitomized its greatness. Indeed, the press was quick to point out that these would be "real fishermen's races," because "all the participants were built as fishermen" long before "racers" were launched to compete in the *Halifax Herald* series.

When the doctor ordered Marty Welch not to race, Manuel Domingoes, another bona fide fishing skipper, replaced him. Domingoes, the managing owner of the United Fisheries Company that owned *Progress,* had worked his way up from the fo'c'sle to command several well-known schooners. He was so respected in the Portuguese community that in 1914 he had been asked to head up United Fisheries. Like the other racing skippers, Domingoes represented the best qualities that Gloucester had to offer. Strong and determined, he was still vigorous and robust at age sixty.

The newspapers made much of such qualities, for they confirmed the popular and heroic images of Gloucestermen depicted in James Connolly's stories and in Kipling's *Captains Courageous.* There was something nostalgic, and at the same time awe-inspiring, reading about men like Charles Vino, the fore-topmast headman aboard *Progress.* Seventy-four years old, Vino had spent more than thirty years at sea. As agile as a cat, he could scramble up the ratlines quicker than some men half his age. A wiry little man, white hair blowing in the wind high above the deck, Vino inspired respect without uttering a word.

The only thing that could have made the races better would have been Clayt Morrissey's participation, and that almost happened. The O'Hara Brothers proposed to enter the *Josephine De Costa* under Morrissey's command, but the crew voted not to lose time and money racing because they were having a good season on the Banks. Even that, though, harked back to an earlier time, when fishermen weighed the chance to race against lost wages, and more often than not opted to stay fishing. The 1929 races became a living testimonial to an earlier generation's values, and a community's affirmation of them. Trawlermen may have controlled the city's economy, but dorymen still held its heart.

The races themselves proved to be a disappointment, with hardly enough wind to make it worthwhile. Still, they had their moments, not the least of which was the performance of the underdog, *Progress*. In the first race, on August 31, she was thirty-seven minutes behind the leader at the first turn. Yet, Domingoes knew what he was doing. As he rounded the first mark, *Progress* caught a breeze and took off. While *Elsie* lay becalmed for awhile, and the *Gorton* and *Story* languished inshore waiting for a land breeze, the little *Progress* charged ahead, turning the second buoy seventeen minutes ahead of *Elsie,* and fifty-one minutes in front of the *Gorton.* The race had already been called by the time Ben Pine reached the second mark with the *Story.*

The next day's race proved to be more of the same. *Story* got off fast, with *Elsie* and *Gorton* close behind, and *Progress* back two and a half minutes. With a nice wind blowing, *Story* built a four and a half minute lead over *Elsie* by the second turn of the first round, *Progress* edging past *Gorton* into third place by three minutes. Domingoes drove his vessel, pulling into second at the third mark. He took the lead when the boats made the first turn of the second lap. Then the wind died. After a two-hour drifting match, the race was called, *Progress* fifteen minutes and ten seconds ahead of *Elsie.*

The third race was on Labor Day, and the holiday crowds were out in force. Ben Pine took the *Arthur Story* around the course smartly, building a lead that he held until the last five miles. As the schooners worked to windward from Thatchers to Eastern Point, the *Story* tacked offshore and lost her wind momentarily.

Domingoes, seeing what had happened, tacked inshore, caught a land breeze, and shot into the lead. He never looked back. *Progress* crossed the finish line ten minutes ahead, greeted by a cacophony of shouts, whistles, and horns from the spectator fleet and onshore gallery. The cheering did not stop until the *Gorton,* bringing up the rear some twenty-one minutes later, tied up at the wharf.

There were big plans for a Labor Day gala that evening at Stage Fort Park. According to the original itinerary, it was to be capped off by the awarding of prizes to the winning skipper and his crew. Unfortunately, there had been only one official race in what was advertised as a best-two-out-of-three event. The Race Committee convened at the Master Mariners' Hall and resolved to terminate the series and declare *Progress* the winner. Officially, the action was justified "in order to restore the fishing industry to normal." Realistically, it was a recognition of the popular sentiment outside the Hall that wanted to get on with the celebration.

When the decision was announced, a cheer went up and a victory parade was quickly organized. With thousands of people lining the street, clapping and shouting, and fire engine sirens blaring, the procession made its way from downtown to Stage Fort Park, the racing crews marching alongside or riding atop the hook and ladder trucks. At the head of the line walked Domingoes and the other skippers. Charles Vino marched beside his captain, smiling proudly and waving to friends in the crowd. When the parade reached the park, it merged with thousands of other spectators who had come early to stake out a place to enjoy the festivities.

As soon as the scene settled down, Captain Henry Hilton, of the Gloucester Fire Department, introduced W. W. Lufkin, acting chairman of the Race Committee. Lufkin wasted no time in bringing Colonel Prentiss on stage to do the honors. With the trophies and cash prizes awarded, the captains got to say a few words.

Domingoes's remarks were simple and to the point, the kind of comment one would expect from a fishing skipper who did not see the need to waste words in needless hyperbole. The outcome of the race was simple enough to understand. "The *Progress* is only a small boat, but good things come in small packages." The speeches over, the firemen lit a bonfire and set off $3500 worth of firecrackers.

After nearly three years without racing, the 1929 event rekindled a desire for international competition. Rumors were strong that the Gloucester races would likely interest the Canadians in reviving the *Halifax Herald* series. At least, that was what the Gloucester folks hoped. What no one seemed to consider were the implications of such a dream. Certainly, the 1929 races had been great fun, but none of the participants could seriously be considered a contender in a race against *Bluenose*. Gloucester would have to build another racer if it wanted to compete internationally, but there had been no serious interest in building a racing schooner since 1923.

Although few people still saw the races as working sport, most were caught up in the spirit of competition and sentimentality that schooners under sail inspired. Of course, this meant publicity and tourism, and Gloucester's civic leaders had no objections to that. So, despite its irrationality, building a new Gloucester contender became almost inevitable. Not surprisingly, though, a new racer, when it came, marked the end of what little remained of the old-style fishermen's races.

9

"Clouds of White Sail": Romanticism and the End of Racing in the 1930s

WITHIN MONTHS OF THE 1929 RACES, A GLOUCESTER SYNDICATE WAS organized to build a racing schooner capable of challenging *Bluenose.* Naturally, Ben Pine was at the heart of the effort, but so too was local businessman Joe Mellow. Mellow had no direct ties to the fishing industry, save for what his daughter later characterized as "a passion for boats and for Gloucester."[1]

The relationship between Pine and Mellow was a case of romanticism making for strange bedfellows. Mellow owned and operated the First Taxi Cab and Limousine Service, which provided transportation to many of the wealthy summer residents of Eastern Point. One of these was Louis Thebaud, the retired head of a New York insurance company. Thebaud and Mellow became friendly during long sightseeing rides around the Cape Ann area. By the summer of 1929, Thebaud was bored, complaining to Mellow, "[There's n]othing to do [in this city] but come down town to shop, then go back home and rest, probably take a ride now and then. Same old stuff day after day."

Not so, responded Mellow, and with that he took Thebaud to the Master Mariners' Hall. After introducing Thebaud around, Mellow was surprised when the millionaire pulled a ten-dollar bill from his pocket and said, "I'm going to like this place here, Joe, take this ten-spot and see if I can take out a membership."

A generation earlier, he would have been laughed out of the room. The Master Mariners' Association was not some private club where someone with a few bucks in his wallet could walk in off the street and join. It was a fraternity of men who had been tested by the elements and won, who had earned the respect and admiration of their crews, their peers, and their community.

They were men, in the words of the Association's annual reports, with a "record of probity, uprightness, and square dealing." That was something that could not be bought. Because of that, even those who later "swallowed the anchor" and became prominent businessmen were still "proud to remember that they were once 'skipper'."[2]

In 1929, however, the Master Mariners' Hall had become a hangout for retired fishing captains who found Thebaud's childlike adoration gratifying. It gave them someone new to regale with their yarns. When Mellow came back with a membership card, he found Thebaud surrounded by old-timers, laughing and having the time of his life. By the time Mellow and Thebaud left, Thebaud had been named to the Race Committee, had donated $2000 to the racing fund, and had been awarded the title of "Captain."

From the Mariners' Hall, the two men walked down to the waterfront, where Mellow introduced the new "skipper" around. They ended up at the Atlantic Supply Company chatting with Ben Pine, who invited Thebaud to go deep-water fishing with him the next day. Thebaud readily agreed, and, with that, a friendship with Pine was cemented.

A few days after the Labor Day Races, Mellow told Thebaud how he wished Gloucester had a legitimate racer to challenge the Canadians. Thebaud concurred. Mellow thought nothing more of it; there were a lot of people in Gloucester expressing the same sentiment.

Then, on September 12, Thebaud showed up at Mellow's garage and asked, "Who shall I make the check out to?"

"What check?" a confused Mellow answered.

"You remember what we were talking about the other day," Thebaud explained. "The fishing boat, one that could race. Don't you remember after the races on Labor Day, when we agreed there wasn't a good racer here in Gloucester? Well, here's $10,000 towards a vessel that *can* race."

Mellow was no fool. It was a dream come true, not only for him, but also for the city he loved. "Make it out to Ben Pine and myself," he responded.

Mellow went to see Pine with the news. After some discussion, they decided to see whether they could buy *Mayflower*. After all, she was the only surviving American racer with the credentials to beat *Bluenose*. The problem was that she was freighting in the West Indies. Her bottom had been coppered to protect her from the marine growth in the Caribbean, and her owners wanted $28,000 to let her go. The price tag was steep, and that did not include the cost of bringing her to Gloucester to be refitted.

Frustrated, Mellow and Pine visited Thebaud and told him what they had learned. Thebaud did not hesitate. He sat at his desk and wrote another check for $20,000, telling the pair to build a new schooner instead.

As they stood to leave, Mrs. Thebaud called them back. "I like to see boat races," she said, "so won't you accept this little gift to help you build a new boat?" With that, she wrote a check for $10,000.

A few years earlier, $40,000 would have bought a decent fishing schooner, with money left over. It certainly would have built a dragger or trawler capable of paying for itself after several trips. However, it was only a start, given what Mellow and Pine had in mind. As Mellow told Thebaud, "[W]e'll build a new one, and it won't be an ordinary fishing schooner, either."

Pine and Mellow commissioned Frank C. Paine of the Boston firm of Paine, Belknap, and Skene to draft plans for the new boat. What they got was a design for a 134½-foot semi-knockabout schooner, with a cut-away forefoot that gave her a sharp bow and strong, yachty lines. The captain's cabin was to be made of solid mahogany, and there were electric lights throughout the vessel. A 180-hp Fairbanks-Morse Diesel provided auxiliary power, and electrical equipment included a deck hoist and Stoddart steerer. The total projected cost for the vessel was $73,000.[3]

If $52,000 to build *Mayflower* had been prohibitive in 1921, $73,000 for a fishing schooner in 1929 was ridiculous. Yet, what Pine and Mellow wanted was a racing yacht that could fish, not a fishing boat that could race. More than any of the earlier racers, this new boat was just that.

Certainly, when compared with *Mayflower*, which had been banned from international competition for being a yacht, the new schooner hardly qualified as a fisherman. With a carrying capacity of 400,000 pounds (600,000 without an engine, if that space was used), *Mayflower* had had one of the biggest holds in the fleet. By comparison, Mellow and Pine's vessel could accommodate only 175,000 pounds of fish. That was 25,000 pounds less than the smaller, more traditionally designed *L. A. Dunton*. If such older, more economically built schooners were having problems making money in the 1930s, it is no wonder that the new schooner never turned a profit.

Equally telling, for a boat built to compete in races that were meant to promote the design of better-built sailing fishing vessels, she never used her sails except to race. Indeed, on one occasion she had to be towed from the fishing grounds by the Coast Guard because her engine broke down and she did not have enough canvas aboard to get home.[4]

All that was in the future, however. Mellow and Pine were on a mission, and nothing was going to stop them from building their racer. Confronted with a $33,000 shortfall, they organized a syndicate of wealthy benefactors.[5] It was the organizers' intention to name the schooner for Mrs. Thebaud, and during the fall of 1929, *Gertrude L. Thebaud*, Inc., was established. Wetmore Hodges of General Seafoods contributed $5000 and solicited his longtime friend and business associate Bassett Jones of New York to join in. Jones wrote back, "I'll always go into anything you suggest, am enclosing a check for $5000." Thebaud relative Robert H. McCurdy and Chandler Hovey chipped in another $5000 a piece. The remainder of the stock was subscribed by Pine and Mellow, who also became managers of the corporation. In December the keel was laid at the Arthur Story Yard in Essex.

Unlike previous racing syndicates, *Gertrude L. Thebaud*, Inc., did not even make the pretense of including fishermen in the enterprise. It was going to be an elite affair done on behalf of Gloucester, rather than in partnership with it.

Ben Pine said as much when the *Thebaud* was launched on March 17, 1930. Noting that a race with *Bluenose* would cost money, Pine told reporters that, although Gloucester residents might not be willing or able to contribute as liberally to the race fund as in years past, the syndicate behind *Thebaud* would step "into the breach financially." Certainly, he and Mellow were doing everything they could to curry favor with those financially able to help. Elizabeth Hovey, an accomplished yachtswoman who the year before had done a respectable job skippering *Oriole* in a series against Germany, christened the new schooner with a thirty-five-year-old bottle of champagne donated by the Thebauds.

June Mellow, Joe's daughter, was five when *Thebaud* was launched, and she spent a lot of time playing on the deck before the schooner slid down the ways. She recalled being aboard during the trials. Although her memory of details is sketchy, her lasting impression of these events was that it was a yachting affair. There were lots of rich and important people about, and no one ever talked about the *Thebaud* as a fishing boat.[6]

Certainly there was nothing in June Mellow's experience to suggest a connection between *Thebaud* and the fishing industry. During an initial trial on April 27, seventy-five guests, representing a fair cross section of the social register, enjoyed a four-hour excursion out passed Thatcher's Island and down to Nahant and back. With only a riding sail, jumbo, and foresail set, *Thebaud* motored out of the harbor, her engines wide open. Even under power, she was quite a sight, white water foaming impressively under her forefoot. As she came up on Marblehead, someone in the crowd wondered what the folks at the Eastern Yacht Club would say if they saw a racing schooner charge into the harbor unannounced.

Never one to miss an opportunity, Pine swung her in toward land without a word. As *Thebaud* entered the harbor, she caught a breeze, her sails filled, and, after circling the harbor, Pine pointed her out to sea. As *Thebaud* made her pass, car horns blared onshore and pedestrians waved and doffed their hats. The schooner acknowledged the greetings with several blasts from her siren. The passengers were duly impressed by the show.

So too was the general public, which seemed anxious for a resumption of international competition.[7] Aware of that, the Marine Committee of the Massachusetts Bay Tercentenary Commission contacted Gloucester's Race Committee, offering to help sponsor an international series in exchange for scheduling it in conjunction with the state's Three Hundredth Anniversary celebration in the fall. Charged with commemorating "the enterprise of the seamen of the Massachusetts Bay Colony" and recognizing "the maritime achievements of their successors—the offshore fishermen of New England," the Marine Committee hoped to use the popular appeal of the fishermen's races to showcase the fishing industry and thereby market one of the state's primary products to a national audience.

Unfortunately, Angus Walters was not impressed. Although the owners of the new America's Cup contender *Yankee*—another Frank Paine design—wanted a private race against *Thebaud*, Walters announced that he had no intention of taking *Bluenose* to Gloucester to race in October. If the Americans wanted an international series, "Let the *Gertrude L. Thebaud* come to Halifax, where the series was broken off and I will race."

The American Race Committee was not so easily dissuaded, however. This was largely the same group of men who had refused to take "no" for an answer when competition was suspended in 1923. They had challenged every year until 1927, when *Columbia* went missing. Pine had even threatened to go north and wait for a race that last year. With a new boat capable of challenging *Bluenose*, there was no way that they were going to give up without a fight.

So, plans for a regatta proceeded apace. Frank E. Davis once again offered a cup. A delegation from the *Thebaud* syndicate, including Joe Mellow and Ben Pine, went to New York to talk to Sir Thomas Lipton about giving a trophy. Lipton was busy with the New York Yacht Club preparing to make yet another challenge for the America's Cup. Still, the affable tea magnate made time for the Gloucester contingent, listening enthusiastically to their plans to resume international racing, then agreeing to donate a cup for the event.

By September, it was clear that there would be a race. Enough money was raised to guarantee a $5000 purse, $3000 for the winner, $2000 for the loser, just as for the *Halifax Herald* Trophy. Frank C. Pearce, Ben Pine, and Wilmot Reed traveled to Nova Scotia to talk to *Bluenose*'s owners about the race specifics. Through sheer determination, Mellow and Pine had managed to keep fishermen's racing alive a bit longer. As *Yachting* magazine commented:

> The interest in the races off Gloucester lie not in the extreme speed of the vessels nor the exhibition of consummate racing tactics, but in the spectacle itself and its traditions—in the fact that the few remaining commercial sailing vessels can still scare up the will and the way to put on a race at all.[8]

The will came from Mellow and Pine's sense of romanticism and public spirit. The way came from the financial backing of the affluent Eastern Pointers who supported them. Neither reflected very much of the original intent and purpose of fishermen's races, but that did not matter to a general public excited by the prospect of once again seeing, in the words of *Boston Globe* Yachting Editor Leonard Fowle a year later, "Schooners with clouds of white sail."[9]

Clearly the races captured the imagination of the public in a way that the practical-minded fishing industry found increasingly irrelevant. A survey of the *Atlantic Fisherman*'s coverage of races after 1923 is particularly revealing.[10] Between 1921 and 1923, detailed reports appeared in each issue about racing plans, personalities, and vessel launchings. By 1929, the first hint that Gloucester was resurrecting racing appeared in a column called "Gloucester Gleanings." Plans by the American Race Committee to raise

$20,000 were given equal play with news that one of the last gasoline auxiliaries, the *Benjamin Wallace*, had blown up, that Captain Tom Benham had launched a new vessel, and that United Sail Loft Company was "busy on reconstruction work." The races themselves got a little more attention in the September issue, with photos and details of each contest covering four pages.

The launching of the *Gertrude L. Thebaud* in March 1930 merited one page in the April edition. That was a far cry from the detailed reports that heralded the launchings of *Mayflower, Puritan, Henry Ford, Columbia, Bluenose, Canadia,* and *Mahaska* in the early 1920s. In those days, readers were provided with sail plans, hull designs, and waterfront opinion about the relative merits of each vessel before it even touched the water.

Plans for the 1930 Lipton Cup Races received equally short shrift amid reports on the dredging of Gloucester's Inner Harbor and a bumper lobster catch in Nova Scotia. The races themselves got three pages in October, but the final results merited a mere column and a quarter, given the same attention as other news from Gloucester.

Coverage of the 1931 races for the *Halifax Herald* Trophy were much the same as that of the 1930 series. Plans for the five-race 1938 affair, meanwhile, received only five paragraphs in September of that year. Six paragraphs on the results appeared in November. Both articles were part of a larger roundup about events on the Gloucester waterfront. All this was significantly less attention than the races received in the popular press, whose coverage remained as enthusiastic in 1938 as it had been in 1920.[11]

Just how far the 1930s races were from the genuine article was reflected in *Thebaud's* prerace trials off Gloucester and Marblehead in 1930. On the first sail, more than one hundred guests were on board, including a large delegation from the North Shore summer colony. With *Thebaud* moving along at a good pace, Ben Pine called Peggy Farrell over and asked her to take the wheel.

The young socialite was delighted. The daughter of summer resident Margaret Farrell and granddaughter of oil magnate James Anthony Brady, Peggy was one of the Eastern Yacht Club's most proficient women sailors. As she steered, old Charlie Harty gave her advice. At seventy-nine years of age, Harty was still spry. More importantly, having logged some time as a yacht master, he knew how to make suggestions gently. He also knew how to stroke the egos of the rich and powerful. Certainly, he had managed to ingratiate himself well enough with J. Malcolm Forbes to get him to build *Fredonia* back in 1889. Now, as Pine took back the wheel, Harty told the crowd that Peggy was "an efficient helmsman." That was high praise from the man who everyone acknowledged was the dean of Gloucester's fishing skippers.

As *Thebaud* came abreast of Marblehead, Commodore Francis B. Crowninshield nudged his *Cleopatra's Barge II* out of the harbor. A beautiful steel-hulled schooner designed and built by Nathaniel Herreshoff in 1917 for Frederick Jacob Brown, she had been bought by Crowninshield and his wife in 1928. Ever since, they had spent every spare day cruising or day-sailing aboard her.[12]

The two vessels fell in together and battled admirably for several miles. The impromptu contest added spice to the outing and was repeated during the next two trials as well. Mrs. Thebaud even got in on the act during the third sail, taking her turn at the wheel along with Peggy Farrell.

Coming as it did at the same time as Lipton's America's Cup challenge, press coverage of the fishermen's race preliminaries was often hard to distinguish from that of the yachting event.[13] The same prattle about sportsmanship characterized both, as did pictures and stories about the rich and famous at play. It was a far cry from the 1892 "Race It Blew" or even Angus Walters's cantankerousness in 1923.

The series itself proved to be the longest international event to date.[14] It was nine days from the first race to the last, and that was only because *Thebaud* swept the series. If *Bluenose* had won one of the races, a rubber match would have been sailed, and given the flukiness of the weather, there is no telling how much longer the series might have lasted. Four races had to be called off in the middle because of weather, and light winds led the race committee to postpone racing outright on two days. It was a long way from the days when races were run as simply as possible to let the boats and crews get back to work.

Indeed, there was something especially telling about the cancellation of the October 15th race. The day began with heavy rain and a freshening thirty-five-mile-an-hour breeze. By 10:30, the weather was so thick that the *Conyngham*, the Coast Guard cutter that served as the press and committee boat, lost sight of the racers.

After a particularly rough ride in which she lost one of her trestle trees and her main boom jaws split, *Bluenose* had made it to where the eighteen-mile mark should have been, but no one aboard could see it. While Coast Guard vessels tried in vain to spot the buoy, Walters jogged the *Bluenose* back and forth, hoping that his mast headman would spy it. Just then, the skies opened up. Rain poured down in sheets, reducing visibility to zero. The judges decided to call off the race because no one could locate the halfway mark.

Walters was livid. "Why don't they let us stay out there until something carries away?" he asked the press. If it does, he continued, "That's our hard luck. We were perfectly satisfied to carry on."

Of course, he was right. The race had, in many ways, been reminiscent of the 1892 "Race It Blew." In fact, if accounts are to be believed, conditions for the latter were significantly worse, with winds well over fifty knots. No one called off that event, and they would not have dared try. Even the original premise behind the *Halifax Herald* series assumed that a real fishermen's race could only happen in a blow, like those that often occurred on the Banks. William Dennis had chortled at the cancellation of a 1920 America's Cup Race when it blew twenty-three knots, knowing full well that fishermen did not think that things got interesting until it was blowing at least thirty-five.

Be that as it may, the Lipton Cup Races succeeded in doing what Pine and Mellow had hoped they would do—rekindle racing fever on both sides of the border. Canadians were excited by the fact that *Bluenose* had handled so well in the October 15th race, and might have won what proved to be the last race on the eighteenth had Walters not been fooled into splitting tacks. As far as they were concerned, the series had proven nothing. After all, the Gloucester races had not been for the official "Fishing Fleet Championship of the North Atlantic." That title belonged only to the holder of the *Halifax Herald* Trophy.[15]

After the results of the Nova Scotia Fisheries Exhibition and Fishermen's Reunion Race off Lunenburg, however, it was not clear that *Bluenose* was the only Canadian schooner with a chance of defending it. Organized in 1929 by the Lunenburg Board of Trade, the Fisheries Exhibition was a three-day gala that brought together fishermen, their families, and exhibitors from all the upper provinces. It was the sort of homecoming celebration that the community looked forward to all year long, and in 1930 a fishermen's regatta was introduced.

Margaret K. Smith, Alsatian, and *Haligonian* were the official entrants in the twenty-eight-mile race.[16] Shortly after the event got underway, however, *Bluenose* sailed into the harbor fresh from the Banks, heavy laden with fish. She joined in the chase. With every stitch of canvas drawing perfectly, *Haligonian* covered the course in four hours, nineteen and a half minutes, eight minutes faster than *Bluenose* and well ahead of the *Smith* and *Alsatian.*

The results left the waterfront abuzz. With *Haligonian* showing real racing speed for the first time in her career, she might be a legitimate contender against *Bluenose,* some believed. At the very least, if national eliminations were held in 1931 to pick a defender of the *Halifax Herald* Trophy, it could prove to be a real horse race. Not likely, others argued. When one considered that *Bluenose* finished only eight minutes behind with her topmasts off and her hold full of fish, it was clear that she was in a class by herself. Popular sentiment was with *Bluenose,* but a little controversy added spice to the festivities, to say nothing about enhancing the betting line and giving the fellows down on the wharves something to argue about all winter.

For their part, the Americans were ecstatic after the Lipton Cup series. They had finally built a schooner capable of beating the mighty *Bluenose.* More importantly, perhaps, international racing had been revived after a seven-year hiatus, and the prospects for future competition looked bright.

The price had been high, but no one in the *Thebaud* syndicate, or in Glouces-ter, doubted that it had been worth it.

Amid this euphoria, the deepening Depression added an air of urgency to the desire to race. By early September 1931, the newspapers were full of reports about a possible *Bluenose-Thebaud* rematch, this time for the *Halifax Herald* Trophy.[17] Quite a few writers went on to imply that if it was going to happen, this was the year. After all, "No one portends what the future will hold out for either of these vessels." Part of the problem was the difficulty in getting competent crews for the schooners. In the United States, age, re-strictive immigration rules, and competition from draggers and trawlers left many schooners tied up for as much as a year. Indeed, *Elsie,* the 1921 Amer-ican challenger, was chartered to the Sea Scouts to avoid that fate and spent the summer of 1931 cruising.[18]

Conditions were so bad in Lunenburg that *Bluenose* did not even go fish-ing in 1931. It was reported early in the season that she would be chartered by the tourist agency Thomas Cook and Son "to take a party of excursion-ists away up north for a thrill cruise." While nothing came of it, efforts to se-cure her for exhibition purposes at the Canadian National Exposition at Toronto were well underway when Gloucester began negotiating terms of its *Halifax Herald* challenge.[19]

In the past, the series had been held in late October or early November because of the length of Lunenburg's fishing season. Now, with *Bluenose* in port anyway, there was talk of scheduling the event for late September or early October. That would draw more people to Halifax for the regatta by taking full advantage of the late-season tourist trade. The starting date was eventually set for October 17, later than initially speculated, but still earlier than any previous International Fishermen's Trophy competition.

In Gloucester, nothing was being left to chance. Ben Pine ordered *The-baud*'s sail plan modified slightly so that she would conform to the Deed of Gift. The changes cut down her rig a bit and gave *Bluenose* an even larger ad-vantage in overall sail area than she had had in 1930. Other modifications proved equally detrimental. Expecting heavy weather for the races off Hal-ifax, Pine and his advisers opted to lay in more ballast. *Thebaud* had been de-signed to sail on a ninety-nine-foot waterline. When the lumpers had fin-ished loading pig iron, her waterline measured 103 feet.

The results were obvious almost immediately. In the tune-up series in early October against *Elsie,* the *Thebaud* looked sluggish. In the races off Hal-ifax, she was beaten two straight, prompting Angus Walters to remark, "I'm sorry it can't be arranged we have company on these schooner races. *The-baud* wasn't any company . . . and a feller don't get much out o' racin' the clock all the time."[20]

For many, *Bluenose*'s triumph marked the end of the age of sail. As *Yacht-ing* magazine put it:

Unless something is done, one of the most picturesque phases of rac- ing under sail will have passed. The fishermen may not be scientific in their racing, and their vessels may not be on a plane with America's Cup contestants for speed, but if you have ever tailed onto a sheet or halliard with a score of fishermen on the deck of a schooner with her cabin house dragging in the water and two men at the wheel, you won't forget it in a hurry.[21]

Even though the 1931 series had not been competitive, such images lived on in the public imagination, making the schooners popular tourist attrac- tions. In light of the history of the all-sail fishing fleet, it was hardly a fitting epitaph, but an appropriate reflection of the times.

Angus Walters knew better than most the promotional value of his vessel. When he received a telegram from R. Y. Easton of Toronto congratulating him on his victory, Walters wired back his thanks, with a promise to take *Bluenose* to Ontario for the 1932 Canadian National Exhibition, "if arrange- ments can be satisfactorily completed."[22] Walters was well aware that a lot of folks in Ontario were clamoring to see his champion fishing schooner, and that that could be turned to advantage. Indeed, had it not been for Toronto's shoal inner harbor, he might have taken *Bluenose* to the exhibi- tion instead of racing her in 1931.

As things turned out, it was not until 1933 that *Bluenose* made it to Toronto, and then only as an afterthought. She and the *Thebaud* were in- vited to Chicago that year for the Century of Progress Exposition as, re- spectively, Canada's and Massachusetts' exhibits.[23] Realizing the potential of the situation, local businessmen organized the Lunenburg Exhibitors Limited to coordinate *Bluenose*'s itinerary. With people willing to pay for an excursion up the St. Lawrence River and through the Great Lakes aboard the "Queen of the North Atlantic Fishing Fleet," *Bluenose* made the trip loaded with passengers.

Arriving in Chicago, she spent the summer and early fall providing pleas- ure sails to hordes of visitors, while making a tidy profit for her investors in the bargain. So popular were the schooners that *Thebaud* and *Bluenose* each hosted some twenty-five hundred visitors a day. When they left in October, the level of interest had not even begun to wane. Sensitive to that, Walters pointed his big salt banker toward Toronto. His buddy, C. H. J. Snider, of the *Toronto Telegram,* had convinced him that the Ontario tourist trade was ripe for a visit. *Bluenose* spent the winter of 1933 and the spring of 1934 in Toronto, giving sightseeing and sailing excursions to eager visitors whenever the weather allowed.

As for the *Thebaud,* she had become something of a goodwill ambassador for Gloucester. With the fishing industry in dire straights, she had taken a contingent of industry leaders, including several prominent skippers, to

Washington before the Chicago World's Fair in 1933. The group hoped to remind the recently inaugurated President not to forget the fishermen in his "New Deal." President Roosevelt was so delighted with the visit that he brought British Prime Minister Ramsey MacDonald to the pier to tour the vessel and meet Ben Pine and his crew. Later, Mrs. Roosevelt hosted the Gloucester delegation at the White House.[24] The appeal of the schooners was so widespread that they seemed to transcend class, politics, and nationality.

That point was made abundantly clear in 1935 when *Bluenose* was invited to England to help celebrate King George V's and Queen Mary's Silver Jubilee.[25] After a record crossing of seventeen days, she arrived in Plymouth to a rousing welcome. Following the Sailpast Review at Spithead, a yacht race was arranged around the Isle of Wight. Angus Walters had the time of his life. Everywhere he went, he was entertained by England's elite. He suppered with earls and spun yarns with members of the Royal Yacht Squadron. The visit proved to be a tour de force for the fourteen-year-old schooner and her captain.

By 1937, however, such glories were all but forgotten. Fish prices remained low, and many owners kept their vessels tied up. Skeleton crews were employed at minimal wage to maintain the craft, but that expense seemed astronomical when no money was coming in. With no end in sight to the Depression, shareholders got restless and often pressured their companies to sell schooners at whatever price the market would bear. Even *Bluenose* was not immune.

The only thing that saved her was Angus Walters's determination. To him, *Bluenose* was a national treasure. She deserved to be retired, floating majestically at a registered berth alongside a government-funded museum. Future generations should be allowed to tread on her decks, reliving some of the most glorious moments in Canadian maritime history. When a significant number of stockholders were not convinced, Walters formed an alliance with two partners and bought out the others.[26]

Meanwhile, in Gloucester, the situation was not much better. *Thebaud* was not likely to make any money on the Banks, so her owners chartered her to Donald B. MacMillan for the summer. MacMillan was an Arctic explorer who was organizing his sixteenth expedition north. A crew of thirty-seven, including professors and college students, left Gloucester on June 24, 1937, bound for Frobisher Bay and adventure. Before they had finished, they had covered some eight thousand miles and nearly lost the vessel in a dramatic drop of tides.[27]

There the story might have ended had it not been for MGM. In 1937, moviegoers flocked to see Spencer Tracy and Freddie Bartholomew star in *Captains Courageous*.[28] Markedly different in many of the particulars from Rudyard Kipling's book, the film managed to capture its essential message.

Spoiled Harvey Cheyne fell off a European-bound steamer, was rescued by Portuguese doryman Manuel, and learned about life aboard the *We're Here*. Sitting on the deckhouse playing his concertina and serenading the fish, Tracy's Manuel was a working-class philosopher. In a simple and gentle way, he taught Freddie Bartholomew's character far more than he had ever learned at his fancy prep school.

Lionel Barrymore, as Disko Troop, was the quintessential Gloucester skipper—tough, proud, and able to think like a codfish. He commanded the respect of his crew with the quiet self-confidence of a man's man. His son, played by Mickey Rooney, knew better than most the special mixture of stern discipline and empathy that made Disko a good father and effective skipper.

Audiences delighted in such images. Hard-working men with a sense of fair play and a stoic pride in themselves embodied the American spirit as surely as any cowboy in the equally popular westerns of the day. Yet, that was only part of the movie's attraction. The stirring climactic race home between the *We're Here* and the *Cushman* showcased the beauty and power of the schooners in a way that had not been done since the 1931 races. With every stitch of canvas aloft, the boats plowed through the water, their decks slanted at a forty-five-degree angle and the sound of water hissing as they went. The majesty and drama of the race was magnified by the danger inherent in the contest, a danger played out melodramatically when *We're Here* lost her mainmast, crippling Manuel and setting up his tragic death scene.

The movie's popular appeal was obvious to the real-life Captains Courageous of Gloucester. At their regular monthly meeting on December 6, 1937, the Master Mariners' Association voted to endorse an international fishermen's race that would attract "the attention of millions in all parts of the country."[29] Deciding to contact Governor Charles F. Hurley to ask his support in getting the Commonwealth of Massachusetts to finance the venture, the Master Mariners argued that the publicity for the event would "increase the markets for fresh and salt fish and thus benefit one of Massachusetts' largest industries."

As plans for the regatta developed, it was decided to make it a best-three-out-of-five series, sailed alternately off Boston and Gloucester, beginning October 9, 1938. The Boston course was a thirty-six-mile race twice around an eighteen-mile triangle. Off Gloucester, the schooners would sail a single thirty-six-mile triangle. The idea of a three-out-of-five series was new, and the October 9 starting date was the earliest on record. Both facts reflected the purposes of the event. A longer series meant more public attention and more tourist dollars. An early start date maximized the number of out-of-towners likely to show up for all or part of the affair.

If there was any question that the races were going to be more image than substance, the hype in the month before the regatta removed all doubt. The most blatant example of playing to public sentiment was the Race Committee's invitation to Spencer Tracy to cruise aboard the steamer *Steel Pier* on September 9. The committee made no secret that it hoped to capitalize on Tracy's popularity as Manuel in the *Captains Courageous* movie "to draw public interest to the race."

The excursion was planned as a round trip between Boston and Gloucester for more than five hundred representatives of state shipping interests and "others identified with port affairs." Although Tracy was unable to make it, the cruise went on anyway. With the steamer decorated fore and aft with pennants and code flags, the fifty-piece Boston Police Post Band, accompanied by the American Legion Band, kept the scene lively with a mix of old standards that everyone aboard enjoyed.

As events turned out, the committee need not have troubled Tracy, for they had in the *Thebaud* crew a homegrown matinee star of their own. Twenty-two-year-old Sterling Hayden, the mainmast headman was, the *Boston Post* trumpeted, "LIKE A MOVIE IDOL." He was six feet five inches, blonde, a "fine masculine specimen" that "scores of women who viewed the vessels . . . inquired [about]. . . ." Yet, he was also more than that. He was the genuine article—a skilled mariner with a healthy dose of wanderlust. The combination of his youth, good looks, and genuine seamanship made him a popular character during the races because he embodied the very ideals that the races had come to represent in the public mind.

Therein lay the irony of the 1938 races. Like Hayden, they were easily characterized in terms of surface features—a nostalgic throwback to the romantic days of sail when fair-haired New England boys stood watch in the trestle trees high above a wildly pitching deck. It was an image the public could understand and appreciate. It was heroic and, as such, gratifying. Yet, underneath the surface, things were not always what they appeared. The image, while true, told only part of the tale.

Reflecting back on his experiences years later, Hayden tried to make sense of what his life had meant during what he called the "Shroud of an Era." In a section of his book *Wanderer* entitled "Requiem. Midnight," he outlined an imaginary conversation he had with a stranger on the evening after the last race. Lying flat against the crosstrees, staring up at the stars, Hayden mused about what he would do now that the races were over. A stranger appeared on the dock reminding him of what the papers had said about him. Hayden was unimpressed. The stranger persisted, reading a passage from the October 24 *Boston Post* detailing his exploits in securing a flaying block on the main gaff in a raging gale. Hayden put up his hand.

"Stop," [he said.] "That's enough."
But there's more.
"I know; I read it all right, don't worry about that; made me feel good, I admit."

The stranger continued to detail the press's love affair with Hayden, quoting an article that claimed his "masculine pulchritude . . . wins by 100 fathoms over fellow members of both crews."

> "Yeah, Yeah. I read that one too, [Hayden observed]. They shouldn't print stuff like that."
> Oh, why not?
> "Because it makes you feel embarrassed. Besides, it's not even true."
> What do you mean?
> "Never you mind what I mean."[30]

Like Sterling Hayden, his crew mates could not help but be flattered by the attention, gratified by the praise. Yet, they also knew that they were not the larger than life heroes the reporters made them out to be. They were ordinary guys with ordinary tastes who ultimately neither understood nor cared about the niceties of romanticism.

Even though the 1938 races were conceived as a publicity gimmick, they were sailed by real fishermen, and that made the event every bit as cantankerous as earlier *Halifax Herald* series. Put simply, although much had changed since 1920, the fundamental tension between the organizers' and the public's fantasies, and the fishermen's realities, had not. This point was obvious from the outset. When *Bluenose* arrived in Boston, Governor Hurley hosted a welcoming luncheon on behalf of the state. Angus Walters declined the invitation. From aboard the deck of his schooner, he remarked, "Let 'em spout. I'm gettin' ready to race."

Down in Gloucester, the mayor discreetly let the saloon keepers on Duncan Street know that he wanted to see some decorum and self-restraint during the races. The owners complied, storing every bit of breakable furniture. When the regular customers surveyed the changes to their favorite watering holes, all they could do was laugh.

It was only the beginning of the absurdities, however. As with previous events, the combination of unpredictable weather and Race Committee stupidity set the tone for most of the races.[31] After *Thebaud* won the first contest on October 9, the second race off Gloucester proved to be a drifting match. Still, the Race Committee persisted, refusing to call the contest until the time limit had expired. The committee did this despite the fact that it was obvious to everyone else that it would be no race when the schooners had covered only twelve miles in three hours, half the time allowed for the entire thirty-six-mile race.

Following a victory by *Bluenose* on the thirteenth, fog and calm conditions kept the schooners tied up for days. When they tried to race again on October 20, exactly one week after the last completed contest, the committee called the race with *Thebaud* in the lead. When the Gloucesterman docked,

her crew was fit to be tied. They charged that the Race Committee was going out of its way to hamstring the *Thebaud*, racing only on days when she would have no wind.

Then rumors began circulating that Angus Walters was shifting ballast, a clear violation of the rules. When he was caught in the act, the Gloucester contingent demanded that *Bluenose* be disqualified. Walters was adamant. As far as he was concerned, it was his ballast and he would do as he pleased with it. The Race Committee did nothing to challenge him.

Bluenose won the next race on the twenty-third to take a two-to-one lead in the series. The following day's contest was held in a driving rain, with twenty-five-mile-an-hour winds and poor visibility. *Thebaud* surged ahead when *Bluenose's* fore-topmast backstay parted. She ran for the finish line nearly unchallenged, but when she got there, the committee boat was nowhere to be found. Apparently, it had gotten lost following the racers and was off station. Not knowing that, *Thebaud's* crew came up with what they believed to be a more plausible explanation—the seasick committeemen had been forced to run into port to appease their stomachs. Not knowing whether the marker should be left to port or to starboard, *Thebaud* crossed the line twice, once on each side, to avoid anyone getting "technical."

The next day, the gale was still howling. As if to legitimize the Gloucestermen's charges that the committee raced only on days with no wind, a "lay day" was declared. The jokes were merciless. As far as the fishermen were concerned, it was proof that Captain Charles M. Lyons, a U.S. steamboat inspector and chair of the Race Committee, had not only gotten lost the day before, but had been seasick as well. The prospects of being out in a storm for a second day in a row, the pundits chortled, was simply too much for him. Whether true or not, the perceptions were heartfelt, and undermined what little credibility the committee had left with the fishermen.

The series finally concluded on October 26. In less than fifteen-mile-an-hour winds, *Thebaud* got across the starting line first, but was quickly headed by *Bluenose*. When it was over, the Lunenburger had won the race and the series by two minutes and fifty seconds.

The contest may have been finished, but not the rhetoric, or the class divisions it represented. With politicians and civic leaders droning on about the heroic feats of the fishermen, the crews of the schooners threw themselves a party in the hold of the *Bluenose*. The affair was by invitation only, and fishermen guarded each hatch to make sure that it stayed that way.

(Opposite) What the public wanted to see, and why the fishermen's races lasted as long as they did: the beauty and romance of two schooners under a full press of sail, battling neck-and-neck for the championship of the North Atlantic fishing fleet. Bluenose, on the left, and the *Gertrude L. Thebaud*, heeling slightly to leeward during the 1938 series. (Photograph courtesy of Mystic Seaport Museum, Rosenfeld Collection, Mystic, Connecticut)

Some ninety men were in the smoke-filled hold, drinking rum, singing and carrying on. Off-color jokes drew periodic bursts of laughter from the clusters of men scattered about. Hymie Rodenhauser, a *Bluenose* mast headman, sat on a keg, blaring away on a trumpet. Then, as Sterling Hayden described it, the politicians intruded.

"All right, you bassards, up, up, everybo'y up on the goddam deck! Hear me? The governor's gonna make us his honorin' speech, an' the mayor wants every friggin' one o' you on th' deck . . . and leave the booze down here . . . and no friggin' noise! Hear?"

No one moves. "Drink up!" roars O'Toole. You can hear the Legion band playing the National Anthem. All rise. When the Anthem expires, they sit. . . .[32]

If the fishermen were reluctant to hobnob with "respectable society," they had good reason. The prize money was not even ready for presentation at the awards ceremony (it took months and the help of lawyers to finally recover it), and some practical jokers stole the *Halifax Herald* Trophy as a prank. It showed up three days later with a poem:

Here's to Angus, good old sport,
Whose challenge sort of takes us
short.
Send us a gale that blows at thirty,
And we'd bet our shirts on little Gerty.

Angus Walters was not amused. He decided to get *Bluenose* home "before she too disappeared." As he made ready to leave, he told reporters, "The *Bluenose,* as long as I live, will never again race in the United States. If *Thebaud* ever wants to come and race in Canada, we'll meet her at the starting line." Ben Pine responded that he would be damned if he would ever challenge again. Given the history of international competition, there could not have been a more fitting ending to it all.

Bluenose arrived home to a grand welcome. Citizens from Lunenburg and the surrounding countryside thronged the waterfront as she came into the wharf. A procession formed, and the crew and captain were escorted through the streets to the shouts and cheers of the admiring crowd. The parade ended at Jubilee Square, where the mayor and other dignitaries made speeches of welcome and congratulations. The heroes were escorted to a sumptuous banquet, guests of the town of Lunenburg.

As the dust settled, Walters resumed his plans to retire his beloved schooner and turn her into a "monument to the sail-propelled fishermen, who are rapidly becoming extinct."[33] Between the lingering Depression and the threat of war in Europe, few people seemed interested. By 1942, Walters had to admit defeat. He sold *Bluenose* into the West Indian freighter trade. She went aground on a coral reef off Haiti and sank in January 1946.

Thebaud's fate was similar.[34] With the American entry into World War II, she was chartered by the Coast Guard as part of the Corsair Fleet and patrolled the East Coast as a submarine spotter. In the spring of 1944, Ben Pine got her back, but he had no use for her. He sold her to William H. Hoeffer of New York as a Caribbean freighter. In February 1948, at La Guaira, Venezuela, she was smashed to bits in a storm.

⛵

Bluenose had meant a lot to the Canadians. They issued a stamp in 1929 bearing her likeness, and their ten-cent piece has borne the image of the Lunenburg salt banker since 1937. Not surprisingly, then, the *Halifax Herald* characterized her passing as a "national sorrow; the ignominy of her death, a national shame."[35]

In Gloucester, sentimentality about the schooners was equally strong. According to one fisherman, "People [just] loved them."[36] On the waterfront, draggermen had an abiding respect for the old vessels and the men who still worked them, although the feeling was never reciprocated. When a schooner came onto the fishing grounds, it was given priority. As one man recalled:

> [A]lmost everybody that was in the fleet [in the 1940s] started in dory vessels and . . . [while] they were a thing of the past . . . nobody really wanted to see them go. . . . [I]f a [dory vessel] was there . . . you gave him a good berth. . . . Guys were really sorry to see them go . . . [even though] they were an anachronism.[37]

That seemed to be a universal sentiment, and it may be the simplest explanation for why the races persisted as long as they did. Regardless of who one was or where one came from, the schooners represented an ideal, a link to a simpler and more heroic past. Average fishermen had either grown up with these vessels or knew someone who did. Citizens of Gloucester and Lunenburg saw their fleets as a source of economic survival and community pride. Middle-class folks from Toronto, Chicago, and elsewhere identified with the simple values fishermen and their way of life seemed to represent. Yachtsmen reveled in the romantic tales of derring-do on the high seas. Perhaps most importantly, it was all eminently marketable.

Between all these positions were wide schisms of perspective, the most glaring perhaps between the fishermen and the sentimental ideal of the general public. Yet, the common link was the vessels themselves. Everyone was touched by the sheer beauty of the schooners. It was something that transcended time and defied reason. Perhaps it was nothing more than romanticism writ large, magnified by nationalism and hyped by public relations. Whatever it was, it kept the mystique of the all-sail fishing fleet alive far longer than any practical concern for dollars and cents would ever have dictated.

Epilogue: Continuing Legacies

Ben Pine died on February 23, 1953, after a long illness. Five years later, the *Gloucester Times* ran a five-part series offering "an appraisal of his contribution to the welfare of Gloucester." The articles were less an assessment of Pine's life than reminiscences about the good old days and a strategy for recapturing them.[1]

Readers were reminded that "nothing ever spread the fame of Gloucester so widely" as the fishermen's races. Tourism was expanded beyond July and August, beginning in March and April when new racers were launched, and extending without interruption until late October. "THOSE WERE THE DAYS!" one article gushed. "Every room in town was rented and the restaurants did a land office business." The lesson from the series of articles was obvious.

Build a fishermen's racer in Gloucester.

From the day that the announcement is made Gloucester will be on the front pages again all over the United States and Canada and if the publicity is properly handled she will stay there for a good many years.

Choose a good trade name for the racer, one that can be copyrighted. Be sure it is distinctive and above all SALTY.

The plan was foolproof because it brought together the city's two primary industries in a complementary way. As the *Times* put it, "THE FISH BUSINESS IS OUR HERITAGE! THE FISH BUSINESS IS OUR DESTINY! LET'S GIVE THE SUMMER RESIDENTS WHAT THEY CAME HERE FOR ORIGINALLY—SUNLIT SAILS!"

Once the decision to build a racing schooner was reached, the public would be told that the shipyard would be open every Saturday and Sunday afternoon with "a capable man on hand" to explain the progress made during the week. Not only would this encourage tourism, but it was educational, because it "would appeal to many school teachers and children and . . . provide many classes with an [instructive] outing."

Funding for the project would come primarily, though not exclusively, from the tourist and fishing industries. The benefits to the former in an expanded tourist season were obvious, but with proper marketing they could be equally significant for the fish firms. With the vessel's name copyrighted

161

and her likeness a trademark, every Gloucester company that qualified would be authorized to use the logo along with their regular brand name. Assuming the widespread publicity the schooner would naturally receive, the trademark would heighten consumer awareness of the products displaying it, and it would come to be accepted as a mark of quality. Since the return on investment would be astronomical, a small fraction of a cent per pound would be contributed to the schooner's racing fund to keep the project economically viable.

Every truck leaving Gloucester would display the schooner logo on its sides. Everett R. Jodrey, the series' author, was convinced that there would be "many requests to have . . . truck[s] stop a moment in various towns through which they pass to enable the children to learn what the fish look like in their natural habitat." A colorful calendar displaying the fish would be produced as well. There was no doubt that such an item would be "in demand all over the country, especially in school rooms, and would further enhance its value to the industry." After all, with "so many fish . . . now being sold in packages, cut up and cooked," children and "for that matter an adult a few miles from Gloucester" had "no idea what the fish looked like before processing."

It was an ambitious proposal for a city whose economic star was in eclipse. As they had in the '20s and '30s, civic leaders were hoping to promote their community by recapturing the glory days of sail. The strategy had worked before, so why not again? The logic made sense and pointed to the lingering hold that the schooners had on the city, and, if Jodrey and others were right, on the general public.

Of course, the dream never came to pass. Money was tight, and the folks of Gloucester were not particularly interested in reclaiming or preserving their past at that moment. The last years of the *Sadie M. Nunan* should have made that point abundantly clear.[2] Built in 1901 at East Boothbay, Maine, the *Nunan* was a pretty little clipper-bowed schooner that spent thirty-seven years fishing out of Cape Porpoise, Maine, and Boston, before being sold to Argentinean adventurer Ewing Parra. Parra renamed her *Expedition* in anticipation of a sail around the world, but disappeared from Gloucester before anything came of his plans.

Joe Mellow, of *Thebaud* fame, acquired the *Nunan*, and over the next 14 years spent some $12,000 to keep her afloat at the State Pier. He used her as a party fishing boat for a while, but by 1952 the costs of upkeep were too much. Her topsides were deteriorating, and Pier authorities wanted her towed away.

Mellow and a small group of local citizens formed the Gloucester Museum Corporation to save the *Nunan* as a museum and a memorial to the fishermen. They bought her at sheriff's auction on August 16, 1952, and she became a receptacle for fishing artifacts over the next several years. Despite bumper stickers imploring Gloucester to "Save Sadie," public apathy proved to be too strong. Faced with mounting bills, the museum sold her to a quahoger, who moved her to East Gloucester, where she rolled on her side. In August 1957 she was badly burned in a fire, and seven months later, just before Jodrey's series appeared, what was left of her was torched to get rid of the unsightly hulk.

In Lunenburg the rationale for a Jodrey-like proposal led to the building of *Bluenose II*.[3] Canadians had long regretted doing nothing to save the original, and Lunenburgers in particular often wondered what might have happened had they backed Walters's plans more enthusiastically.

There was certainly interest in *Bluenose,* even fourteen years after her demise off Haiti. Captain Spurgeon Geldert of the Lunenburg Tourist Information Centre observed that seven thousand Canadian and American tourists came to Lunenburg in the summer of 1959, many specifically to see *Bluenose.* "It's surprising how many people don't know she's not here," he noted. "They do know that this was her home port, and they want to look at her."

For years folks had talked off and on about building a new *Bluenose,* but nothing came of it until 1960. Between May and August of that year, the Smith and Rhuland shipyard, which had launched the original *Bluenose,* was busy building a replica of the HMS *Bounty* for a forthcoming MGM movie about the mutiny. Thousands of people visited the yard to watch the construction. It occurred to more than a few locals that such a turnout proved the viability of a *Bluenose II* project. As Geldert put it, "Most everybody wanted to see the *Bounty* and were well pleased with her. If the *Bluenose* were here, she'd be a great drawing card."

Committees to study the idea were set up, and men associated with the first *Bluenose* were consulted. Bill Roue said, "[V]isitors still look for the *Bluenose* in Lunenburg. If they want to, they should be able to see what she was like. . . . I bet she'd be good for a tourist attraction and to take people out for sails. She'd probably almost support herself, being out every day with twenty-five or thirty people on her."

Angus Walters agreed. "If they build another, why she'd pay and repay for herself!" However, he warned, this was the "last chance they'll ever have to build another, while interest and feeling is as it is now. There's a different class of people—new generations—and I think she should be built while the fellows are still around who know how she should go." He was right. Of all the shipwrights that had worked on *Bluenose,* only three were still around in 1960.

The public relations potential of building a second *Bluenose* seemed limitless. As Lunenburg Mayor R. G. A. Wood noted, "I think that for the town it would be a wonderful idea, if it were pursued correctly and with proper promotion. . . . If they build her . . . it would be a marvelous thing not only for Lunenburg, but for Nova Scotia, and all of Canada."

The only problem was money. Fred Rhuland estimated the cost of construction at $200,000. Several options were batted around, including a nationwide drive by schoolchildren to contribute a dime apiece, and the plan Walters had proposed to save the first *Bluenose*—selling "ownership" certificates in the vessel for a dollar each. However, none of these schemes seemed adequate to raise the amount of capital realistically needed to fund *Bluenose II*. As it had in Gloucester with Jodrey's proposal and the *Nunan,* it appeared that a lack of cash would doom the idea.

Then serendipity intervened. Oland and Sons Brewery had plans in the works to build a Nova Scotian fishing schooner to promote its new Schooner Beer. When company executives learned of the rumblings in Lunenburg, they offered to build the *Bluenose II* instead. Organizers of the reconstruction project readily agreed.

On February 27, 1963, *Bluenose II's* keel was laid at the Smith and Rhuland yard. On July 24 she was launched. Since then, she has taken passengers on daily summer cruises, worked the charter trade in the Caribbean, and served as a Canadian and Nova Scotian goodwill ambassador.

Ironically, given its history and the legacy of men like Ben Pine, Gloucester has only recently attempted to capitalize on its past. The old *Adventure,* the last dory trawler, came home to Cape Ann in 1986, after 32 years in the Maine "dude trade."[4] Her owner, Captain Jim Sharp, who had skippered her out of Camden, Maine, since 1964, gave her to the Gloucester *Adventure* Corporation on condition that she would be "cared for, prominently displayed as a monument to the history of Gloucester, and used for the education and pleasure of the public." Sharp understood, as he wrote in the "Foreword" of Joe Garland's history of the vessel, that even when she was a windjammer, *Adventure* represented "a monument to fishing tradition . . . Her spirit infects thousands of enthused, experienced and inexperienced sailors who, through her, have been steeped in the kind of voyaging our forefathers did when wind was the only power."

Previous generations had lived the experience vicariously through novels like *Captains Courageous* and the stories of James Connolly. They had identified with Spencer Tracy as Manuel or delighted in the stories of Ben Pine's sportsmanship or Sterling Hayden's acts of derring-do. Somehow the impulse to keep alive the mystique was passed from generation to generation down to the late-twentieth century. Certainly, how else does one account for the widespread appeal of boats like *Adventure* and *Bluenose II?* As Garland put it:

> [I]f you have an unexplainable yen to know how it was to feel the slanting deck of a Gloucester schooner under your feet, to experience the

push and the thrill of the wind and the sails and the heft of the spars that drove these great vessels out to the Banks and back in the best and the worst of the weather, to sway up canvas and haul sheets the way the horny-handed gang did in the old days, to spit to leeward and rub up against the life and the hardness and the camaraderie of the dorymen profanely plying their oars and hauling their trawls with a glance at the lowering clouds—then there is only one route left in all creation, and that is down the gangplank of the schooner *Adventure* out of Camden on the coast of Maine.

Those who had sought to preserve the schooners in the racing years instinctively understood this appeal. Faced with the challenges of draggers and trawlers and changing economic times, they had clung to the certainty of an older world represented by the schooners. The general public beyond Gloucester and Lunenburg reveled in the nostalgia. Of course, good marketing added to the popular appeal and economic benefit for local business.

Remarkably, the same equation, minus the fishermen, defined the logic behind Jodrey's proposal in 1958, the building of *Bluenose II*, and the return of *Adventure* to Gloucester. Unfortunately, nostalgia costs money, and that can be a hit-or-miss proposition. Gloucester was lucky in 1930 when Louis Thebaud and other monied interests decided to foot the bill for the *Gertrude L. Thebaud*. The city was less fortunate in the '50s when it lost the *Nunan* and there were no takers for Jodrey's scheme. *Bluenose II* became a reality, but only because Oland and Sons saved the project.

In the 1920s and 1930s, support could be more readily counted on because the past was still so immediate. Back then, there had been no question that Gloucester and Lunenburg would get behind the fishermen's races. It was part of their heritage. Now the linkages between past and present are not so obvious. World events, economics, and the passage of time have seen to that.

Yet, despite it all, a sense of tradition still persists in these communities, and, for that matter, in the public at large, albeit in an often overly romanticized view of the ships and the men who sailed them. Certainly, the romanticism that clouded public perceptions of international racing still accounts for a large part of the popularity of *Bluenose II* and *Adventure*.

Although this romanticism may have helped perpetuate an interest in the workaday life of the fishermen far longer than was possible for nonmaritime laborers, it has gotten us no closer to a real understanding of their experience. Fishermen were not romanticized caricatures, but men very similar to workers who labored in less exotic settings. Indeed, James Connolly's words on the passing of the Gloucestermen could serve as an equally fitting epitaph for most skilled workers during the early-twentieth century. "To linger sighing over the industrial current of the times is a waste of time perhaps . . . but nonetheless, these were great men . . . and what men knew . . . them but will continue to wish everyone else could have known them for who they were?"[5] The irony of Connolly's words is that the only way to truly know these men is to disabuse ourselves of the romantic images that Connolly and others like him helped to create. Perhaps this book is a small step in that direction.

Notes

INTRODUCTION: ROMANTICISM AND REALITY: FISHERMEN AS WORKERS AND HEROES

1. Much has been written about the changes in labor-management dynamics in the late-nineteenth and early-twentieth centuries. At the heart of most of the redefinition of work was the introduction of new technology that made skill obsolete and management's search for efficiency a high priority. New corporate structures, vertical and horizontal integration, and the time-and-motion studies of Frederick Winslow Taylor all contributed to the workers' loss of power and control in the workplace. When similar changes upset the traditional relationships in the fishing industry, fishermen reacted in much the same way as their counterparts in other industries. For a good overview of the changing realities throughout industrial America at the time, see Harry Braverman, *Labor and Monopoly Capital: The Degradation of Work in the Twentieth Century* (New York: Monthly Review Press, 1974); David Brody, *Workers in Industrial America: Essays on the 20th Century Struggle* (New York: Oxford University Press, 1980), chapter 1; Alfred D. Chandler, Jr., *The Visible Hand: The Managerial Revolution in American Business* (Cambridge, Mass.: Belknap Press, 1977); Alfred D. Chandler, Jr., "The Emergence of Managerial Capitalism," *Business History Review* 58 (Winter 1984): 473–503; Richard Edwards, *Contested Terrain: The Transformation of the Workplace in the Twentieth Century* (New York: Basic Books, 1979); David Montgomery, "Worker Control of Machine Production in the 19th Century," *Labor History* 17 (Fall 1976): 485–509; David Montgomery, *Workers' Control in America: Studies in the History of Work, Technology, and Labor Struggles* (Cambridge: Cambridge University Press, 1979); David Nelson, *Managers and Workers: Origins of the New Factory System in the United States, 1880–1920* (Madison: University of Wisconsin Press, 1975); Daniel T. Rodgers, *The Work Ethic in Industrial America, 1850–1920* (Chicago: University of Chicago Press, 1974); Benson Soffer, "A Theory of Trade Union Development: The Role of the 'Autonomous' Workman," *Labor History* 1 (Spring 1960): 141–63. There are also some excellent industry-specific studies. See, for example, Cecelia F. Bucki, "Dilution and Craft Tradition: Bridgeport, Connecticut, Munitions Workers, 1915–1919," *Social Science History* 4 (Winter 1980): 105–24; David Nelson, "Taylorism and the Workers at Bethlehem Steel, 1898–1901," *Pennsylvania Magazine of History and Biography* 101 (October 1977): 487–505; Robert Ozanne, "Union-Management Relations: McCormick Harvesting Machine Company, 1862–1886," *Labor History* 4 (Spring 1963): 132–60; Robert Ozanne, *A Century of Labor-Management Relations at McCormick and International Harvester* (Madison: University of Wisconsin Press, 1967); Katherine Stone, "The Origins of Job Structures in the Steel Industry," *The Review of Radical Political Economics* 6 (Summer 1974): 61–95.

2. Quoted in Brody, *Workers in Industrial America*, 9.

3. Herbert Gutman explored this theme in several case studies. See Gutman, "Two Lockouts in Pennsylvania, 1873–1874," *Pennsylvania Magazine of History and Bi-*

ography 83 (July 1959): 307–326; Gutman, "An Ironworkers' Strike in the Ohio Valley, 1873–1874," *Ohio Historical Quarterly* 68 (October 1959): 353–70; Gutman, "Trouble on the Railroads in 1873–1874: Prelude to the 1877 Crisis?" *Labor History* 2 (Spring 1961): 215–35; Gutman, "The Worker's Search for Power: Labor in the Gilded Age," in *The Gilded Age: A Reappraisal*, ed. H. Wayne Morgan, (Syracuse, N.Y.: Syracuse University Press, 1963), 38–68; Gutman, "Class, Status, and Community Power in Nineteenth Century American Cities—Paterson, New Jersey: A Case Study," in *Work, Culture, and Society in Industrializing America: Essays in American Working Class and Social History* (New York: Vintage Books, 1977), 234–60. Other historians have found similar patterns. See, for example, Irwin M. Marcus, "Labor Discontent in Tioga County, Pennsylvania, 1865–1905: The Gutman Thesis, a Test Case," *Labor History* 14 (Summer 1973): 412–22; John T. Cumbler, "Labor, Capital, and Community: The Struggle for Power," *Labor History* 15 (Summer 1974): 395–415; Cumbler, "The City and Community: The Impact of Urban Forces on Working Class Behavior," *Journal of Urban History* 3 (August 1977): 427–42; Nick Salvatore, "Railroad Workers and the Great Strike of 1877: The View From a Small Midwest City," *Labor History* 21 (Fall 1980): 522–45; Michael W. Santos, "Community and Communism: The 1928 New Bedford Textile Strike," *Labor History* 26 (Spring 1985): 230–49; David J. Walkowitz, *Worker City, Company Town: Iron and Cotton Worker Protest in Troy and Cohoes, New York, 1855–84* (Urbana: University of Illinois Press, 1978).

    4. Francis G. Couvares, *The Remaking of Pittsburgh: Class and Culture in an Industrializing City, 1877–1919* (Albany: State University of New York Press, 1984); Michael W. Santos, "Between Hegemony and Autonomy: The Skilled Iron Workers' Search for Identity, 1900–1930," *Labor History* 35 (Summer 1994): 399–423.

    5. Rudyard Kipling, *Captains Courageous: A Story of the Grand Banks* (New York: Century, 1897).

    6. For an excellent discussion of the introduction of beam trawling to New England, see Andrew W. German, *Down on T Wharf: The Boston Fisheries As Seen Through the Photographs of Henry D. Fisher* (Mystic, Conn.: Mystic Seaport Museum, 1982), chapter 7; Andrew W. German, "Otter Trawling Comes to America: The Bay State Fishing Company, 1905–1938," *American Neptune* XLIV (Spring 1984): 114–31.

    7. *Fishing Gazette*, 3 February 1912, as quoted in German, "Otter Trawling Comes to America," 121.

    8. For more on the steel industry, see David Brody, *Steelworkers in America: The Nonunion Era* (Cambridge: Harvard University Press, 1960); Couvares, *The Remaking of Pittsburgh;* John A. Garraty, "The United States Steel Corporation versus Labor: The Early Years," *Labor History* 1 (Winter 1960): 3–38.

    9. *Fishing Gazette*, 3 February 1912, as quoted in German, *Down on T Wharf,* 110, and German, "Otter Trawling Comes to America," 121.

    10. U.S. Bureau of Fisheries, *Report of the United States Commissioner of Fisheries for the Fiscal Year 1914*, Appendix VI, by A. B. Alexander, H. F. Moore, and W. C. Kendall (Washington, D.C.: Government Printing Office, 1915), 49.

    11. Ibid.

    12. John A. Fitch, *The Steel Workers*, vol. 3 of *The Pittsburgh Survey*, (New York: Russell Sage Foundation, 1910), 232–33.

    13. *Fishing Gazette*, 3 February 1912, as quoted in German, *Down on T Wharf,* 110, and German, "Otter Trawling Comes to America," 121.

    14. Most of the books written about *Bluenose* and the international fishermen's races begin with the premise that the fishermen followed the America's Cup Series closely and could not believe that a race was canceled because of a twenty-three-knot wind. The incident became scuttlebutt in every fo'c'sle from Lunenburg to Gloucester, and eventually prompted Dennis to offer a cup for a "real race." This story makes good reading but is not quite the truth. A more accurate version of the events sur-

rounding the first *Halifax, Herald* series is given by Fennie Ziner, *Bluenose: Queen of the Grand Banks* (Halifax, Novia Scotia: Nimbus Publishing, 1970), chapter 3. See also *Boston Evening American,* October-November 1920; *Boston Globe,* October-November 1920; *Boston Herald,* October-November 1920; *Boston Post,* October-November 1920; *Boston Traveller,* October-November 1920; *Gloucester Times,* October-November 1920; *Rudder,* December 1920; George Story Hudson, "How *Esperanto* Won the Fisherman's Race," *Yachting,* December 1920, 296–98.

15. *The Evening Mail,* 21 October 1920, as quoted in R. Keith McLaren, *Bluenose and Bluenose II* (Willowdale, Ontario: Anthony R. Hawke, 1981).

16. Hudson, "How *Esperanto* Won the Fisherman's Race," 298.

17. For more on Tom McManus, see W. M. P. Dunne, "Thomas Francis McManus (1856–1938): An Irish Immigration Success Story" (Ph.D. diss., State University of New York at Stony Brook, 1990); W. M. P. Dunne, "The McManuses of Boston: Champions of Safety and Performance," *WoodenBoat,* May/June 1993, 72–89; W. M. P. Dunne, *Thomas F. McManus and the American Fishing Schooners: An Irish-American Success Story* (Mystic, Conn.: Mystic Seaport Museum, Inc., 1994).

18. Thomas F. McManus to the Editor, *Atlantic Fisherman,* December 1922, 10.

19. William Martell, interview by Gary Adair, Nancy d'Estang, and Erik Ronnberg, Jr., tape recording, Gloucester, Mass., February 1991, Mystic Seaport Museum Oral History Collection (hereafter MSMOHC), G. W. Blunt White Research Library, Mystic Seaport Museum, Mystic, Conn.

20. Robert Merchant, interview by Virginia Jones, tape recording, Stonington, Conn., 1 April 1978, MSMOHC.

21. George Wesley Pierce, *Goin' Fishin': The Story of the Deep-Sea Fishermen of New England* (Salem, Mass.: Marine Research Society, 1934; reprint, as *Going Fishing: The Story of the Deep-Sea Fishermen of New England,* Camden, Maine: International Marine Publishing Co., 1989), 181; James B. Connolly, *The Book of the Gloucester Fishermen* (New York: John Day, 1927), 285–86; Walter Furlong, interview by R. Wayne Anderson, transcript, Charlestown, Mass., 10 June 1982, Northeastern University Oral History Project (hereafter NUOHP), G. W. Blunt White Research Library, Mystic Seaport Museum, Mystic, Conn.

22. Leo Hynes, interview by Gregory J. Fulham, tape recording, Nashua, N.H., 29 April 1980, MSMOHC; Robert O'Brien, interview by R. Wayne Anderson, transcript, Watertown, Mass., 2 March 1982, NUOHP; Pierce, *Going Fishing,* 166. The point is implicit in much of Raymond McFarland, *The Masts of Gloucester: Recollections of a Fisherman* (New York: W. W. Norton Inc., 1937).

23. United States Commission of Fish and Fisheries, *The Fisheries and Fishery Industries of the United States,* by George Brown Goode et al., Section II (Washington, D.C.: Government Printing Office, 1887), 137, 143–45; William S. Webber, Jr., *Waterfront: Around the Wharves of Gloucester in the Last Days of Sail* (Manchester, Mass.: Cricket Press, 1973); James B. Connolly, *The Port of Gloucester* (New York: Doubleday, Doran, 1940), chapter XXVI.

24. O'Brien, interview. This point was also made by R. Barry Fisher, interview by Gary M. Adair, tape recording, Mystic, Conn., 13 January 1992, MSMOHC; Connolly, *Book of the Gloucester Fishermen,* 296–97.

25. O'Brien, interview.

26. Joseph R. Gusfield, "The Sociological Reality of America: An Essay on Mass Culture," in *On the Making of Americans: Essays in Honor of David Reisman,* eds. Herbert J. Gans, Nathan Glazer, Joseph R. Gusfield, and Christopher Jencks (Philadelphia: University of Pennsylvania Press, 1979), 41–62; Couvares, *The Remaking of Pittsburgh,* Chapter 8.

27. Charles F. Sabel, *Work and Politics: The Division of Labor in Industry* (Cambridge: Cambridge University Press, 1982), 89. In a study of machinists in Bridgeport, Conn.,

between 1915 and 1919, Cecelia Bucki found a similar tendency. Many craftsmen, concerned with exclusivity and fearing that organization of the less skilled was a concession to employer attacks on their craft, found it difficult to accept industrial unionism. As a result, where organization reinforced craft power, the skilled men acted alone. See Bucki, "Dilution and Craft Tradition." The control issue is also addressed in Montgomery, "Worker Control of Machine Production;" Montgomery, *Workers' Control in America;* Santos, "Between Hegemony and Autonomy;" Michael W. Santos, "Brother Against Brother: The Amalgamated and Sons of Vulcan at the A. M. Byers Company, 1907–1913," *Pennsylvania Magazine of History and Biography* 111 (April 1987): 195–212.

28. Howard I. Chapelle, *The American Fishing Schooners, 1825–1935* (New York: W. W. Norton, 1973), 311.

29. See, for example, Brian Backman and Phil Backman, *Bluenose* (Toronto, Ontario: McClelland and Stewart, 1965); Claude Darrach, *Race to Fame: The Inside Story of the Bluenose* (Hantsport, Nova Scotia: Lancelot Press, 1985); G. J. Gillespie, *Bluenose Skipper* (Fredericton, New Brunswick: Brunswick Press, 1955); R. Keith McLaren, *Bluenose and Bluenose II;* Andrew Merkel, *Schooner Bluenose* (Toronto, Ontario: The Ryerson Press, 1948); Dana Story, *Hail Columbia! The Rise and Fall of a Schooner* (Gloucester, Mass.: Ten Pound Island Book Co., 1985); Ziner, *Bluenose.*

30. See, for example, Chapelle, *The American Fishing Schooners;* Joseph E. Garland, *Adventure: Queen of the Windjammers* (Camden, Maine: Down East Books, 1985); German, *Down on T Wharf;* German, "Otter Trawling Comes to America;" *Sea History* 49 (Spring 1989); U.S. Bureau of Fisheries, *Reports of the United States Commissioner for the Fiscal Years 1912–1915* (Washington, D.C.: Government Printing Office, 1912, 1913, 1914, 1915); U.S. Commission of Fish and Fisheries, *The Fisheries and Fishery Industries of the United States,* by George Brown Goode et al. (Washington, D.C.: Government Printing Office, 1887).

31. Joseph E. Garland, *Down to the Sea: The Fishing Schooners of Gloucester* (Boston: David R. Godine, 1983), chapter 12.

32. Dunne, "Thomas Francis McManus;" Dunne, "The McManuses of Boston;" Dunne, *Thomas F. McManus and the American Fishing Schooners.*

CHAPTER 1: COMPETITION AND WORKING-CLASS TRADITION AMONG THE GLOUCESTERMEN

1. Connolly, *Book of the Gloucester Fishermen,* 296.

2. Fisher, interview.

3. Captain John Francis, interview by Nancy d'Estang, tape recording, Mystic, CT, 19 October 1987, MSMOHC.

4. These points were repeated countless times in interviews. See Captain Lawrence Allen, interview by John Kochiss, tape recording, Lunenburg, Nova Scotia, 11 November 1969; Frank Mitchell, interview by Fred Calabretta, tape recording, Reading, Mass., 24 July 1992, MSMOHC; Al Edmunds, interview by R. Wayne Anderson, transcript, East Boston, Mass., 20 June 1982; Furlong, interview; O'Brien, interview; Uno Peterson, interview by R. Wayne Anderson, transcript, Chelsea, Mass., 9 June, 16 June 1982, NUOHP; Hubert Cluett, interview with David Masters, tape recording, Gloucester, Mass., 15 March 1978, Gloucester Arts and Humanities Program, (hereafter GAHP), G. W. Blunt White Research Library, Mystic Seaport Museum, Mystic, Conn. Lunenburg fishermen described similar situations, a point worth noting because many Gloucestermen started life in Lunenburg. See Peter

Barss, *Images of Lunenburg County* (Toronto, Ontario: McClelland and Stewart, 1978), 19–24.
5. O'Brien, interview.
6. Cluett, interview.
7. Peterson, interview. These points were also made by O'Brien, interview; McFarland, *Masts of Gloucester*, 74.
8. These points were made several times by Merchant, interview; O'Brien, interview; Peterson, interview.
9. Barss, *Images of Lunenburg County*, 20.
10. O'Brien, interview.
11. Edmunds, interview.
12. Peterson, interview.
13. Furlong, interview; Martell, interview.
14. Quoted in Brody, *Workers in Industrial America*, 3–4.
15. Sabel, *Work and Politics*, 92.
16. Connolly, *Book of the Gloucester Fishermen*, 245.
17. Pierce, *Going Fishing*, 164.
18. Connolly, *Book of the Gloucester Fishermen*, 285–86; Robert Merchant, interview by Virginia Jones, tape recording, Gloucester, Mass., 16 November 1977, MSMOHC.
19. Furlong, interview; Merchant, interview, 16 November 1977.
20. *Atlantic Fisherman*, September 1922.
21. *Ibid.*, December 1922.
22. Pierce, *Going Fishing*, chapter 15.
23. *Ibid.*, 179–84.
24. Jeremiah Digges, *In Great Waters: The Story of the Portuguese Fishermen* (New York: McMillan, 1941), xii.
25. Peter Brown, telephone conversation with author, 15 October 1993.
26. Charlton L. Smith, "Who's Who Among the Skippers," *Atlantic Fisherman*, March 1922, 9.
27. Gillespie, *Bluenose Skipper*, 116.
28. I could not locate a copy of the *Atlantic Fisherman* in which Herreshoff's letter appeared. Fortunately, it was reproduced in L. Francis Herreshoff, *An L. Francis Herreshoff Reader* (Camden, Maine: International Marine Publishing Co., 1978), 259–65.
29. *Atlantic Fisherman*, March-April 1922.
30. Pierce, *Going Fishing*, 166–67.
31. *Atlantic Fisherman*, August 1922.
32. McFarland, *Masts of Gloucester*, 175–81.
33. German, *Down on T Wharf*, chapter 3; Connolly, *Book of the Gloucester Fishermen*, 297.
34. Gloucester Master Mariners' Association, *Yearbook* (Gloucester, Mass.: Gloucester Master Mariners' Association, 1917), 12.

CHAPTER 2: CLASS, COMMUNITY, AND THE FISHERMEN OF GLOUCESTER

1. Gutman, "Two Lockouts in Pennsylvania"; Gutman, "An Ironworkers' Strike in the Ohio Valley, 1873–1874;" Gutman, "Trouble on the Railroads in 1873–1874;" Gutman, "The Worker's Search for Power;" Gutman, "Class, Status, and Community Power in Nineteenth Century American Cities."

2. *Gloucester Times*, 17 April 1889.

3. This description has been pieced together from the narrative in the *Gloucester Times* and from Dana Story's account of a "typical" launch at an Essex shipyard. See *Gloucester Times*, 17 April 1889; Dana Story, *Frame-Up! The Story of Essex, Its Shipyards, and Its People* (Barre, Mass.: Barre Publishers, 1964), 64–65.

4. Dana Story contends that early photographs in his collection show "many vessels being launched with hardly a soul bothering to take notice." Joe Garland disagrees. He notes that, though launchings were commonplace, they were occasions for great excitement in Gloucester. Likewise were trial trips, especially when a highly regarded vessel was involved. The *Gloucester Times* for the late-nineteenth century bears him out. See Story, *Frame Up!*, 65; Garland, *Down to the Sea*, chapter 3; *Gloucester Times*, 1888–1900.

5. *Atlantic Fisherman*, May 1931.

6. Story, *Frame-Up!*, 101. These points are reiterated in Dana Story, *Growing Up in a Shipyard: Reminiscences of a Shipbuilding Life in Essex, Massachusetts* (Mystic, Conn.: Mystic Seaport Museum, 1991), chapter 1; Dana Story, interview by author, tape recording, Essex, Mass., 16 November 1993.

7. Frank E. Davis, Vertical File: Biography, Cape Ann Historical Association, Gloucester, Mass.

8. German, *Down on T Wharf*, chapter 4; Garland, *Down to the Sea*, Chapter 2.

9. Manuel F. Domingoes, Jr., interview by Linda Brayton and David Masters, tape recording, Gloucester, Mass., n.d., GAHP.

10. For more on Mesquita, see Digges, *In Great Waters*, 173–87.

11. *Atlantic Fisherman*, February 1923.

12. Brief biographical sketches of these and other captains are included in Gordon W. Thomas, *Fast and Able: Life Stories of Great Gloucester Fishing Vessels* (Gloucester, Mass.: Gloucester 350th Anniversary Celebration, 1973), 203–10. More on Sol Jacobs can be found in Pierce, *Going Fishing*, chapter XV.

13. Benjamin A. G. Fuller, "Blue Collar Yachting" (paper presented at the Yachting History Symposium, Mystic Seaport Museum, Mystic, Conn., 1995).

14. For more on the East Gloucester Yacht Club, see Joseph E. Garland, *Eastern Point: A Nautical, Rustical, and Social Chronicle of Gloucester's Outer Shield and Inner Sanctum, 1606–1950* (Peterborough, N.H.: William L. Bauham, 1971), chapter 37.

15. Descriptions and plans of modified fishing boats appeared as early as 1905 in *Rudder*. In a 1910 issue of *Yachting*, mention is made of a New York yachtsman who built an offshore cruiser on fishermen's lines. After 1912, articles and plans for such vessels were common in the yachting literature. Interestingly, when draggers began to displace schooners in the fishing industry, attention shifted to modified beam trawler designs. See *Rudder*, 1905–38; *Yachting*, 1907–38. For more on the influence of yacht design on the fishing schooners, see Chapelle, *American Fishing Schooners*, chapters 4–8.

16. Dana Story recalled that the James Yard was more active in yacht building than the Story Yard. He speculated that that may have been because his father did not want "yachty types under foot." Dana Story, interview by Maynard Bray, John Gardner, and John Kochiss, tape recording, Essex, Mass., 10 September 1969, MSMOHC.

17. For more on Burgess and the Eastern Yacht Club's involvement with the 1885–1887 America's Cup Races, see Joseph E. Garland, *The Eastern Yacht Club: A History From 1870–1985* (Marblehead, Mass.: The Eastern Yacht Club, 1989), chapter 2; Charles H. W. Foster, *The Eastern Yacht Club Ditty Box, 1870–1900* (Norwood, Mass.: Plimpton Press, 1932), 130–31.

18. W. P. Stephens, *Traditions and Memories of American Yachting* (1939–1946; rev. ed., Brooklin, Maine: WoodenBoat Publications; 1989), 201–2, as quoted in Dunne, *Thomas F. McManus and the American Fishing Schooners*, 151.

19. Dunne, *Thomas F. McManus and the American Fishing Schooners*, chapter 8.

20. For more on the 1889 race see Garland, *Eastern Yacht Club*, 50; Foster, *Eastern Yacht Club Ditty Box*, 121–22.

21. For more on Bohlin's participation in the 1905 race, see Connolly, *Book of the Gloucester Fishermen*, 147–69.

22. For more on the development of Eastern Point, see Garland, *Eastern Point*, chapter 18.

23. Peterson, interview.

24. Julian Hatch, interview by author, tape recording, Naples, Fla., 25 October 1993.

25. Captain Seymore Harnish, interview by Peter Parsons and Peter Anastas, in *When Gloucester Was Gloucester: Towards an Oral History of the City* (Gloucester, Mass.: Gloucester 350th Anniversary Celebration, 1973), 25–27.

26. McFarland, *Masts of Gloucester*, 201–3.

27. *Gloucester Times*, 1888–1920; Digges, *In Deep Water*, 63–65; Fisher, interview.

28. Quoted in Digges, *In Great Waters*, 65.

29. See the *Gloucester Times* for 1889 for the ongoing debate over prohibition. The "Fishermen's Club House" idea was one solution to the problem, and letters advocating it were especially prevalent in April of that year.

30. Gloucester Fishermen's Institute, *First Annual Report* (Gloucester, Mass.: Cape Ann Breeze, 1893), 5.

31. Gloucester Fishermen's Institute, *Second Annual Report* (Gloucester, Mass.: Cape Ann Breeze, 1894), 5.

32. Gloucester Fishermen's Institute, *Fifth Annual Report* (Gloucester, Mass.: Cape Ann Breeze, 1897), 3.

33. Digges, *In Great Waters*, 64.

34. Gloucester Fishermen's Institute, *Second Annual Report*, 3; Gloucester Fishermen's Institute, *Third Annual Report* (Gloucester, Mass.: Cape Ann Breeze, 1895), 3.

CHAPTER 3: THE EARLY RACES, 1886–1913

1. Dunne, "Thomas Francis McManus;" Dunne, "The McManuses of Boston;" Dunne, *Thomas F. McManus and the American Fishing Schooners*.

2. U.S. Commission of Fish and Fisheries, *The Fisheries and Fishery Industries of the United States*, by George Brown Goode et al., Section II (Washington, D.C.: Government Printing Office, 1887), 177.

3. The McManuses and Lawlor were not the only ones interested in vessel safety. Captain Joseph Collins of the U.S. Commission of Fish and Fisheries was instrumental in having the government launch the deep-drafted research schooner *Grampus* in 1885. For more on the campaign to build safer schooners, see Chapelle, *The American Fishing Schooners*, chapter 4; Garland, *Down to the Sea*, chapter 1.

4. An old skipper recalled the events leading up to the first race in an article for *Yachting* a few months after Tom McManus died. See Charlton L. Smith, "The First Fishermen's Race," *Yachting*, January 1939, 64–65, 212.

5. Dunne, "Thomas Francis McManus," chapter 8; Dunne, "The McManuses of Boston," 81–82; Dunne, *Thomas F. McManus and the American Fishing Schooners*, Chapter 8.

6. For more on the *Phillips's* design innovations, and comparisons to other schooners, see Chapelle, *American Fishing Schooners,* chapter 5. Also see Dunne, "Thomas Francis McManus," chapter 8; Dunne, "The McManuses of Boston," 81–82; Dunne, *Thomas F. McManus and the American Fishing Schooners,* chapter 8.

7. *Gloucester Times,* 19 October 1888.

8. For more on the 1889 race, see Garland, *Eastern Yacht Club,* 50; Foster, *Eastern Yacht Club Ditty Box,* 121–22.

9. For more on Hovey, see Garland, *Eastern Yacht Club,* 50–53.

10. The events leading up to and including the 1892 race are documented in *Gloucester Times,* August 1892; Connolly, *Book of the Gloucester Fishermen,* chapter 5; Garland, *Down to the Sea,* chapter 12; Pierce, *Going Fishing,* chapter 17; Story, *Hail Columbia!,* 19–21. Details on the *Nannie C. Bohlin, Caviare,* and *Grayling* appear in Thomas, *Fast and Able,* 10–18.

11. Foster, *Eastern Yacht Club Ditty Box,* xix, 141–42.

12. Garland, *Eastern Yacht Club,* 53.

13. For more on Rouse and the aborted 1899 race, see Garland, *Eastern Point,* 213–14.

14. For more on Lawson, see Garland, *Eastern Yacht Club,* 120.

15. The events leading up to and including the 1901 race are well documented in *Gloucester Times,* 1 August–4 September 1901.

16. O'Brien, interview.

17. For more on the *Independence,* see Thomas, *Fast and Able,* 65–67.

18. The events leading up to and including the 1907 race are well documented in *Gloucester Times,* 31 July–4 August 1907; *Rudder,* November 1907; James F. McNally, "The Fisherman's Race," *Yachting,* November 1907, 273–75; Digges, *In Great Waters,* 206–9. The Lipton Cup is on display between June and October at the Provincetown Heritage Museum, and during the rest of the year, at the Pilgrim Monument Museum. A half-scale model of the *Rose Dorothea* is housed on the second floor of the Provincetown Heritage Museum.

19. For more on the *Helen B. Thomas, Ingomar, Frances P. Mesquita, Rose Dorothea,* and *Clintonia,* see Thomas, *Fast and Able,* 83–85, 91–94, 108–9, 113–14, and 135–36, respectively.

20. The events of August 20, 1907, are discussed in greater detail in Digges, *In Great Waters,* 201–12. Connolly also mentions the incident, but gets Perry's name wrong, calling him Captain Santos. Connolly, *Book of the Gloucester Fishermen,* 239–40.

21. What little documentation on the Brittain Cup Races that I have found comes from an article in *the Shelburne Gazette and Coast Guard,* 4 November 1920. The cup itself is housed at the Maritime Museum of the Atlantic, Halifax, Nova Scotia.

CHAPTER 4: "BUCKING THE INEVITABLE": THE VIEW FROM THE UNITED STATES

1. *Atlantic Fisherman,* March 1926.

2. For more on the *Gould,* see Thomas, *Fast and Able,* 57.

3. Chapelle, *American Fishing Schooners,* chapter 7.

4. Ibid., chapter 8.

5. Giles M. S. Tod, "The Passing Gloucestermen," *Motor Boating,* March 1958, 90, 92.

6. Edward W. Sloan, "'Vulcan Now Rides in Neptune's Barge': Steam Propulsion and Seafaring Enterprise in Post-Civil War America," in *American Industrialization,*

Economic Expansion, and the Law, eds. Joseph R. Frese and Jacob Judd (Tarrytown, N.Y.: Sleepy Hollow Press and Rockefeller Archive Center, 1981), 55–84; Edward W. Sloan, "The Evolution of Seagoing Steam: Stages in a Maritime Revolution," *Log of Mystic Seaport,* Winter 1992, 87–98.

7. Martell, interview.

8. Sabel, *Work and Politics,* 89–92.

9. *Fishing Gazette,* 18 May 1912, as quoted in German, *Down on T Wharf,* 110, and German, "Otter Trawling Comes to America," 121.

10. German, *Down on T Wharf,* 109.

11. O'Brien, interview.

12. Domingoes, interview.

13. Sabel, *Work and Politics,* 89.

14. German, "Otter Trawling Comes to America," 123–25.

15. German, *Down on T Wharf,* 109.

16. German, "Otter Trawling Comes to America," 125.

17. O'Brien, interview.

18. Montgomery, "Worker Control in the 19th Century"; Montgomery, *Workers' Control in America,* chapter 1.

19. Soffer, "A Theory of Trade Union Development."

20. Frank H. Wood, "Trawling and Dragging in New England Waters," part 1, *Atlantic Fisherman,* January 1926, 23.

21. *Atlantic Fisherman,* January 1926.

22. Connolly, *Book of the Gloucester Fishermen,* 13, 241.

23. A nice overview of dragging and trawling in this period is given in Wood, "Trawling and Dragging in New England Waters," parts 1 and 2, *Atlantic Fisherman,* January 1926, 1, 11–14, 23; February 1926, 11–14, 23–24, 28, 30.

24. German, *Down on T Wharf,* chapter 2.

25. Wood, "Trawling and Dragging in New England Waters," part 1, 11.

26. *Gloucester Times,* 30 January 1926; *Atlantic Fisherman,* February 1926.

27. *Atlantic Fisherman,* May 1931.

28. Louis Skinner, interview by Nancy d'Estang, George Emery, and Jonathan Shay, tape recording, Mystic, Conn., 29 June 1984, MSMOHC.

29. Domingoes, interview. This point was also made by Lorraine Louanis, interview by Fred Calabretta and Julie Goodrich, tape recording, Reading, Mass., 18 July 1992, MSMOHC.

30. Jeannie Auditore, interview by David Masters, tape recording, Gloucester, Mass., n.d.; Domingoes, interview; Leo and Rosalie Favaloro, interview by David Masters, tape recording, Gloucester, Mass., n.d., GAHP.

31. Fisher, interview. This point was also made by Francis, interview.

32. Fisher, interview.

CHAPTER 5: "BUCKING THE INEVITABLE": THE VIEW FROM CANADA

1. *Atlantic Fisherman,* March 1926.

2. U.S. Bureau of Fisheries, *Report of the United States Commissioner of Fisheries for the Fiscal Year 1914,* Appendix VI, by A. B. Alexander, H. F. Moore, and W. C. Kendall (Washington, D.C.: Government Printing Office, 1915), 49.

3. *Atlantic Fisherman,* March 1930.

4. German, "Otter Trawling Comes to America," 120.

5. For more on the changes in the Lunenburg fisheries during this time, see B. A. Balcom, *History of the Lunenburg Fishing Industry* (Lunenburg, Nova Scotia: The Lunenburg Marine Museum Society, 1977), chapter 6.

6. Allen, interview.

7. Quoted in Barss, *Images of Lunenburg County*, 45–46.

8. Detailed coverage of the struggle over otter trawling in Canada appeared in the *Atlantic Fisherman*, July 1929–May 1938.

9. The profiles of life in Lunenburg at this time are drawn from Barss, *Images of Lunenburg County*, 9–11, 19–24, 76–83.

10. Quoted in Gillespie, *Bluenose Skipper*, 117.

11. Details on the strike are drawn from *Atlantic Fisherman*, January-February 1938.

CHAPTER 6: "BONA FIDE FISHING VESSELS": THE EARLY RACES FOR THE *HALIFAX HERALD* Trophy, 1920–1921

1. For more on the sinking of the *Esperanto* and the effort to salvage her, see *Gloucester Times*, June-July 1921; *Atlantic Fisherman*, June-July 1921.

2. *Atlantic Fisherman*, February 1921.

3. For more detail on the *Esperanto*, see Thomas, *Fast and Able*, 124–27.

4. For more on the controversy surrounding the *Mayflower*'s eligibility in 1921, see *Atlantic Fisherman*, February-October 1921; *Boston Evening American*, February-September 1921; *Boston Globe*, February-September 1921; *Boston Herald*, February-September 1921; *Boston Post*, February-September 1921; *Boston Traveller*, February-September 1921; *Gloucester Times*, February-September 1921; *Rudder*, October 1921, December 1921; *Yachting*, May-November 1921; Story, *Hail Columbia!*, 34–39; Merkel, *Schooner Bluenose*, chapter 3.

5. For more on *Esperanto*'s selection and the events surrounding the 1920 international series, see Connolly, *Book of the Gloucester Fishermen*, 246–61; Pierce, *Going Fishing*, 229–34; *Boston Evening American*, October-November 1920; *Boston Globe*, October-November 1920; *Boston Herald*, October-November 1920; *Boston Post*, October-November 1920; *Boston Traveller*, October-November 1920; *Gloucester Times*, October-November 1920; *Rudder*, December 1920; Hudson, "How *Esperanto* Won the Fisherman's Race."

6. Thomas, *Fast and Able*, 126.

7. Story, *Frame-Up!*, 65; Story, interview, 16 November 1993.

8. For more on the building and launching of *Mayflower*, see *Atlantic Fisherman*, February-April 1921; *Boston Evening American*, February-April 1921; *Boston Globe*, February-April 1921; *Boston Herald*, February-April 1921; *Boston Post*, February-April 1921; *Boston Traveller*, February-April 1921; *Gloucester Times*, February-April 1921; *Rudder*, April 1921; *Yachting*, April-May 1921.

9. A comparative table of specifications for *Bluenose*, *Mayflower*, and *Canadia* appears in *Atlantic Fisherman*, March 1921, and is the basis for the analysis in the text.

10. Quoted in Merkel, *Schooner Bluenose*, 24.

11. For more on the effort to build *Bluenose*, see Backman and Backman, *Bluenose*, 15, 23–24; McLaren, *Bluenose and Bluenose II*; Merkel, *Schooner Bluenose*, chapter 2.

12. *Boston Globe*, 19 October 1921.

13. For more on the *Canadia*, see *Atlantic Fisherman*, February-April 1921, August 1921; *Shelburne Gazette and Coast Guard*, 7 April 1921.

14. *Boston Globe*, 14 October 1921.

15. For more on the *Arthur James, Elsie,* and *Elsie G. Silva,* see Thomas, *Fast and Able,* 104–06, 148–50, 176–78, respectively.

16. For more on the 1921 international series, and the continuing debate over what constituted a "bona fide fishing schooner" that followed it, see *Atlantic Fisherman,* September-October 1921; *Boston Evening American,* September-October 1921; *Boston Globe,* September-October 1921; *Boston Herald,* September-October 1921; *Boston Post,* September-October 1921; *Boston Traveller,* September-October 1921; *Gloucester Times,* September-October 1921; *New York Herald Tribune,* October 1921; *New York Times,* October 1921; C. H. J. Snider, "The Fisherman's Race," *Rudder,* December 1921, 3–6, 44–45; Frederick William Wallace, "The International Fisherman's Race," *Yachting,* November 1921, 213–15, 255–56.

CHAPTER 7: FORGETTING PRINCIPLE: NATIONALISM, CIVIC PRIDE, AND THE QUEST FOR THE TROPHY, 1922

1. For more on the *Puritan* syndicate, see *Boston Evening American,* October-November 1921; *Boston Globe,* October-November 1921; *Boston Herald,* October-November 1921; *Boston Post,* October-November 1921; *Boston Traveller,* October-November 1921; *Gloucester Times,* October-November 1921; *New York Herald Tribune,* October-November 1921; *New York Times,* October-November 1921; Story, *Hail Columbia!,* 43–44.

2. Charlton L. Smith, "Who's Who Among the Skippers," *Atlantic Fisherman,* October 1922, 12. Ben Pine's personality and background were also discussed by Hatch, interview.

3. This story was told by Eric Ronnberg, Jr., during the Martell interview.

4. Captain John Francis, interview by Nancy d'Estang, tape recording, West Franklin, N.H., 13 April 1987, MSMOHC.

5. Ronnberg, during Martell interview.

6. For more on the contrasts between *Puritan* and *Mayflower,* see Chapelle, *American Fishing Schooners,* 300–02; Herreshoff, *L. Francis Herreshoff Reader,* 259–65; *Atlantic Fisherman,* March 1922.

7. For more detail on the building and launching of the *Ford,* see *Atlantic Fisherman,* March-April 1922; *Boston Evening American,* March-April 1922; *Boston Globe,* March-April 1922; *Boston Herald,* March-April 1922; *Boston Post,* March-April 1922; *Boston Traveller,* March-April 1922; *Gloucester Times,* March-April 1922; *New York Herald Tribune,* March-April 1922; *New York Times,* March-April 1922; Thomas, *Fast and Able,* 185–87.

8. For more on the loss of *Puritan,* see *Boston Evening American,* 24 June-10 July 1922; *Boston Globe,* 24 June-10 July 1922; *Boston Herald,* 24 June-10 July 1922; *Boston Post,* 24 June-10 July 1922; *Boston Traveller,* 24 June-10 July 1922; *Gloucester Times,* 24 June-10 July 1922; Garland, *Adventure,* 23–27; Thomas, *Fast and Able,* 188–90.

9. For more on Pine's acquisition of and plans for the *Howard,* see *Gloucester Times,* July 1922.

10. For more on the *Howard,* see, Chapelle, *The American Fishing Schooners,* chapter 8.

11. Garland, *Adventure,* 27.

12. For more on the *Yankee,* see Chapelle, *American Fishing Schooners,* 292–93.

13. Felix William Hogan, interview by Nancy d'Estang, tape recording, Mystic, Conn., 22 October 1984, MSMOHC.

14. For more on the continuation of the *Mayflower* controversy in 1922, see *Atlantic Fisherman*, August-September 1922; *Boston Evening American*, August-September 1922; *Boston Globe*, August-September 1922; *Boston Herald*, August-September 1922; *Boston Post*, August-September 1922; *Boston Traveller*, August-September 1922; *Gloucester Times*, August-September 1922.

15. For more on the American elimination races and the events leading up to the international series, see *Atlantic Fisherman*, October 1922; *Boston Daily Advertiser*, October 1922; *Boston Evening American*, October 1922; *Boston Evening Transcript*, October 1922; *Boston Globe*, October 1922; *Boston Herald*, October 1922; *Boston Post*, October 1922; *Boston Traveller*, October 1922; *Gloucester Times*, October 1922; *New York Herald Tribune*, October 1922; *New York Times*, October 1922.

16. *Boston Daily Advertiser*, 16 October 1922; *Boston Evening American*, 16 October 1922; *Boston Evening Transcript*, 16 October 1922; *Boston Globe*, 16 October 1922; *Boston Herald*, 16 October 1922; *Boston Post*, 16 October 1922; *Boston Traveller*, 16 October 1922; *Gloucester Times*, 16 October 1922; *New York Herald Tribune*, 16 October 1922; *New York Times*, 16 October 1922.

17. For more on the 1922 *Halifax Herald* series, see *Atlantic Fisherman*, October-December 1922; *Boston Daily Advertiser*, October 1922; *Boston Evening American*, October 1922; *Boston Evening Transcript*, October 1922; *Boston Globe*, October 1922; *Boston Herald*, October 1922; *Boston Post*, October 1922; *Boston Traveller*, October 1922; *Gloucester Times*, October 1922; *New York Herald Tribune*, October 1922; *New York Times*, October 1922; C. H. J. Snider, "The International Fishermen's Race," *Rudder*, December 1922, 3–5; Herbert L. Stone, "How *Bluenose* Won the Fishermen's Race," *Yachting*, November 1922, 229–33, 258. Most of the books about the races devote only two to three pages to the 1922 series. The exceptions are Merkel, *Schooner Bluenose*, chapter 4; Story, *Hail Columbia!*, chapter 3.

18. For an interesting description of that meeting, see Garland, *Eastern Point*, 361–63.

19. The incident aboard *Ford* on October 25 was reported in *Boston Globe*, 26 October 1922.

20. Charlton L. Smith, "Who's Who Among the Skippers," *Atlantic Fisherman*, March 1922, 9.

21. The Deed of Gift is reproduced in its entirety in Darrach, *Race to Fame*, Appendix C; and McLaren, *Bluenose and Bluenose II*.

22. Thomas F. McManus to the Editor, *Atlantic Fisherman*, December 1922, 10.

23. Quoted in *Boston Globe*, 26 October 1922.

CHAPTER 8: BOOSTERISM, SENTIMENTALITY, AND WORKING-CLASS SPORT: RACING BETWEEN 1923 AND 1929

1. For more on the events leading up to and including the 1923 Anniversary Race, see *Boston Evening American*, May-August 1923; *Boston Globe*, May-August 1923; *Boston Herald*, May-August 1923; *Boston Post*, May-August 1923; *Boston Traveller*, May-August 1923; *Gloucester Times*, May-August 1923; William J. Deed, "*Henry Ford* Wins Fishermen's Race," *Rudder*, October 1923, 18–19.

2. For more on the controversy over *Columbia*, see *Boston Evening American*, September-October 1923; *Boston Globe*, September-October 1923; *Boston Herald*, September-October 1923; *Boston Post*, September-October 1923; *Boston Traveller*, September-October 1923; *Gloucester Times*, September-October 1923.

3. For more on the 1923 American eliminations, see *Atlantic Fisherman*, October 1923; *Boston Evening American*, October 1923; *Boston Globe*, October 1923; *Boston Herald*, October 1923; *Boston Post*, October 1923; *Boston Traveller*, October 1923; *Gloucester Times*, October 1923; *New York Herald Tribune*, October 1923; *New York Times*, October 1923.

4. For more on the 1923 International Races and their aftermath, see *Atlantic Fisherman*, November 1923; *Boston Evening American*, October-November 1923; *Boston Globe*, October-November 1923; *Boston Herald*, October-November 1923; *Boston Post*, October-November 1923; *Boston Traveller*, October 1923; *Gloucester Times*, October-November 1923; *New York Herald Tribune*, October-November 1923; *New York Times*, October-November 1923; *Rudder*, December 1923; Merkel, *Schooner Bluenose*, 40–46; Story, *Hail Columbia!*, chapter 6.

5. Gillespie, *Bluenose Skipper*, chapter 12.

6. *Rudder*, December 1923.

7. For more on the role of sports in American society, see John Rickards Betts, *America's Sporting Heritage: 1850–1950* (Reading, Mass.: Addison-Wesley, 1974); Allen Guttman, *From Ritual to Record: The Nature of Modern Sports* (New York: Columbia University Press, 1977); Steven A. Reiss, *Touching Base: Professional Baseball and American Culture in the Progressive Era* (Westport, Conn.: Greenwood Press, 1980).

8. For more on Babe Ruth, see Robert W. Creamer, *Babe: The Legend Comes to Life* (New York: Simon and Schuster, 1974); Associated Press Sports Staff, *The Sports Immortals* (Englewood Cliffs, N.J.: Prentice-Hall, 1972), 42–47.

9. For more on Jack Dempsey, see Associated Press Sports Staff, *Sports Immortals*, 54–59.

10. Leonard Fowle, Sr., to Leonard Fowle, Jr., 2 November 1923, "Yachting Scrapbooks," Vol. 3, No. 5, Leonard Fowle Collection, Museum of Yachting, Newport, R.I.

11. For an excellent biography of Walters, see Gillespie, *Bluenose Skipper*.

12. *Atlantic Fisherman*, September 1922.

13. Ibid., October 1923.

14. For an excellent assessment of the confusing decade that was the 1920s, see Frederick Lewis Allen, *Only Yesterday: An Informal History of the Nineteen-Twenties* (New York: Harper and Row, 1931); William E. Leuchtenburg, *The Perils of Prosperity, 1914–1932* (Chicago: University of Chicago Press, 1958).

15. F. Scott Fitzgerald, *The Great Gatsby* (1925; reprint, New York: Charles Scribner's Sons, 1953), 182.

16. For more on the futile efforts to organize international races between 1924 and 1926, see *Boston Evening American*, September 1924, September 1925, July-October 1926; *Boston Globe*, September 1924, September 1925, July-October 1926; *Boston Herald*, September 1924, September 1925, July-October 1926; *Boston Post*, September 1924, September 1925, July-October 1926; *Gloucester Times*, September 1924, September 1925, July-October 1926; Story, *Hail Columbia!*, 128–135.

17. For more on the sale of *Columbia* and Pine's efforts to buy her back, see *Gloucester Times*, January-March 1926; *Atlantic Fisherman*, January-March 1926.

18. Barss, *Images of Lunenburg County*, 117–23.

19. For more on the 1926 Gloucester Races, see *Boston Evening American*, September-October 1926; *Boston Globe*, September-October 1926; *Boston Herald*, September-October 1926; *Boston Post*, September-October 1926; *Gloucester Times*, September-October 1926; Story, *Hail Columbia!*, chapter 8.

20. Alfred Elden, "Fishermen Machinists," *Rudder*, May 1926, 26–28.

21. For more on the *Bluenose-Haligonian* races, see Merkel, *Schooner Bluenose*, 46–48.

22. For more on the plans for a 1927 challenge and the loss of *Columbia*, see *Boston Evening American*, September-October 1927; *Boston Globe*, September-October 1927; *Boston Herald*, September-October 1927; *Boston Post*, September-October 1927; *Gloucester Times*, September-October 1927; Story, *Hail Columbia!*, 151–59.

23. For more on the events leading up to and including the 1929 races, see *Atlantic Fisherman*, August-September 1929; *Boston Evening American*, August-September 1929; *Boston Globe*, August-September 1929; *Boston Herald*, August-September 1929; *Boston Post*, August-September 1929; *Gloucester Times*, August-September 1929; Edmund Gilligan, "Schooner *Progress* Wins Fisherman's Race," *Yachting*, November 1929, 57, 104.

24. For more on the *Thomas S. Gorton* and *Elsie*, see Thomas, *Fast and Able*, 118–19, and 149–50, respectively.

25. *Rudder*, April 1930.

CHAPTER 9: "CLOUDS OF WHITE SAIL": ROMANTICISM AND THE END OF RACING IN THE 1930s

1. June Mellow, interview by author, tape recording, Gloucester, Mass., 18 November 1993. Mellow's and Pine's role in building the *Gertrude L. Thebaud* is also discussed in great detail in Frank Jason, "Avast Ye Lubbers! Taxi Man May Win Fishermen's Races in Gloucester," *Boston Post*, 16 March 1930, B-4.

2. Gloucester Master Mariners' Association, *Yearbook* (Gloucester: Gloucester Master Mariners' Association, 1917), 12.

3. For more on the *Thebaud*, see Thomas, *Fast and Able*, 199–202.

4. Tod, "The Passing Gloucestermen," 89.

5. For more on the organization of the *Thebaud* syndicate and the building and launching of *Thebaud*, see *Atlantic Fisherman*, April-May 1930; *Boston Evening American*, March 1930; *Boston Globe*, March 1930; *Boston Herald*, March 1930; *Boston Post*, March 1930; *Gloucester Times*, March 1930.

6. Mellow, interview.

7. For more on the *Thebaud*'s sea trials and the efforts to resume international racing, see *Atlantic Fisherman*, May-June 1930; *Boston Evening American*, April-September 1930; *Boston Globe*, April-September 1930; *Boston Herald*, April-September 1930; *Boston Post*, April-September 1930; *Gloucester Times*, April-September 1930.

8. William H. Taylor, "Gloucester Once More Holds Fishermen's Championship," *Yachting*, December 1930, 81, 108.

9. *Boston Globe*, 9 October 1931.

10. See *Atlantic Fisherman*, February 1921–December 1923, for detailed coverage of racing events in the early years of international competition. Contrasts with the later years are startling. See *Atlantic Fisherman*, August-September 1929, April 1930, October 1930, November 1930, October-November 1931, September-November 1938.

11. For a representative sample of the type of coverage given the races in the popular press, see *Boston Daily Advertiser*, October 1922; *Boston Evening American*, October 1920–October 1930; *Boston Evening Transcript*, October 1922; *Boston Globe*, October 1920–November 1938; *Boston Herald*, October 1920–November 1938; *Boston Post*, October 1920–November 1938; *Boston Traveller*, October 1920–October 1923; *Gloucester Times*, October 1920–November 1938; *New York Herald Tribune*, October 1921–October 1930; *New York Times*, October 1921–November 1930.

12. For more on Crowninshield and *Cleopatra's Barge II*, see Garland, *Eastern Yacht Club*, 176–78.

13. For a sense of the press coverage devoted to the fishermen's race preliminaries and the America's Cup, see *Boston Evening American*, 1 September-8 October 1930; *Boston Globe*, 1 September-8 October 1930; *Boston Herald*, 1 September-8 October 1930; *Boston Post*, 1 September-8 October 1930; *Gloucester Times*, 1 September-8 October 1930; *New York Herald Tribune*, 1 September-8 October 1930; *New York Times*, 1 September-8 October 1930.

14. For more on the Lipton Cup Races, see *Atlantic Fisherman*, October-November 1930; *Boston Evening American*, 9 October-19 October 1930; *Boston Globe*, 9 October-19 October 1930; *Boston Herald*, 9 October-19 October 1930; *Boston Post*, 9 October-19 October 1930; *Gloucester Times*, 9 October-19 October 1930; *New York Herald Tribune*, 9 October-19 October 1930; *New York Times*, 9 October-19 October 1930; Taylor, "Gloucester Once More Holds Fishermen's Championship;" Backman and Backman, *Bluenose*, 46–49; Merkel, *Schooner Bluenose*, 53–55.

15. *Atlantic Fisherman*, November 1930.

16. For more on the race, see *Atlantic Fisherman*, November 1930; Backman and Backman, *Bluenose*, 20–21.

17. For more on the events leading up to the 1931 series, see *Atlantic Fisherman*, September-October 1931; *Boston Globe*, 1 September-17 October 1931; *Boston Herald*, 1 September-17 October 1931; *Boston Post*, 1 September-17 October 1931; *Gloucester Times*, 1 September-17 October 1931.

18. *Atlantic Fisherman*, June 1931.

19. Ibid., September 1931.

20. For more on the 1931 races, see *Atlantic Fisherman*, November 1931; *Boston Globe*, 18 October-22 October 1931; *Boston Herald*, 18 October-22 October 1931; *Boston Post*, 18 October-22 October 1931; *Gloucester Times*, 18 October-22 October 1931; William H. Taylor, "*Bluenose* Still Queen of the Fleet—Beats Gloucester Schooner *Thebaud* in Straight Races," *Yachting*, December 1931, 39–40, 110; Merkel, *Schooner Bluenose*, 56–58.

21. Taylor, "*Bluenose* Still Queen of the Fleet," 110.

22. *Atlantic Fisherman*, September 1931, November 1931.

23. For more on *Bluenose*'s appearance at the Century of Progress Exposition and her stay in Toronto, see Darrach, *Race to Fame*, chapter 4; Merkel, *Schooner Bluenose*, chapter VII. For more on the *Thebaud* at Chicago, see Thomas, *Fast and Able*, 201.

24. *Gloucester Times*, April 1933.

25. Backman and Backman, *Bluenose*, 18–19; Darrach, *Race to Fame*, chapter 4; Merkel, *Schooner Bluenose*, chapter 7.

26. Darrach, *Race to Fame*, 47–48.

27. Thomas, *Fast and Able*, 201.

28. Metro-Goldwin-Mayer, *Captains Courageous*, 1937; available on videocassette, New York: MGM/UA Home Video, 1985.

29. For more on prerace activities, see *Atlantic Fisherman*, December 1937, June-September 1938; *Boston Globe*, June-September 1938; *Boston Herald*, June-September 1938; *Boston Post*, June-September 1938; *Gloucester Times*, June-September 1938.

30. Sterling Hayden, *Wanderer* (London, England: Longmans, Green, 1963), 223–24.

31. For more on the 1938 races, see *Boston Globe*, 9 October-5 November 1938; *Boston Herald*, 9 October-5 November 1938; *Boston Post*, 9 October-5 November 1938; *Gloucester Times*, 9 October-5 November 1938; Alfred F. Loomis, "The Last of the Fishermen's Races," *Yachting*, December 1938, 31–32, 108; Darrach, *Race to Fame*, 48–60;

Hayden, *Wanderer,* chapters 42–43; McLaren, *Bluenose and Bluenose II;* Merkel, *Schooner Bluenose,* 58–62.
32. Hayden, *Wanderer,* 223.
33. *Atlantic Fisherman,* December 1938.
34. Thomas, *Fast and Able,* 201–2.
35. Quoted in Backman and Backman, *Bluenose,* 15.
36. Fisher, interview.
37. Ibid.

EPILOGUE: CONTINUING LEGACIES

1. *Gloucester Times,* 14 April-18 April 1958.
2. For more on the *Nunan* and the attempt to save her, see Thomas, *Fast and Able,* 71–72; Mellow, interview; Joseph Mellow obituary, *Boston Globe,* 19 January 1969.
3. For more on the campaign to build *Bluenose II,* see Backman and Backman, *Bluenose,* 13–29; McLaren, *Bluenose and Bluenose II;* Brown, telephone conversation.
4. For more on *Adventure,* see Garland, *Adventure;* Garland, "Gloucester's *Adventure,*" *Sea History* 49 (Spring 1989): 16; Thomas, *Fast and Able,* 195–98.
5. Connolly, *Book of the Gloucester Fishermen,* 288–89.

Selected Bibliography

THE ORGANIZATION OF THIS BIBLIOGRAPHY IS A BIT UNORTHODOX. IT REflects the current state of the literature, which tells bits and pieces of the fishermen's story in the last days of sail, but does nothing to synthesize the experience into a coherent whole. That, I hope, is the unique contribution of this book.

Certainly, the results of the fishermen's races have been well documented elsewhere, as have the controversies. The stories of vessels and skippers that were part of the fishermen's folklore have been recorded and retold countless times. We know what it was like to fish aboard a dory trawler, and we have a good sense of the special relationship that existed between communities like Gloucester and Lunenburg and their fleets. We even understand the economic dislocations created by the introduction of steam trawlers and, later, diesel-powered draggers. Although by no means exhaustive, this bibliography is designed to provide a representative sampling of works in the field, in the hope of leading readers to additional material on issues that I have found especially interesting.

Of course, some sources defy categorization, and by necessity the choice to place them in one or another section was somewhat arbitrary. Usually such works deal with more than one issue, so I have grouped them according to the topic on which they shed the most light. Certainly, newspapers, oral histories, and archival sources do not allow for such decisions, because they cover a wide array of issues. I have therefore placed them into their own categories, after the topical sections. To further assist readers, each section gives a brief survey of the literature related to the topic, before listing the sources.

THE FISHING INDUSTRY

The launching of *Spray* in 1905 was the single biggest event in the history of the North Atlantic Fisheries in the twentieth century. By successfully introducing beam trawling, *Spray* revolutionized the industry and marked the beginning of the end for the schooners. Andrew German does an excellent job of tracing the introduction of the otter trawl from 1905 to its acceptance as *the* means of fishing in the 1920s and 1930s. His study of T Wharf goes well beyond that story, though, giving us a social and visual history of the New England Fisheries as they were practiced in Boston. The Bureau of Fisheries *Reports* for 1912 through 1915 document the U.S. government's response to the new technology.

Goode et al.'s investigation of the nineteenth-century fisheries remains a classic work on the industry, vessels, workers, methods, and communities that made their living from the sea. Church and Connolly's work gives the reader a visual tour of the industry through Church's photos. Everything from building schooners to the nature of work in the various fisheries is documented, with a brief narrative by Connolly giving context for the pictures.

Church, Albert Cook, and James B. Connolly. *American Fishermen.* New York: W.W. Norton, 1940.

German, Andrew W. *Down on T Wharf: The Boston Fisheries As Seen Through the Photographs of Henry D. Fisher.* Mystic, Conn.: Mystic Seaport Museum, 1982.

———. "Otter Trawling Comes to America: The Bay State Fishing Company, 1905–1938." *American Neptune* 44 (Spring 1984): 114–31.

U.S. Bureau of Fisheries. *Reports of the United States Commissioner of Fisheries for the Fiscal Years 1912–1915.* Washington, D.C.: Government Printing Office, 1912, 1913, 1914, 1915.

U.S. Commission of Fish and Fisheries. *The Fisheries and Fishery Industries of the United States,* by George Brown Goode et al. Washington, D.C.: Government Printing Office, 1887.

THE FISHERMAN'S LIFE

Books by fishermen about their lives are rare. Theirs was an oral tradition. For that reason, James Connolly's work is helpful. He knew these men, listened to their stories, and recorded the more interesting ones, though he also sometimes embellished the yarns. I have been careful in this book to reference only those Connolly stories that were confirmed by other sources to be part of fishermen's lore.

McFarland's work is particularly helpful because the narrative is based on three trips he made aboard his uncle's mackerel seiner, *Yosemite,* in the 1890s. Pierce was a fisherman as well. Five generations of his family fished, and he began shore fishing as soon as he was "old enough to climb into a boat." He wrote his book in 1934 because he was aware that much of the "information concerning New England's first industry is rapidly becoming a thing of the past and likely to be forgotten." Both books are invaluable.

Digges's study focuses mostly on the Portuguese fishermen in New England. He obviously knew the men he wrote about, having both sailed and talked extensively with them. He supplemented this personal knowledge with research of the local press, and he produced a valuable book on one of the industry's key ethnic groups.

Stanford's pictorial history brings together a wonderful set of photographs depicting the men and their work. There are shots of baiting up, casting off dories, mending nets, and working aboard beam trawlers. The collection brings to life the experiences described by McFarland, Pierce, and Connolly.

Kipling's *Captains Courageous* is a quick and easy read, but it provides a remarkably good sense of the rhythms and dynamics of shipboard life. It was a significant accomplishment for someone who got seasick the only time he sailed aboard a Gloucesterman. The film version of *Captains Courageous* is also an enjoyable way to vicariously experience shipboard life.

Connolly, James B. *The Book of the Gloucester Fishermen*. New York: John Day, 1927.

Digges, Jeremiah. *In Quiet Waters: The Story of the Portuguese Fishermen*. New York: MacMillan, 1941.

Kipling, Rudyard. *Captains Courageous: A Story of the Grand Banks*. New York: Century, 1897.

McFarland, Raymond. *The Masts of Gloucester: Recollections of a Fisherman*. New York: W. W. Norton, 1937.

Metro-Goldwin-Mayer. *Captains Courageous*, 1937. Available on videocassette, New York: MGM/UA Home Video, 1985.

Pierce, George Wesley. *Goin' Fishin': The Story of the Deep-Sea Fishermen of New England*. Salem, Mass.: Marine Research Society, 1934; Reprint, as *Going Fishing: The Story of the Deep-Sea Fishermen of New England*, Camden, Maine: International Marine Publishing Co., 1989.

Stanford, Alfred. *Men, Fish, and Boats: The Pictorial Story of the North Atlantic Fishermen*. Jersey City, N.J.: Morrow, 1934.

HISTORIES OF GLOUCESTER AND ESSEX

The towns of Gloucester and Essex were intimately intertwined in the age of sail. According to Dana Story, Essex shipyards have launched more than four thousand vessels since the town was settled in 1637, most of them for the fishing trades. This relationship, as well as life in a small boat-building community, is nicely chronicled by Story, who mixes personal experience (as the son of A. D. Story) and historical research to tell his tale.

Garland's overview of Gloucester's fishing industry is the best single source on everything from the evolution of vessel design, to the structure of shipboard life, to the social and economic realities of the community in the schooner days. Parsons and Anastas's volume is a nice collection of edited oral histories that capture snatches of life in Gloucester "once upon a time."

Webber's, Thomas's, and Hoyt's works are largely pictorials of Gloucester, and they provide a visual sense of the times. Webber's narrative gives the
reader a sort of "walking tour" of Gloucester at the end of the sailing era,
and Hoyt chronicles the transformation of the waterfront due to draggers
and trawlers.

Connolly and Kenny provide general histories from the discovery of Cape
Ann to the twentieth century. They are not the most objective works on the
subject, but they do provide a handy thumbnail sketch of Gloucester's evolution and its sense of its past.

The Gloucester Master Mariners' Association's *Yearbook* gives a listing of
fishing vessels, public buildings, and summer homes. Perhaps the most interesting part of the document is the prefatory "Gloucester and the Master
Mariner," which sheds some light on how these men perceived their role in
the community, and vice versa. The Gloucester Fishermen's Institute's *Annual Reports* offer an interesting look at the goals and achievements of one
of the city's most important efforts on behalf of the fishermen.

Connolly, James B. *The Port of Gloucester.* New York: Doubleday, Doran, 1940.

Garland, Joseph E. *Down to the Sea: The Fishing Schooners of Gloucester.* Boston: David
R. Godine, 1983.

Gloucester Fishermen's Institute. *Annual Reports.* Gloucester, Mass.: Cape Ann
Breeze, 1893–1897.

Gloucester Master Mariners' Association. *Yearbooks.* Gloucester, Mass.: Gloucester
Master Mariners' Association, 1917; 1925–1930; 1937–1938.

Hoyt, William D. *Hanging On: The Gloucester Waterfront in Change, 1927–1948.*
Gloucester, Mass.: Chisholm & Hunt Printers, 1987.

Kenny, Herbert A. *Cape Ann: Cape America.* Philadelphia: J. B. Lippincott, 1971.

Parsons, Peter, and Peter Anastas. *When Gloucester Was Gloucester: Towards an Oral History of the City.* Gloucester, Mass.: Gloucester 350th Anniversary Celebration, 1973.

Story, Dana. *Frame-Up! The Story of Essex, Its Shipyards, and Its People.* Barre, Mass.: Barre
Publishers, 1964.

———. *Growing Up in a Shipyard: Reminiscences of a Shipbuilding Life in Essex, Massachusetts.* Mystic, Conn.: Mystic Seaport Museum, 1991.

Thomas, Gordon W. *Wharf and Fleet.* Gloucester, Mass.: Nautical Reproductions of
Gloucester, 1977.

Webber, William S., Jr. *Waterfront: Around the Wharves of Gloucester in the Last Days of
Sail.* Manchester, Mass.: The Cricket Press, 1973.

Histories of Lunenburg

Peter Barss gives us an intimate picture of the everyday lives of Lunenburg's common folk. Based on sixty-two interviews with fishermen, the book
captures their way of life and community by allowing the interviewees to

speak for themselves. Barss organizes his chapters topically and chronologically, keeping the narrators' wording, syntax, and the substance of their comments intact, editing only to delete boring or repetitive material, and combining statements where several speakers say essentially the same thing. The result is a first-rate social history of Lunenburg County in the first decades of this century.

Balcom's study is a good overview of Lunenburg's fishing industry from 1753 to 1933. Of particular interest for this book is his discussion of changing economic and technological realities and their impact on the evolution of fishing in Lunenburg County from 1870 to 1933.

Barnard's book provides a basic overview of the Nova Scotia and Lunenburg fisheries from colonial times to the 1980s. It is a bit overgeneralized, but as a primer for someone unfamiliar with the story, it is a good place to begin.

Balcom, B. A. *History of the Lunenburg Fishing Industry.* Lunenburg, Novia Scotia: Lunenburg Marine Museum Society, 1977.

Barnard, Murray. *Sea, Salt, and Sweat: A Story of Nova Scotia and the Vast Atlantic Fishery.* Halifax, Nova Scotia: Four East Publications and the Nova Scotia Department of Fisheries, 1986.

Barss, Peter. *Images of Lunenburg County.* Toronto, Ontario: McClelland and Stewart, 1978.

VESSEL HISTORIES AND DESIGN

The history of fishing under sail and the evolution of schooner design is a fascinating story that dates back to the early Chebacco boats and heel tappers of the colonial period. By the mid-nineteenth century, sharp shooters and clipper-bowed schooners were making fast trips to and from the Banks, but often at the cost of their crews. Tom McManus, Dennison Lawlor, and Joe Collins pioneered designs to build vessels that were both fast and safe. As architect of some 450 boats, McManus's impact on fishing schooner design was perhaps the most significant. All this is authoritatively documented in Howard Chapelle's seminal work on the schooners. Bill Dunne's research is destined to be the definitive word on McManus.

L. Francis Herreshoff was not convinced about the design integrity of the Gloucestermen, and he voiced his opinion in no uncertain terms in an article comparing *Puritan* and *Mayflower.* That piece, along with several articles he wrote for *Rudder* in the 1940s and 1950s, appear in the *Herreshoff Reader.*

As a pictorial history, O'Hearn's book provides a nice visual sense of the evolution of fishing schooners, from the sharp shooters to the racers. However, there are several factual errors. The most glaring of these include a tendency to confuse the *Halifax Herald* series and Lipton Cup Races, a claim that *Thebaud* lost to *Bluenose* in 1923, and the assertion that *Columbia* was built in 1924 and sank in the mid-1930s.

One of the best books about the schooners is Thomas's collection of seventy-six short histories of selected vessels from 1874 to 1930. Each boat receives a two- to three-page overview detailing its career, skippers, and fate. Joe Garland's study of *Adventure* chronicles that vessel's life as the last dory trawler and "Queen of the Windjammers."

Tod's article is an interesting reminiscence of the last days of sail and the intrusion of power by someone who grew up in Gloucester and shipped aboard the *Thomas S. Gorton* as a youngster. The Spring 1989 issue of *Sea History* is devoted to the Gloucestermen, with articles on the art of Thomas Hoyne, the evolution of the schooner, and efforts to preserve the remaining all-sail fishing vessels.

Chapelle, Howard I. *The American Fishing Schooners, 1825–1935*. New York: W. W. Norton, 1973.

Dunne, W. M. P. "Thomas Francis McManus (1856–1938): An Irish Immigration Success Story." Ph.D. diss., State University of New York at Stony Brook, 1990.

———. "The McManuses of Boston: Champions of Safety and Performance." *WoodenBoat*, May/June 1993, 72–89.

———. *Thomas F. McManus and the American Fishing Schooners: An Irish-American Success Story*. Mystic, Conn.: Mystic Seaport Museum, 1994.

Garland, Joseph E. *Adventure: Queen of the Windjammers*. Camden, Maine: Down East Books, 1985.

Herreshoff, L. Francis. *An L. Francis Herreshoff Reader*. Camden, Maine: International Marine Publishing, 1978.

O'Hearn, Joseph C. *New England Fishing Schooners*. Milwaukee, Wis.: Kalmbach Publishing, 1947.

Sea History 49 (Spring 1989).

Thomas, Gordon W. *Fast and Able: Life Stories of Great Gloucester Fishing Vessels*. Gloucester, Mass.: Gloucester 350th Anniversary Celebration, 1973.

Tod, Giles M. S. "The Passing Gloucestermen." *Motor Boating*, March 1958, 38–40, 89–96.

RACERS AND RACING

There are several sources on the races, most of them by Canadians, and focused on *Bluenose*. Although essentially accurate, these works tend to be a bit too romantic about the "Queen of the North Atlantic Fishing Fleet." They perpetuate the common folklore that the races began when William

Dennis decided to oblige the fishermen, who were clamoring for a "real race" after a 1920 America's Cup contest was canceled because of a 23–knot breeze. Ziner's book is the only one that details Dennis's more extensive role in initiating the races. There is also a common misperception that *Thebaud* was built by "Boston interests." McLaren and the Backmans do a nice job of outlining the connections between *Bluenose* and *Bluenose II*. All of these works give good race-by-race and year-by-year accounts of the international series.

Dana Story's history of *Columbia* is the only book-length study about one of the American racers. It documents the late-nineteenth- and early-twentieth-century races as well as the pre-1923 *Halifax Herald* events, before unfolding the story of Ben Pine's pride and joy.

Hayden's autobiography is an interesting introspective look at the wanderlust and searching for self that led him to sea. Of particular interest are chapters 42 and 43, dealing with the 1938 races.

⚓

Backman, Brian, and Phil Backman. *Bluenose*. Toronto, Ontario: McClelland and Stewart, 1965.

Darrach, Claude. *Race to Fame: The Inside Story of the Bluenose*. Hantsport, Nova Scotia: Lancelot Press, 1985.

Gillespie, G. J. *Bluenose Skipper*. Fredericton, New Brunswick: Brunswick Press, 1955.

Hayden, Sterling. *Wanderer*. London, England: Longmans, Green, 1963.

McLaren, R. Keith. *Bluenose and Bluenose II*. Willowdale, Ontario: Anthony R. Hawke, 1981.

Merkel, Andrew. *Schooner Bluenose*. Toronto, Ontario: Ryerson Press, 1948.

Story, Dana. *Hail Columbia! The Rise and Fall of a Schooner*. Gloucester, Mass.: Ten Pound Island Book Co., 1985.

Ziner, Feenie. *Bluenose: Queen of the Grand Banks*. Halifax, Nova Scotia: Nimbus Publishing, 1970.

YACHTING INFLUENCES

One of the most interesting aspects of the fishermen's races is the love/hate relationship between yachtsmen and fishermen. The cross-class connections between the Gloucester waterfront and the affluent residents of Eastern Point were long-standing, and they did much to shape the community dynamic in which the schooners raced. Joe Garland's history of Eastern Point documents the evolution of that area from farmland and a departure point for fishermen to a summer resort and artist colony. The ebb and flow of contact between the super rich and Gloucester's average citizens is particularly intriguing, as are Garland's biographical vignettes of wealthy Eastern Pointers.

The Eastern Yacht Club, a short distance away at Marblehead, was intimately involved in the fishermen's races since their beginnings in 1886. Garland's history is excellent, and Foster's book, though quirky, is an interesting collection of letters, reminiscences, photographs, and other club-related documents.

Foster, Charles H. W. *The Eastern Yacht Club Ditty Box, 1870–1900*. Norwood, Mass.: Plimpton Press, 1932.

Garland, Joseph E. *Eastern Point: A Nautical, Rustical, and Social Chronicle of Gloucester's Outer Shield and Inner Sanctum, 1606–1950*. Peterborough, N.H.: William L. Bauham, 1971.

———. *The Eastern Yacht Club: A History From 1870–1985*. Marblehead, Mass.: Eastern Yacht Club, 1989.

MUSEUMS AND HISTORICAL SOCIETIES

There is surprisingly little material on the races in archives or special collections besides what is contained in newspaper accounts of the day. In fact, most of the holdings I have uncovered are scrapbooks of news articles about the events. These include the McInnis and Welch papers at the Cape Ann Historical Association and the Fowle scrapbooks at the Museum of Yachting. Cape Ann also has a smattering of vertical files containing random press clippings pertaining to the lives of certain Gloucester citizens. Additionally, the Shelburne County Museum has copies of articles from the local newspaper—*The Shelburne Gazette and Coast Guard*—that deal with the 1912–13 Brittain Cup Races.

Other museums have artifacts from the races. The Maritime Museum of the Atlantic is home to the Brittain Cup. The Provincetown Heritage Museum displays the 1907 Lipton Cup between June and October, after which it spends the rest of the year at the Pilgrim Monument Museum. On the second floor of the Provincetown Heritage Museum is a half-scale model of the *Rose Dorothea*. The Fisheries Museum of the Atlantic has videos of the Lunenburg area, photographs, vertical files with biographical data on the skippers, and old newspapers.

Fisheries Museum of the Atlantic, Lunenburg, Nova Scotia.

Fowle, Leonard. "Yachting Scrapbooks." Leonard Fowle Collection. Museum of Yachting, Newport, R.I.

Maritime Museum of the Atlantic, Halifax, Nova Scotia.

McInnis, W. J. Scrapbook. "Fisherman's Races—Gloucester and Boston." W. J. McInnis Collection. Cape Ann Historical Association, Gloucester, Mass.

Pilgrim Monument Museum, Provincetown, Mass.

Provincetown Heritage Museum, Provincetown, Mass.

Shelburne County Museum, Shelburne, Nova Scotia.

Welch, Captain Martin. Untitled Scrapbook on the 1920 Race. Captain Martin Welch Papers. Cape Ann Historical Association, Gloucester, Mass.

NEWSPAPERS, JOURNALS, AND MAGAZINES

The most useful sources on the races are the daily newspapers. Along with descriptions of the contests, they provide a host of related stories about personalities and sidelights. The tone of the coverage is also instructive for the insights it gives into popular depictions of the races. *Yachting* and *Rudder* are helpful on that issue as well. The *Fisherman* was a publication of the Gloucester Fishermen's Institute; it provides interesting information on the Institute's goals, objectives, and missionary work. By far the best source about goings-on in the industry during the 1920s and 1930s is the *Atlantic Fisherman*.

Atlantic Fisherman, February 1921–December 1938.

Boston Daily Advertiser, October 1922.

Boston Evening American, October 1920–October 1930.

Boston Evening Transcript, October 1922.

Boston Globe, July 1920–November 1938.

Boston Herald, October 1920–November 1938.

Boston Post, October 1920–November 1938.

Boston Traveller, October 1920–October 1923.

Fisherman, January 1895–December 1901.

Gloucester Times, June 1888–April 1958.

Nautical Gazette, December 1905–August 1907.

New York Herald Tribune, October 1921–October 1930.

New York Times, October 1921–November 1930.

Rudder, January 1905–December 1938.

Shelburne Gazette and Coast Guard, 4 November 1920, 7 April 1921.

Yachting, November 1907–December 1938.

ORAL HISTORIES

Researchers for the Gloucester Arts and Humanities Program, Mystic Seaport Museum's Oral History Collection, and the Northeastern University

Oral History Project conducted a host of interviews with dory fishermen and others connected with the schooners. These are part of the holdings at the G. W. Blunt White Research Library, Mystic Seaport Museum, Mystic, Conn. Additionally, I spoke with people who had insights into the personalities or events under study. Oral history is a valuable tool, a means of getting at the facts and feelings behind the headlines, and of humanizing the story being researched. Few of the interviews listed below deal exclusively with the races, and a majority do not address them at all. However, as a way of understanding the day-to-day lives of the fishermen, their values, and their perspective, they are invaluable.

Gloucester Arts and Humanities Program

Auditore, Jeannie. Interview by David Masters. Tape recording. Gloucester, Mass., n.d.

Cluett, Hubert. Interview by David Masters. Tape recording. Gloucester, Mass, 15 March 1978.

Domingoes, Manuel F., Jr. Interview by Linda Brayton and David Masters. Tape recording. Gloucester, Mass., n.d.

Favaloro, Leo and Rosalie. Interview by David Masters. Tape recording. Gloucester, Mass., n.d.

Mystic Seaport Museum Oral History Collection

Allen, Captain Lawrence. Interview by John Kochiss. Tape recording. Lunenburg, Nova Scotia, 11 November 1969.

Beatteay, Captain Walter. Interview by David Littlefield. Tape recording. Concord, Mass., 21 April 1993.

Fisher, R. Barry. Interview by Gary M. Adair. Tape recording. Mystic, Conn., 13 January 1992.

Francis, Captain John. Interview by Richard Rudis. Tape recording. West Franklin, N.H., 3 March 1987.

Francis, Captain John. Interview by Nancy d'Estang. Tape recording. West Franklin, N.H., 13 April 1987.

Francis, Captain John and Ruth. Interview by Nancy d'Estang. Tape recording. Mystic, Conn., 19 October 1987.

Hogan, Felix William. Interview by Nancy d'Estang. Tape recording. Mystic, CT, 22 October 1984.

Langworthy, Maxon. Interview by Thomas Parker. Tape recording. Noank, Conn., January 1976.

Louanis, Lorraine. Interview by Fred Calabretta and Julie Goodrich. Tape recording. Reading, Mass., 18 July 1992.

Martell, William. Interview by Gary Adair, Nancy d'Estang, and Erik Ronnberg, Jr. Tape recording. Gloucester, Mass., 11 December 1990.

Martell, William. Interview by Gary Adair, Nancy d'Estang, and Erik Ronnberg, Jr. Tape recording. Gloucester, Mass., February 1991.

Merchant, Robert. Interview by Virginia Jones. Tape recording. Gloucester, Mass., 16 November 1977.

Merchant, Robert. Interview by Virginia Jones. Tape recording. Stonington, Conn., 1 April 1978.

Mitchell, Frank. Interview by Fred Calabretta. Tape recording. Reading, Mass., 24 July 1992.

Peterson, Edward. Interview by Barry Thomas. Tape recording. Mystic, Conn., 28 October 1973.

Skinner, Louis. Interview by Nancy d'Estang, George Emery, and Jonathan Shay. Tape recording. Mystic, Conn., 29 June 1984.

Stephens, Bruce. Telephone conversation with Nancy d'Estang. Transcript. 12 May 1986.

Story, Dana. Interview by Maynard Bray, John Gardner, and John Kochiss. Tape recording. Essex, Mass., 10 September 1969.

Tibbo, Winston. Interview by Gary Adair, Nancy d'Estang, and R. Hambidge. Tape recording. Mystic, Conn., 6 May 1986.

Northeastern University Oral History Project

Edmunds, Al. Interview by R. Wayne Anderson. Transcript. East Boston, Mass., 20 June 1982.

Furlong, Walter. Interview by R. Wayne Anderson. Transcript. Charlestown, Mass., 10 June 1982.

Hynes, Leo. Interview by Gregory J. Fulham. Transcript. Nashua, N.H., 29 April 1980.

O'Brien, Robert. Interview by R. Wayne Anderson. Transcript. Watertown, Mass., 2 March 1982.

Peterson, Uno. Interview by R. Wayne Anderson. Transcript. Chelsea, Mass., 9 June, 16 June 1982.

Personal Interviews

Brown, Peter. Telephone conversation with author. 15 October 1993.

Hatch, Julian. Interview by author. Tape recording. Naples, Fla., 25 October 1993.

Mellow, June. Interview by author. Tape recording. Gloucester, Mass., 18 November 1993.

Story, Dana. Interview by author. Tape recording. Essex, Mass., 16 November 1993.

INDEX

Page references to illustrations are in italic type.

202   INDEX